Job Coach-Life Coach-Executive Coach-Branding-Letter & Resume-Writing Service

Job Coach-Life Coach-Executive Coach-Branding-Letter & Resume-Writing Service

Step-by-Step Business Startup Manual

Anne Hart

ASJA Press
New York Lincoln Shanghai

Job Coach-Life Coach-Executive Coach-Branding-Letter
& Resume-Writing Service
Step-by-Step Business Startup Manual

Copyright © 2005 by Anne Hart

ASJA Press
an imprint of iUniverse, Inc.

iUniverse books may be ordered through booksellers or by contacting:

iUniverse
2021 Pine Lake Road, Suite 100
Lincoln, NE 68512
www.iuniverse.com
1-800-Authors (1-800-288-4677)

ISBN-13: 978-0-595-37100-6
ISBN-10: 0-595-37100-0

Printed in the United States of America

CONTENTS

FOREWORD

So You Want to Be a Job/Career Coach, Life Coach, or Executive Coach and Write Resumes with Business Letters in Your Online, Home-based Business

Here's how to start your personal service business. As a job or career coach, an executive coach, or a life coach, you will be presenting and classifying your client's competencies, writing resumes, cover letters, and creating a wide variety of business correspondence including sales letters, news releases, and direct mail copy. You will be planning events for your clients and their prospective employers. You'll need to really work a room to find clients as well as niches or jobs for clients when networking at professional associations and trade shows. Most frequently, you'll be asked to write, evaluate, and repackage resumes, cover letters, and other summaries of qualifications of your clients. Develop an icon, logo, and motto for your coaching clients.

A resume is a summary of qualifications. A career coach helps clients find success by taking step-by-step detailed, concrete strategies that solve specific problems, get results, and reach a defined goal. A resume writing business online can be combined with a career coaching enterprise. The steps are outlined here for you to follow in chronological order to open and operate a resume-writing service business and also a career coaching enterprise, online from your home, mobile location, or office. You can telecommute online and still help people find direction by offering information, training, or consulting services.

Here's how to open an online business at home presenting and packaging your clients' competencies. Make your living writing resumes, business letters, and being a job coach. Help clients obtain appoints for interviews that may eventually lead to finding work. Write and repackage resumes and all types of business correspondence—from cover letters and follow-ups to direct mail or trade show sales letters. Write news releases for employee newsletters about people in key positions. Be a job coach and consultant with employees and employers with a goal of matching people. Even help place public speakers with corporations hosting events such as conventions.

You don't have the packaging, postage, and handling expense of mailing the resumes or letters. Your client does the mailing of any letters you write online or on resume paper. Save every correspondence on disc for your files and turn over or email to your client a copy of your master disc or CD. Your client may return in the future for more copies or updates.

All you do online at home is write resumes, business letters, and other business correspondence, repackage the material and save it on a disk and in your computer files. Then you email the finished writing as an attachment saved in Microsoft Word, Rich Text, or any other file format, to your client. To expand your resume and letter-writing business, consider training as a job coach and help your client make more connections, find niche markets, hidden resources, or emphasize certain skills.

The client opens the document file, saves it on a disc, such as a CD, and keeps copies. The client prints out the files, and mails them to prospective employers or partners. You can also send copies of discs and paper-text copies of the resumes or letters to your client along with a CD, if requested. Always keep master copies. Your client may not be able to open a file sent as an attachment by email, may lose the files, or want another copy mailed by regular mail.

This book contains step-by-step how-to techniques about how to open and operate a resume-writing and business letter writing enterprise, including sample letters and resumes as guides or templates. There is growing evidence that a well-written cover letter that introduces you and highlights your best abilities may be more of an attention-grabber than sending unsolicited resumes to organizations. The book you're reading discusses the craft of well-written cover (and follow-up) letters as well as resumes. It also shows you ways to learn more about yourself in relation to a job so you can analyze your motives for wanting to be in the computer industry.

This book is designed to help you write penetrating cover and follow-up letters to top resumes that won't be tossed in inactive files or thrown away as so many are. These tips will help you from going in the wrong direction. You need to stand out in a crowd of paperwork and get the kind of attention you want from employers.

Don't spend too much time looking for a job in the same industry you left. Unusual jobs for computer personnel exist in other industries. Creative expression jobs in the computer industry exist as do computerized, technical jobs in the entertainment, biotech, or food industry, for example.

In your search for a job, you'll meet many leads along the road. You'll meet vendors who valued your business when you were employed now getting contracts from the person who replaced you in your former job. These vendors may not return your calls or do lunch until you're back in business.

Contact new groups for luncheons, such as a wide variety of professional associations, your local chamber of commerce and convention bureaus, event planners, and support groups. Your companions from the last place you worked or school alumni aren't going to lunch with you now, unless they're close friends.

Along the road you may find outplacement firms focusing on career counseling and redirection, not on finding a job for you. Perhaps your former employer hired them for psychological counseling to ease stress. Some employers use outplacement firms as preventative measures to lessen the chances of workplace trauma after termination or out of an employer's own guilt.

Employment agencies you stop at along the road may represent the employer who paid them the fee, not you, unless you pay their fee. Their job market coverage may be narrow, with emphasis on finding many more lower-level jobs by cold-calling employers listed in the Yellow Pages, business directories, and classified ads in the daily newspaper.

If you're a manager traveling this road, your chances of being hired in a new job as a manager are slimmer if you target employment agencies without realizing which agencies specialize in referring rank-and-file workers to employers with specific preferences.

Temporary services may be helpful for shorter-term work if you're a contingency professional or are seeking temporary technical or clerical jobs. Use temporary services to tide you over, meet people, and earn survival money.

There's always the chance you'll be picked for a staff job, especially in lower-level and clerical jobs. This is a good route for emergency work in the case of displaced homemakers seeking entry-level clerical, healthcare technician, word processing, and desktop publishing jobs. It's also a good road for technical writers and illustrators seeking to break into the computer industry through overflow work on a temporary basis.

If you're an out-of-work executive, along the job search road, you'll see ads for executive search firms (for people who earned more than $25,000 or $30,000 annually) that say they know exactly what the employer wants. Sometimes the employer pays them to make a good match. Some head hunters ask you to pay a fee.

Make sure you know what services your fee will buy. You may be paying them in advance for advice and packaging. You may not fit what their leads want. If you want to spend the money, go ahead. You might beat the odds.

But why try to beat odds, when you can seek alternatives and ideas from software in your own computer? You may wish to brainstorm, or use brainstorming software such as IdeaFisher, published by IdeaFisher Systems, Inc., Irvine, California, to come up with alternatives and ideas. The software contains 700,000 associative connections and over 5,900 problem solving questions. I highly and objectively recommend it to make you think of all the possibilities you could put to work for you.

Along the job hunter's road, you'll learn that the first step in sending any communication is to keep anger out. Protect your reputation.

To find a compassionate ear willing to listen to your troubles without amplifying the stress, join, volunteer, and focus your services in support groups designed for the unemployed person in your field. To locate job leads and meet more business associates, join professional organizations associated with the computer industry and call their recorded telephone job referral lines.

Be prepared to take a year or more to find the type of work you want, assuming your goals are realistic. Focus on saving as much money as you can while you're out of work.

If you want to find out how to break into the computer industry, you're better off joining a professional association of trainers of computer personnel than scrambling around people not in the information management industry.

To get more information on data processing and information management training, for example, join a professional association such as TASC, Trainers' Association of Southern California. When you talk to the people who develop training in any area or industry, you get a finger on the pulse of the entire industry, even if you're not a trainer yourself. Trainers have a broad overview of the entire industry's needs from a perspective very different from personnel workers.

Look for new directions and purposes for your skills. Don't overlook 'intrapreneurial' opportunities, or entrepreneurial roads into temporary, contingency professional work that may lead to your own business opportunity in a new technology.

If you're listing new ideas, remember that the last 10 ideas are usually the best on any long list. Best of all, feel committed to anything new you try on your road to success. It's physically healthier to stay an optimist. At the end of this book, you'll be an optimist who knows how to combine excellence with common sense.

INTRODUCTION

Clients come to a career/job coach, an executive coach, or a life coach because they want to feel dignified. Colleges are turning out more graduates to compete for fewer positions. Fear of competition and scarcity of employment are driving clients to seek help writing, editing, or evaluating their resumes and business correspondence.

According to the U. S. Department of Labor, between 1994 and the year 2005, "the number of college graduates will outpace the number of available jobs by 20% each year." The number of older, laid-off workers returning to college is increasing as well as the number of younger college graduates—despite fewer people in their twenties in the population.

Competition is increasing. It's important to target several closely-related fields for flexibility as well as specialty. People are seeking careers in high-growth areas such as healthcare. Job seekers are afraid of appearing stupid. Employers want more than logic.

Here's how to be a job coach. Be inventive. Seek out cooperative programs where companies test out employees still in school by hiring them for a semester.

Some of your clients will be older workers not in school. They'll want you to create for them a telephone marathon to find them appointments for job interviews.

As a job coach, you may plan events and even fundraisers. You'll being calling alumni associations, asking alumni for job referrals instead of donations. If the companies can't offer jobs, they make look twice when you offer a client you have 'branded' with a powerful leader image.

Fundraisers for cultural and college alumni organizations know exactly how to ask for money from business owners. Fundraisers use persuasion techniques to sell "the teamwork attitude" as a benefit and ask for money in return.

In this book, you'll learn to use professional fundraising techniques to repackage your resume for the computer industry, (also known as the information industry). Your goal is to persuade employers to offer you an interview and ultimately, a job.

A career or 'job' coach is part of the information industry, known as an "enabling technology." To open an online, home-based business as a job coach, life coach, executive coach, spiritual coach or 'mentor' coach relies on the teamwork attitude.

Clients will ask you to find better ways to harness their resume, cover letter, energy, knowledge, and experiences. As a coach, you'll mentor clients to grow more interactive and user-friendly.

Look at your resumes, cover letters, interviews, and follow-up letters as windows of opportunity to free your client's inner voice. A resume is a way of "clicking in." It gives your clients permission to free their spontaneous self through work.

A resume verifies that an individual is recognized, valued, and discovered. The act of writing resumes for clients and then evaluating those drafts plugs your client into his or her own inner energy. That one page also connects clients to employers. It's a mirror that reflects your client's self-esteem.

The latest way to market client's resumes is electronically via the Internet and through international video-conferencing. Internet-based and satellite video conference systems now link U.S. job-search firms with those overseas.

Most people find jobs through friends, relatives, professional association members they know and worked with, and through former co-workers. Companies still obtain resumes by advertising, employee-referral incentives, college recruitment, tuition reimbursement, direct mail, Internet ads, and employment or outplacement agencies.

Ironically, the last place an employer looks for a resume is to the individual who contacts the company without first being asked. Job coaches contact members of professional associations. Therefore, by contacting organizations to do volunteer work on the national professional and trade associations' newsletters and speakers' panels (for meetings and conventions), your client would have a better chance of being remembered when a job opens. Associations also are swamped by a rush of resumes from members. Your job as a career coach would be to help your clients stand out from the crowd in a positive manner.

When all resumes begin to blur, employers finally hire the job applicant with the most enthusiasm, energy, and charisma.

When employers ask for "a good closer" they're talking about enthusiasm for the company and the product or service. A great resume doesn't "close the sale." Your client's pitch at the oral interview is the real closer. That one-line pitch summarizes advantage your client can offer the company.

Resumes measure how much people believe in themselves. As a job coach, how much do you believe in what you do? Can you be a ghostwriter when it comes to writing resumes and cover or follow-up letters for your client and then write sales letters, news releases, or brochures and flyers for your own business and corporate clients? Can you plan events so your client will be present when people with the power to hire your client are present at that event?

Can you be a catalyst and bring people together? A job coach is a matchmaker and a publicist.

Here's how to open and operate an online or in-person job coach business that also includes writing resumes, cover letters, follow-up letters, and other business correspondence.

Showcase the strength within your client. Finding a job interview for someone else is all about repackaging information in new ways. Now let's look at how to repackage your client's competencies to achieve results. Before you open your doors or email as a job coach, first you need to write a business plan with a time budget as well as a money budget.

Branding your client is a network activity. You need to be forward-thinking as a career coach, executive coach, life coach, spiritual coach, or image coach.

You're not only a ghostwriter, editor, critic, evaluator, event planner, resume writer, business letter editor, publicist, and strategy coach. You're also a behind-the-scene advertising cross-media specialist with the ability to unify messages for the media and corporations. Most of all, you have to *measure your results* to show to employers. That's how you find new clients. Your unemployed client may be "behind the curve."

The main benefit you're offering clients is efficiency. You start by contacting network organizations—corporations cooperating to deliver services to their consumers. Remember the career coach motto: The big corporation learns from the small company. Teachers learn from student feedback. Retailers learn from consumer demand. Welcome to job coach training 101.

CHAPTER 1

How to Write Your Business Plan as a Home-Based Online Entrepreneur, Writer, and Information Re-packager

Develop an icon, logo, and motto for your coaching clients before you write any resumes or letters for them. Before you take on clients, you need a business plan for yourself and for them—a plan that includes a time budget and a money budget. Here is how you develop and write a business plan before your open your online home-based business as a job coach.

This plan helps to enable you to make an informed decision about which type of online writing and information repackaging business is right for you. You can combine resume writing with writing business correspondence, write grant proposals, or a wide variety of business and personal letters.

The first step is to outline the product or service you may be interested in marketing. Ask yourself what need the service satisfies. Write down a physical description of the product; how and where are you going to create it? Can you describe it for potential customers? How and where are you going to run your business?

One of the most important elements of a business plan is assessment of the competition. By studying your competitors, you can discover how your product or service will represent an improvement over existing products and services. You can create variations that fill a community or national need.

Your idea may be something entirely new. Include in your plan the imaginative services you have created. For example, suppose you want to write pet eulogies and sell the poetry on framed plaques to pet cemeteries and pet owners. This is one way you could generate an innovative product on your word processor. If you have designed a product, such as mailing lists compiled at nine cents a name, and feel your low-cost service does the same job as a more expensive service, use this as your selling point.

Market Research

Your writing and information packaging online enterprise or home-based business plan should include the methods and the results of the research as well as sources of information used to determine whether or not a market exists for your product. You may use a good marketing-research software program in your computer, one that composes questionnaires and surveys and tabulates data and other information necessary to a marketing plan. Your program should be able to give you figures regarding the competition and the number of potential users for your product or service. Are there customers out there who need what you're selling? Is the field swamped with businesses doing the same thing?

Market research should back up your sales projections. After you have written a marketing research plan, create a marketing plan. Here you explain how your product is to be sold. Are you going to have a sales force working for you, or are you working at home alone, using your word processor and telephone? Will you have distributors working on commission or on salary putting your product in the stores? What kind of advertising and promotion program are you going to develop for your business? Have any clients given you orders in advance? These are all questions to consider and research carefully.

Staffing

Marketing plans need to include your background and that of anyone working with you, such as business partners or salespersons. Include here all the information that normally goes into the resumes of your key people and yourself. Particularly important is experience. You or key people in your business have been able to run projects and garner profits, for example, or have performed fund-raising or leadership for volunteer work. Generate on your word processor an organizational chart that graphically shows areas of responsibility. Indicate how each person relates to others in your business.

Financial Statements

Create profit-and-loss statements and cash flow projections for the next five years. Computer programs exist that can work up this information for you from data you supply. You will then be able to judge how much money you will need to run your business. This type of forecasting may prevent you from risking undercapitalization in the first or second year of your business.

These figures will also tell you when you can expect the business to break even and how profits will grow over a period of time. Software is available that can show you the potential growth of your business, based on three sets of sales assumptions: low, expected, and better-than-planned.

Check your computer printouts with your accountant or with a programmer with an accounting background for ways in which your program can be individualized or customized to your business. The business plan should be printed out on your computer using a word-processing program. You can package it in a loose-leaf binder.

A disclaimer on your first page should state that this is your business plan and not a brochure or a prospectus to sell stocks or other securities in your company. The Securities and Exchange Commission requires special treatment of prospectuses and imposes penalties on anyone distributing unregistered prospectuses in the mail.

If your business plan is going to be used to obtain financial backing, you should contact your backers in person. Include a table of contents in your business plan and divider tabs for the various sections.

Do You Really Need Bankers Lawyers Accountants, And Insurance Agents To Start A Business?

The person working alone, with only the investment in a personal computer, printer, telephone, and paper supplies, may not be able to afford professional services in the beginning. Software programs exist for bookkeeping. Computer-theft insurance costs are low. Bankers may help you start a pension plan even though they may not agree to loan you money yet.

A credit union may be able to help you with a small loan to buy equipment. The best way to locate experts is to find satisfied customers and ask them to recommend professionals who have done good work over a long period of time. You should be aware of the services you require for your individual needs. Comparison-shop until you find professionals hired by businesses similar to yours.

Do you need special services from an attorney? Are you planning to incorporate? It's very important to explore the tax and legal ramifications of starting your own business as well as your personal liability before you open your doors. Are you going to be the sole owner or a partner? Would you prefer to incorporate and have limited liability?

Ask your attorney questions such as these: What methods can I use to raise money? Can I issue stock? What's the best location for my business for tax purposes if I incorporate? What should I know about bankruptcy laws? Do I need agreements drawn up for financing? You can find a lawyer through The Martindale-Hubbell Legal Directory, which rates attorneys and describes their specialties. The Small Business Administration is a source of free information. It will also refer you to attorneys.

If you need an accountant, you should expect service that clears up your questions about how much money is coming in and going out. You will be asked to provide the figures needed for a balance sheet. The accountant's experience is financial. He or she cannot give you legal advice or advice on marketing or running your business, but you can expect assistance in preparing your business plan.

Profit-and-loss projections based on estimates of future revenues can be prepared by your computer using accounting software programs or can be prepared manually by an accountant for an hourly fee of $75 to $100. The accountant can set up your payroll, prepare your tax returns, and provide financial advice, but you have the option of purchasing software programs that also do payroll and prepare tax returns.

Software can't certify your statements were prepared by an accountant or give you financial advice regarding hiring salaried employees or independent contractors. Accountants can advise you on the best use of your money. Tax-preparation software or an accountant is also tax deductible, but you'll have a hard time deducting a $500 computer tax program this year if last year you spent $40 to have a tax-preparer do your tax return. You can ask the society in your state that certifies accountants to recommend one if you choose not to do your own accounting.

You will also need to know how to plan a budget. Your computer is capable of creating spread sheets—the process of organizing figures in columns so calculations can be made logically. Spread-sheeting on computers is useful for budgeting, but it can handle more tasks.

You may use electronic spread-sheet programs to determine the return on investments, including stocks, bonds, and real estate, or to monitor power consumption on home energy-management devices. A change in one area on a spread-sheet automatically triggers a recalculation of every related value. You can work up sales forecasts, long-range product plans, income tax, and home budgeting on spread sheets.

Other accounting functions may be performed on your computer. You can generate ledger reports, pay employees, and keep track of accounts receivable and payable as well as inventory. Data-base management is defined as keeping track of information; data-base management software can handle any task from the location of coins in a coin collection to the tracking of information in the personnel files of a corporation. A data-base program can act as your "accountant," track articles published in magazines, or chart inventories in warehouses.

Your banker can help you to increase your credibility as a borrower of money. A banker provides advice about obtaining loans and capitalization, establishing credit, starting checking accounts, preparing tax and financial reports if you don't have an accountant, and finding computerized banking services, automatic payroll services, and corporate cash management.

Insurance agents can sell you theft insurance for your computer and peripheral equipment and insure your software programs against damage or loss. Your insurance agent can counsel you about workman's compensation, social security, and state disability. He or she can help you prepare for your changing insurance needs in health insurance, employee benefits, and casualty insurance. Personal referrals are the best way to select an insurance agent.

Where to Get Free Business Advice and Low-Interest Loans

The Small Business Administration may be able to assist you in setting up your business. This organization offers management assistance, checklists, and free booklets. Management-assistance conferences are run frequently, and individual counseling programs are offered. The SCORE organization, made up of retired executives, can help with individual business advice and counseling sessions. You can find a local office by checking your telephone book under "United States Government: Small Business Administration." The headquarters is located at 1441 L Street NW, Washington, DC 20416.

In addition to offering advice, the Small Business Administration grants loans to retail businesses and service companies. SBA offers different loan programs with varying interest rates. Types of loans offered include direct loans, guaranty loans, and economic opportunity loans. Direct loans are based on a company's track record, a good business plan, rejection notices from two banks or finance firms, and the fact that your own money is invested in your business. The SBA usually loans up to four times what you already have invested in your business.

A guaranty loan comes from a commercial bank, but 90 percent of it is insured by the SBA Economic Opportunity Loans are loans to disadvantaged persons, who can borrow a maximum of $50,000 to be repaid within fifteen years with interest below what is charged by most banks. Due to a shortage of funds, there is great competition for these loans and may take several months to process.

The Office of Minority Business Enterprise of the U. S. Commerce Department assists small minority-owned businesses. This organization offers workshops on how to prepare a business package and other management or technical issues. Its headquarters is located at the U. S. Department of

Commerce, Main Commerce Building, 14th and Constitution Avenue NW, Washington, DC 20230.

The Economic Development Administration of the U.S. Commerce Department maintains a dozen EDA research centers to provide management and technical assistance to small businesses. You can obtain free help there in putting together loan packages or finding capital.

To find the center nearest you, contact the EDA regional offices in your state. You should also check with your state commerce departments and city chambers of commerce, which conduct free business seminars.

Publications

Publications are a good source of information. The "Standard Rate and Data Service" publishes the title, *Business Publication Rates and Data*. This monthly publication lists all industry periodicals by type of business.

Dun and Bradstreet issues business-credit publications; key business ratios; analyses of the cost of doing business for corporations, partnerships, or proprietorships; failure records; and accounts of the pitfalls in small-business administration. Write to Dun and Bradstreet, Department of Public Relations and Advertising, 99 Church Street, New York, NY 10007.

Also check out SAIC codes on the Internet. These codes are a guide to other businesses that may be hiring. Check their hiring processes and their expansion data to find out which direction they are growing. Expansion of similar businesses and the demography of their customers may help you focus your business plan on a target market or niche customer base/audience.

In the private sector venture-capital groups invest equity and become part owners in your business. Small Business Investment Companies are licensed by the Small Business Administration to invest money and provide management services.

Some of these venture-capital groups can be found through banks. The Small Business Investment Companies grant long-term loans, purchase debt securities, or combine equity and loan financing. One of these companies may purchase equity in your firm, but it will own part of your business.

Sell Solutions to Problems

Steps to Marketing Your Business to the Digital Media as You Sell Reports Offering Solutions to Problems

1. In order to find out which trade journals are being published so you can sell your new business information to them, go to your Alta Vista search engine and type in "Standard Industrial Codes."

You'll find a list of Web sites full of databases of Standard Industrial Codes for industries of varying dates and locations. You want to begin searching your local area for Standard Industrial Codes (SICs) for the current year. Many of the codes on the Web are not yet current because they come from the databases of a variety of sources from different universities' databases to private research firms.

Use your Internet search engines. At the Lycos search engine, you'll come up with the Standard Industrial Classification Search where you can search the 1987 version SIC manual by keyword, to access descriptive key words. However, what happened in 1987 won't be relevant to the new media today.

For more current data, click onto the Standard Industrial Classifications at the U.S. Small Business Administration approved SIC codes put online by the Wilkins Group, Inc. Unfortunately, many of the SIC Codes on the Web received its 8(a) Certification from the Small Business Administration (SBA) in 1993. Look for databases online that have many years of the SBA's participation.

Still, online Web sites for SIC codes may not be in the location you want, or the company you're seeking may have less than 50 employees and will not be listed in the SIC Codes. You might want to try CSGSD SIC Codes. The CSGSD SIC Codes Standard Industrial Classification Codes (SIC Codes) is a small, online woman-owned corporation as classified by the Small Business Administration. It's on the Web and can be found by a Lycos or Yahoo research engine search. Rather than give you the Web site here, because it may change, it's more current to find its location by doing a Yahoo search.

I recommend using the Standard Industrial Classification Code Finder on the Web. I found it through a Yahoo search. You also can reach it at the University of Virginia gopher in their social science department. If you'd prefer a timely SIC update, try the private company databases such as Vivamus Concepts Inc. for SIC Index Standard Industrial Codes. Vivamus offers a "Numerical Order" for its SIC codes which is a common method of classifying businesses or industries by type.

You even can see the old 1987 Standard Industrial Classification Codes there. What's nice about Vivamus Concepts Inc. is their Alphabetical SIC Index, the Vivamus Concepts Inc. Alphabetical SIC Index Standard Industrial Codes in Alphabetical Order. I like looking up codes alphabetically as compared to other databases that list by numerical codes. Alphabetical codes are a common method of classifying businesses or industries by type. The alphabetical format follows the 1987 Standard.

Checkout the Major Divisions and Groups within the SIC Codes. Not only businesses of 50 or more employees are listed by their standard industrial classification codes on the Web. You can find the same information the old fashioned way at your public library. Librarians can be of tremendous help.

What if you don't want business classification codes for selling your writing to the new media because you write sports articles or books? If you write about athletes or sports, you might try the Athlete Agent; Codes and Standards, Division of; Commercial Coach Plan Approval (Dept. Housing & Com. Dev.); Exemption Permits (Industrial Relations); Factory Built Housing Plan Approval.

When you do a Yahoo search under "Standard Industrial Codes," what also comes up on the menu is the "Athlete Agent, Codes and Standards". So on the Web, you can find under the SIC menu, codes and standards for commercial coach plan approvals from the Department of Housing and Commercial Development. If you're writing for the athletic trade journals, it's a good source to search out on the Web to find publications for your writing.

In beginning a search to market writing for the new media, the first step is to find the **Standard Industrial Code (Sic)**. For every industry there's a standard industrial code. You look up the SIC code number in the library. The code numbers tell you what companies have 50 or more employees.

You find the companies in your city or any other city that way. From then, you find out whether any of the companies in your specialty or niche writing focus has a publication or subscribes to a trade journal. If there is no trade journal and there's a business with more than 50 employees in it listed, here's your chance to start a digital trade journal or work with another person who might start one, with you doing the writing either at home or elsewhere.

Your first step would be to find all the new trade publications for the digital media and companies in the online media. Some have "house organs" which are employee newsletters. Many employee newsletter publications hire freelance or staff writers, whereas other house organs publish magazines for the digital media equipment and software user.

Library-located industrial publications and related volumes have always been in databases on disks since libraries became computerized. Look up the Standard Industrial Codes for each type of business in the new media. From the Standard Industrial Codes, you can find out whether each type of business listed has its own trade journal yet.

If the industry, occupation, or niche does not have its own trade journal, you can either create your own new media or print trade newsletter or journal, or find out which trade journals accept freelance articles by querying the editor. There are thousands of industrial codes for each business type listed, and within each type of business are the lists of trade journals.

Most of those trade journals and newsletters or other periodicals representing doing business will buy timely, up front material with sales and how-to tips and strategies. That's the first way most businesses learn about what the competition is doing in real time.

Job coaches are writers and also ghostwriters. Let your reader choose which solution they want to use as a marketing tool for their own new media business or interest. Write about the benefits and advantages of value to the readers. The editors of any new media publication have similar goals. They want articles or books that show the writer can define the problem. Then you solve the problem. Define the problem for which you'll solve the problem. Research all your niches. If you're a generalist who can't solve any type of problem in the new media, then find experts to interview who have solved current problems or who can offer quotes that solve problems for readers.

Stick with the niches. Every writer needs a tag name. It's like a tag line in a romance novel. "She said, with a sneer of disdain," (how she said it—the body language—is your tag line). In a nonfiction article or book chapter, your tag line identifies how you manage risk within your paragraph. You define the arrangements rather than the body language. The arrangements include equipment, supplies, and customized services that your expert discusses and solves problems within your article.

To market media writing, position yourself as a job coach and writer specializing in a niche within a niche. For example, suppose you used to be a nurse, medical records clerk, physician, lawyer, or teacher who now wants to write full time for the new media. You position yourself as a writer of books and e-zines, or interactive media specializing in writing about computer problems that law offices, medical offices, or schools have. You interview consultants with expertise. What you're marketing about your niche is that you have a name and a tag that always will work for you as you gain experience writing about a very narrow niche—at least at first.

Your goal is to get finely honed experience marketing new media pieces about a small specialty i.e., how medical offices can use specialty software. The former medical records clerk or technician now can write for two dozen hospital and medical trade journals from emergency medical care to running the medical office in terms of economics, solely by specializing in interviewing computer consultants who focus on telling doctors how to solve their computer software and hardware problems in running their office or department.

Read magazines such as Home Office Computing. These specialty niche magazines and trade publications help you build your reputation, if you can write for them. To find people to interview, seek referrals from former clients of computer consultants. Market yourself as a speechwriter, and develop speeches for computer and new media consultants. Approach their colleagues and clients and offer to write their speeches too, for presentations or publication.

Query the new media publications of national associations and organizations where the clients of consultants join and attend trade shows and conferences.

You attend also. Your market research as a writer would be to analyze press releases from companies about whom you want to write. When you interview people for the new media, it's a little different than when you interview for the print media.

Listen and question with the goal of turning opportunities into business. In the coaching media you compose your interview questions with the goal of:

1. Diagnosing problems—one question at a time.

2. Ask your interviewee how that person designed the solution. Most people who solve problems for a living focus on thinking rather than feeling and they use the logic to design the solution. Most people who solve relationship problems use feeling, but they don't design the solution, they solve it through placing a quality of worth on the solution, as in "Is it worth it?" Degrees or values of how much it's worth in terms of well being or feelings solve problems.

Ask the person you're interviewing how the work was delivered. In the new media, anyone you interview will try to debrief you after you finish the interview. Be aware of this. What helps most is to keep a profile of people you interview. They are your clients.

Return to your interviewee profile now and then to ask the people who talked to you and saw your article in print to tell you who else they know who might be interested in having their problems solved by a new interview with the same person or other colleagues that person recommend you interview.

To market your new media writing, ask questions. Don't talk. Ask the person you interview if the individual is aware of the many magazines (name them) who might be interested in articles about their business with new angles.

If you don't like your editor's contract, use your own contract documents. It may work with a few, new media publications that are beginning to startup. Keep a journal about the new media.

Use buzzwords. Forget the early 1990s overuse of words such as 'rocket-pack' and 'cyberspace.' Editors are so tired of buzz words such as cyberspace, e-scribes, hypertext, hyperspace, new media, listen-up, and rocket scientists. How about using easily understood, solid, and standard buzz words such as "help desk?" Define your buzzwords in the first paragraph of your article, script, interactive introduction, or book chapter. Buzz words, like tag lines, define your writing and reveal the timeliness and freshness of your information.

If you're trying to market your writing to a new media publication, it's better to show up in person at the editor's office, even if it's only to hand a query letter with a sample article to the receptionist. In the world of email where you must send your article across the globe, showing up in person at a publisher's business still works better than faxing, emailing, or snail mailing. If you're relatively nearby, show up in person dressed appropriately, and hand your material to a live person. Always hand in both a paper and a disk copy of what you write. Nobody likes to retype your material to disk.

The job coach writer is hired for people skills and technical knowledge. You're paid for what problem you can solve, for how you can think. A problem to be solved for the writer is how to market information about the new media when you have a non-technical education, such as a broad liberal arts education with a degree in creative writing or fiction writing. To solve this problem, get the name of the editor who has the power to buy your writing or assign you something to write. Call the receptionist and ask for the mailing address. The (role not the person) or job of a receptionist is "sensing-judging" (SJ)—to get the right messages to the right people at the right time. The secretary's job (the role, not the person) is to screen you out from reaching the editor and bothering the person. It's a protective, guardian role.

The job of the editorial assistant is also to screen out the slush pile and protect the editor-in-chief from having to wade through the masses coming over the transom. Therefore, after you have the mailing address and have asked the receptionist for the correct spelling of the editor's name, ask to leave a message in the editor's voice mail. "When may I come in person to interview you for my feature on the new media?"

It's important to note that the term "secretary" or "receptionist" as a sensing judging type refers to the ROLE in the job, not to the personality of the person in the role or on the job. Any personality type can work as a secretary or receptionist. What is meant is that the role of receptionist is a sensing/judging role whose goal is to get the right message to the right party at the right time, and the role of the secretary is as guardian and protector of the boss and conservator of the employer's time. The screening out role played by the secretary is to allow his or her boss to make the most efficient use of time during the workday and to prioritize the boss's time and her/his own.

The best way to meet an editor in person is to interview that person for another publication or for a chapter in a book or pamphlet you're writing— even if you're self-publishing the pamphlet on the Internet on your own Web page. Every new media writer needs a personal Web page to feature articles and showcase editors of publications you want to write for as your goal. Interview new media book publishers for magazine articles online or in print.

Interview magazine publishers and editors-in-chief for books and pamphlets or trade newsletters. Interview a general magazine editor for an article you write for a niche specialty trade journal. Interview a trade journal editor for a chapter in a book or in a general readership magazine unrelated to the editor's publication. For example, the editor of a new media magazine on fixing widgets is 80 years old and working 60 hours a week. Interview that person for a magazine such as Modern Maturity on the joy of being in the new media at 80, "Life Begins Online at 80" for this editor who loves her work.

If you write about career or executive coaching, life coaching or spiritual coaching, your bread and butter is studying how human resources use technology. Write about turnover in the Internet Industry, or the problems ad agencies have of copywriters and Web designers working together and how they solved them.

You need insight, support, and specifics wrapped up by showing how a problem was solved. Your solution needs to show results along with insight, foresight, and hindsight—revealing the pitfalls to avoid.

Most new media problems are universal, even when unique, individual, and practical. Get to the concrete through the universal and show the details. Read between the lines and give the big picture in the first paragraph and the trees rather than the forest in each descending paragraphs. Then sum up with applications to the digital, interactive, or new media fields with showing how the Internet, DVD camcorders, telephony, or other industrial applications fitted in to solve the problem.

CHAPTER 2

How to Pre-sell Your Resume-Writing or Information Repackaging Service

Check out the Web site called ResumeWriters.com at: http://www.resumewriters. com/. It's the largest network of certified professional resume writers on the Internet, according to the company's Web site. Combine being a job coach with writing resumes and business letters for your clients. There are thousands of business letters that clients are eager to see samples and templates showing them how to write these types of letters. Compile such letters you create and market them to your clients who need specific types of business writing. Again, writing letters and resumes can be combined with consulting—being a job coach online. The coaching part emphasizes analyzing skills and preferences with a goal of fitting the right person to the job that is the best fit for both your clients.

Employers as well as job applicants are equally your clients. If you had to choose between employer and job applicant as your bread and butter, your most important client would be the job applicant. That's the individual paying you for writing and coaching. You're like a book doctor working on one person's resume at a time.

When you first open an online home-based business of any type, it's important to get orders for your product before you open your business. This will help you get credit, a loan, or equipment. Graphics-design, resume-writing, and word-processing firms often can take some job orders before buying equipment and opening for business. It's important for publishers, writers, and coaches, to get clients in advance so that advertising contracts can be signed.

You pre-sell your service by doing thorough marketing research to find out how much of a need exists for your business in any given community. First, telephone a representative sample of potential customers and ask whether they would buy your product.

Calling about one hundred people for a small home-based business would give you a clear idea of the attitude toward your business. A mailing list of persons who might be interested in your product can be purchased or rented from a mailing list broker.

Mailing lists in specified categories such as senior citizens, teenagers, persons of a certain religion or ethnic origin, persons with incomes over $100,000 annually, and many other categories are for sale from list brokers. Know your prospective customer base and their buying preferences before you outline a business plan.

Next, a mailing-list survey of five thousand letters announcing your service could bring anywhere from a 5-percent to 15percent response in certain communities and as little as 1 percent in others. The rate of response depends upon your target audience and how deep the need is for your product.

If your business will be generating individualized diets by computer using the tremendous variety of software available for nutritionists, a good target audience would be the mailing list of support groups for persons with ailments such as diabetes, allergies, or hypertension, that demand special diets. You could pre-sell your service to physicians, clinics, diet centers, social clubs, hospitals, and health-food chains. The point is, before you open any type of business, the audience must first be gauged.

Other means of pre-selling your service are free classified ads in newsletters of business associations, religious organizations, and social clubs. Some community newspapers offer free personal classified ads. Use shopping newsletters, daily papers, and radio announcements.

Visibility

To gain visibility, send out a press release, a statement of your goals and objectives, to all the media announcing your forthcoming business. Along with visibility, you will have to earn credibility. To prove yourself, offer benefits and advantages.

Personalize your proving ground. How will you incorporate infomercials into your business plan, if you choose to use them in varying formats? Will you use the new media, print, or a combination of the World Wide Web, print, voice, and visuals?

Have a grand-opening party or raffle off a small prize, such as theater tickets, and print your message on entry ballots. Have people return coupons by mail, so you can obtain a head count of how many people might buy your product. Before you open your doors or invest deeply, recognize that the most important part of your business is your customer. Without market research, you'll have no way of knowing if you are filling a real need.

The Small Business Administration, the Better Business Bureau, chambers of commerce, convention and visitors' bureau, and business associations for people in similar trades have directories and other business aids to help you pre-sell your service before you invest in applications software to run your business.

Magazines such as *Entrepreneur* and organizations like the American Entrepreneurs Association, 2311 Pontius Avenue, Los Angeles, CA 90064, publish business manuals that can teach you to run a tremendous number of businesses, many of them home-based and utilizing your personal computer. Their very affordable manuals can save you a great deal of money because the AEA has already gathered information about running a particular business.

For example, computer their manual in print way back in 1983-84 on how to run a software search business predicted that your average net profit before taxes would have been back then $47,000 with a minimum cash investment of $12,000 with publications today predicting profit. Today, find out whether profit is growing or shrinking. That's one way to practice helping clients solve problems when writing resumes or repackaging their work-style information. Back in the eighties, the manual also noted that the average cash investment would be $25,000 and the high net profit before taxes would be over $85,000. Their profit-potential analysis then also gave an above-average risk factor to opening a software search business.

What would the figures today be like on a similar software search business? Compare average of profit before taxes with your interest area of business with what figures were like ten to fifteen years ago. Will your business plan be for a low-tech or tech-oriented business, or low-tech using software to keep records? Or do you plan a business with use of very little technology? How will you keep your records and do cross-references? What risk factors will influence the writing of your business plan? Despite risk factors, however, your biggest concern initially will be where the money will come from and how it will flow into your business.

How Will Cash Flow Into Your Business?

One of the inevitable dilemmas of running a business is that your suppliers will ask you to pay your bills right away, but your customers usually take months to pay. Some won't pay at all. Checks may bounce. When they do, you should call the customer immediately. If nothing happens, turn the bad check over to a collection agency that specializes in collecting unpaid bills.

The correct cash-flow balance in a business requires that you have the money to pay your bills. You must be able to pay your bills before your customers pay you for your services to them. By doing a cash-flow analysis on your computer, you may be able to tell how much cash you will have on hand. Clients frequently may not pay you on time.

You may prepare a cash-flow sheet for the first three months of your business or do a month-by-month projection for the first year using a cash-flow software program on your computer. Your goal is to determine an actual cash balance. In this way you can see whether you have enough cash to pay off your bills and buy inventory for your business.

You'll need to have cash on hand to buy equipment and supplies and to pay utility bills. A cash-flow statement allows you to see whether you'll need a loan to cover expenses if months pass between the time you must pay for equipment purchased and the date money is due from the charge customers. This is called collections on receivables. The only way you will observe when and where to cut back on expenses is to look at your cash-flow sheet for any particular date. Your computer can generate these reports for any month.

The cash-flow statement is divided into sections that give the source, we, and schedule of cash. Label the first section "Cash Sources." Include here money brought into the business by sales, payments by charge customers, money earned on interest, and money derived from loans. The second section should be called "Cash Utilization." In this category list any inventory, equipment, or supplies you bought for the business. Include any loan payments and loan interest, salaries, and other payments that come out of your cash resources.

The third section can be called "Cash Barometer." List whether your business has been bringing in more or less money on certain days of the month. If the cash coming in is growing less, your computer calendar program should remind you that it's time to take drastic action to see whether you're mismanaging the business or are undercapitalized—the two greatest causes of business failure.

The Internet and your personal computer can help you to manage your time efficiently by the use of a good calendar program. Time management is the most important part of a good business plan because the market is always shifting

We live in a visually oriented society where initial judgments are made on the basis of how the written word appears in print, on the World Wide Web of the Internet, through extranets that reach out to consumers and other businesses, through intranets that reach employees within a single business, and through advertising on television and all the other visual or sound communication formats. That makes your person-to-person direct sales letter keyboarded from a word-processing software program the foremost instrument for selling yourself.

A business plan also tells the world that there's a gold mine in your personal computer's applications software that you can use to operate, measure, and market your business long before you open your doors. Before you write your business plan, track your potential customers' suggestions, needs, and requests. Use feedback.

A business plan also develops, manipulates, combines, or acts on any one or more businesses that most closely match your preferences and work styles to the needs of your audience. All businesses are in a way, show business. The right business plan won't lead you into danger. It works for you.

*   *   *

Market Research on the Internet

So important is doing market research on the Internet, that financier George Soros more than a decade ago, announced plans to fund a new project for developing the Internet in Russia. The $1.5 million Internet plan at that time would link hospitals, museums, schools, and scientific institutes across Russia to the global computer network.

Elsewhere, market research on the Internet has become the ax that breaks ice on a frozen sea of commerce. Before you conduct business or start a company, you do market research. Eight of the nation's largest newspaper companies in the United States soon after the Internet became widely available to the public, began a venture, New Century Network to help newspapers get on the Internet. Goals focused on doing more marketing research, selling more advertising, and reaching more customers. The venture provided consulting assistance and software to newspapers that wished to start electronic services.

The Internet is now an extension of your newspaper and uploads ad rates, deadline schedules, advertising information, along with high-profile news and features. In the marketing research world, New Century Network aimed to help newspapers get advertising, track usage, and bill customers—the key economic incentives for distributing information electronically in the name of market research. The marketing research help is open to all newspapers.

The venture filled a leadership void in the industry, and that's the purpose of doing market research on the Internet-to fill leadership voids, whether by people, products, or services. For more information on New Century Network, research market research history at Cox Newspapers, Inc., or at Advance Publications, Inc., Gannett Co. Inc., Hearst Corp., Knight-Ridder Inc., Times Mirror Co., and the Washington Post Co.

Fax and audio services complement Internet access, but anyone doing market research wants reports fast by E-mail. The phenomenal growth of the World Wide Web has led to new thinking about how information providers can repackage and sell timely market research on the Internet in the form of made-to-order market reports, trade publications, international business newsletters and other publications, abstracts, articles, and numerical tables.

Phone books formerly put on CD have now expanded to the world-wide Web (WWW). On the Internet, there are only virtual storage space problems that formerly surrounded thick phone books and CD holders. NYNEX expanded its online Yellow Pages service to include any business in the United States with a listed phone number. At "The New Interactive Yellow Pages" at: http://www.niyp.com, anyone can access its directory of 16.5+ million businesses that include description about the type of company, name, address, and telephone numbers. Advertising from businesses pays for the Internet-accessible directory. Weblinks to sites of listed companies also are offered.

Use Internet-based research to create market opportunities. At http:www. thenet.com/~CEMA/, you can find out how to identify customers or rank sales opportunities. Learn how to track marketing trends and forecast future trends. Find out how to use and trace distribution channels, or access CEMA's job hotline.

Market research on the Internet refers to a process rather than a product. The transformation of desktop publishing into multimedia centers on the information highway is another growing trend. In 1994, the government didn't even track multimedia as a job category. Today, venture capital funding is being directed to fledgling new media developers. More than a decade ago, a survey in the San Jose Mercury News reported millions of dollars of VC funding going to titles publishers such as Crystal Dynamics, Rocket Science Games, and Starpress Multimedia.

Marketing money is funneling into content companies. Publications such as The Red Herring, a Woodside, California-based financial magazine, are focusing on emerging technologies. More than a decade ago, Paul Dali, of Menlo Park's Nazem & Co. had been called the "godfather of the multimedia venture capital industry." Small developers pay contract workers for contributions to projects, but staff employees are few. In a typical Internet-based multimedia marketing company there's a writer and producer, a graphic designer, a programmer, and a production assistant to scan and process images that eventually go up on the Web or onto a CD or DVD.

Look at market research from a decade in the past. Market research is used a lot by inventors. Visualize an inventor's dream come true. Research the marketing history of these types of inventions. They will help you to understand how marketing works and how marketing changes over the decades.

What if you, as an inventor or a sales representative in search of a product to market, or as a market researcher want made-to-order market reports? Look at the excellent Web site titled Thomson Business Intelligence at:

http://www.profound.com. There's a business solutions market trends site directly on the Internet. Read the excellent, timely market research reports, news, business, and financially information by subscription to those with Web browsers.

If you're selling timeliness to competing companies, you can cash in on various newswire stories or start a marketing business of your own selling newswire stories or summarizing and abstracting breaking news stories on the timeliest wire services. I also recommend to *journalists*, News Release Wire, Broadcast Interview Source, Inc. 2233 Wisconsin Ave. N.W. Washington, DC 20007. The company's Web site is at: newsreleasewire@yearbook.com.

Doing market research on the Internet becomes a viable home based business, should you care to open one, where you could offer market research reports, company profiles and articles, briefings of corporations or industries, nation's briefings. A small marketing business might offer only quotes electronically, not quotes for stocks, but historic quotes, or quotes of the leaders of business, or commercial quotes in general to executives who give many speeches and writers.

There's always a marketing angle if you look deep enough. You can open at home online an **electronic clipping service that market researchers need to track for clients. Sell marketing reports online.** Marketing reports are pricey because without the Internet, finding the most current marketing report on a hard-to-find company—when you want it—becomes complex. Until recently, consulting reports weren't online with the major database services such as DIALOG at http://www.dialog.com/. Trademark and patent searches had been on the database services for years. Your business can specialize in searching Thomson & Thomson files and Dun&Bradstreet's. You can search the same files with DIALOG.

You also can open an online home-based public relations service. Your enterprise can thrive on collecting news clippings because customer's frequently don't pay unless they see something in print about their business in the media. The AutoSearch and WorldSearch offers marketing researchers "a power search." Market research reports are on Researchline. Consulting reports at Companyline has corporate profiles. Digging deeper, you can access Disclosure and financial information. There are also Companyline, Brokerline, Newsline, Countryline, and Briefings, for market researchers who need a brief overview of a particular industry such as paper or convenience stores.

Off clients newswire stories in tabloid format as an additional service besides writing resumes and business letters or repackaging business information. Generate reports in PDF or other document format. It's interesting to note that if you choose to open your own business on the Internet specializing in providing articles to businesses, perhaps a collection of timely trade journal articles, the current rate for such articles from freelance businesses is around $20 to $40 per article and more than $4,000 for a full consulting report. You can specialize in providing medical or business reports for a variety of niche businesses or industrial specializations. Look at the array of trade and academic journals on every subject from DNA-driven genealogy to trade publications on digital imaging.

You can sell two pages of market intelligence as a freelancer on the Internet for $25 each. For example, you can buy two pages of market intelligence from Packaged Facts or Frost & Sullivan at a cost of under $50. So if you're searching the Internet for a business of your own, you might take inspiration from the marketing report and research firms online and startup your own pre-packaged marketing information businesses catering to trade journal readers or specific industries as your target audience. There's a lot of money to be made in writing and packaging consulting reports or articles related to marketing research for specific industries and companies.

Many marketing research firms are devoted to analyzing television shows for advertising agencies whose clients want feedback on their commercials between shows. A free shareware, movies-only version of TV Now's database at www.tvnet.com/TVNow/tvhow.html lets you select movies by director or actor in addition to the more usual "what's on" queries.

Market researchers are frequently involved in tracking what people watch, especially former customers of a business whose television watching preferences influence what they buy later. To start a marketing business that relates to this, try offering sneak previews of upcoming movie scripts by Gopher server. Use excerpts from scenes, like trailers do.

Marketing research and other shareware can be accessed at http://www.shareware.com/help-download.html or at http://www.shareware. com. Macintosh software can be downloaded at http://www.interlog.com/~qd/ mac.html. IBM shareware software is at http://silver.ucs.indiana.edu/ ~nouyang/ IBM.html, nicely organized into categories. You can post your own brochures in a Gopher server menu to build loyalty of customers. If your customers skate, maybe they also ski. So you can market all types of related gear.

Internet marketing is profitable when it comes to self-marketing or marketing one's visibility and credibility online. Market researchers whose clients sell or distribute household cleaning products will be pleased to know that home pages exist that share cleanup hints. Collected stain-removing tips useful to marketers are on the Internet at DuPont's home page, http://www.dupont.com/including the mills that make the latest styles.

Shiadeh, at http://www.orientalrugs.com/, an oriental rug dealer in Ardmore, Pennsylvania offered a stain-removal table listing source and carpet fiber cleaning tips such as using mustard to clean acrylic fibers and beer to clean wool rugs. They also trained you to differentiate Mideast and Asian rugs. Crayola, Inc., at http://www.crayola.com/marketed its products by showing you how to remove crayon scribbles from all types of surfaces by spraying with WD-40 lubricant followed by liquid detergent and using paper towels to pick up stains.

More cleanup hints for marketers trying to advertise their products and for anyone else are at http://www.ces.msstate.edu/pubs/is 1436.htm, the Mississippi State University Cooperative Extension, and at: <http://www. ag.uiuc.edu/~robsond/solutions/consumer/stain.html>, the University of Illinois Cooperative Extension Services, and at the World Wide Quilting Page at http://www.ttsw.com/Quilt.html, with the Frequently Asked Questions (FAQ) page containing stain removal information.

Marketing researchers often provide car rental information, supply banking information, answer fitness machine or bicycling questions, offer safety and security tips, or maintain Telnet sites for their representatives. They promote universities through home pages that feature pictures of campuses and tuition information, provide insurance information, and offer home-repair advice all in the name of obtaining consumer feedback.

Marketing information even extended to individuals protesting rate hikes. Another way market researchers can reach their audiences to track them and sell products could be through greeting cards on the Internet, particularly greeting cards that move other products or services. On-line cards for a variety of holidays, like online post cards, are excellent marketing tools as are corporate gift baskets..

Sell articles for a fee. Offer researchers advice or help business owners find answers to start-up questions. Let users search through ads for small businesses for sale across the United States with the weekly updates Help researchers identify businesses to do market research or purchase or investigate. For a fee, let users download the contact name and number that accompanies a listing. You can charge a dollar per search or whatever the market will bear favorably.

Look at publications such as American Demographics, Computerworld, Forbes, Harvard Business Review, Journal of Small Business Management, Marketing News, Nation's Business, and Small Corporation Update. What other marketing publications will help you? Does your computer operating system have a search icon that lets you access every publication on DataTimes? Look at magazines such as Business Week, Forbes, and Fortune. You can access transcripts from ABC, NBC, and CBS broadcasts. Local newspapers are there and specific industry news sources such as Hazardous Waste News, and European Cosmetics Markets.

TRW Business Credit Reports are online there, and other financial information. Market researchers will like the Disclosure and Standard & Poor's profiles of corporations, investment house reports from the largest stockbrokerage firms, and investment strategies.

Today's RSS news feeds and MP3 audio file podcasts and icons monitor news wires and sources. Research information online such as that offered by DataTimes. Look for news media sources from Reuters or the Federal News Service. Offer market researcher's basic tools or industry profiles. Offer prepackaged and executive reports in niche areas not covered by the larger market research services online. If someone already is doing stock searches, for example, find a niche where you can offer industry reports or business directories in another line not covered. What about niche groups surfing the Internet or people over age 70? Who reaches and researches children surfing the Internet?

Market researchers encourage parents to link the entire family to the Web in order to create a smart home within a smart community. Marketers who want to sell more tickets to live theater plays have Web pages. What about organizing groups of local artists online? Offer calendars, ticket information, membership services, press releases, education components, histories, behind-the scenes peeks, surveys, interviews, live chats with directors, crafts people, and cast are on the Internet, all designed to sell tickets to live actor theatrical plays. Theaters are putting costume design sketches, stage notes, and scripts online too, all to market their plays to more theater-goers. So find your niche.

Drama classes and patrons are tuning in to the home pages, and more ticket sales are the goal. Research online ethnic communities that want people outside it's neighborhoods to know about its ethnic food and music. It's a market researcher's dream to find all this unique feedback, customized and individualized on the Internet.

Super cyber cities that link to the future creating "the smart community" is the dream of market researchers. They'd like customers to be able to pay for tickets on the Internet, print out shopping lists at Internet-access consoles in supermarkets, or buy licenses at a convenience store that's linked to the Web. In a smart community, market researchers can obtain instant access to schools, government, medical facilities, consumers, and business all linked electronically to the Internet.

Market research on the Internet done from tele-centers and video-conferencing from desktop computers linked to the Internet make this possible now. National university in 1996 began using its video-conferencing facility for continuing education programs, so students a long drive or bus ride away wouldn't have to travel to class. It's up and running in Chula Vista, California, for now. The public schools in Chula Vista are wired for computers. Juarez-Lincoln Elementary School has its own home page on the Web, and soon all schools in the district will have their own home pages on the Web, too.

You can establish an Internet site connecting an area's homes with schools for electronic mail, homework, and school news. Write to your city and ask the people with the authority to connect the entire community to find baby sitters or make reservations. All this "smart community" access makes marketing researcher easier for those in the profession of collecting information about marketing to "smart communities (well-connected electronically, marketers say)." Start a smart communities-type Web site in your local community. To inspire ideas, look at the Web site of the *World Foundation for Smart Communities* at: http://www.smartcommunities.org/.

Contact your city's local marketing association. The San Diego American Marketing Association is a local chapter of the American Marketing Association. See their Web site at: http://sandiego.marketingpower.com/. Is there an American Marketing Association Chapter in your city? Look at the job hotline. Network, and make contacts at meetings. The national association, American Marketing Association's Web site is at http://www.ama.org/.

How many ways can marketing researchers create money-making opportunities from their Internet connections? Marketing researchers and communicators can make money on the Internet by sending updated price and product information to customers. Instead of creating a news group, create an income-generating feedback group where customers who use your product can exchange how-to tips and other useful information about the product.

Offer free technical support by E-mail. Provide tips by auto-response E-mail, including supplementary information such as timely articles and updates. Send reminders to regular customers. Gift marketers and florists could target birthdays and holidays. Dentists send post-cards when to come in for a checkup. Try E-mail, too. Track customized commercial activity on the Internet. Offer current reports and updates. Take online seminars in marketing.

Here's how to use market research on the Internet to increase profits for your business or to start a new business online, using everything the Internet offers. Create a different drummer newsletter. Share company stories with customers to strengthen relationships and include them in your company's family. Generate fan mail and testimonials by asking your customers what they like about your product or service. Use E-mail.

An electronic suggestion box can help you brainstorm new ideas for marketing or opening a business. Publish the E-mail addresses of executives so they can be reached for detailed feedback. Announce new products on the

Internet and by individual E-mail. Publishers can reach readers with lists of new books. Offer technical information on the Internet by a series of auto-replay mailboxes. Use an E-mail address where people can write for more information about a product.

Market researchers like to do customer surveys by E-mail because it saves postage. Surveys are designed to get feedback for tracking customer responses to your product or service. It's a way of improving advertising at low cost.

If you offer direct service, it's cheaper. Too many lawyers try to market their business by spending days trying to figure out what potential clients need. Later, data is constantly re-entered. Save time by E-mailing your service directly. Distribute news releases. Anyone in the media loves the Internet.

Send electronic news releases to customers and the media. It's to the Internet what video news release was to television and radio in the eighties. Most journalists like to get news releases by E-mail to save storage space and paper recycling chores. E-mail targets your best prospects. Most high-level executives are hard to reach by phone or postal mail. Keep the queries brief.

If you're a financial marketer, send money-related information to lists of stockholders. They'd appreciated being updated about the company where their money is invested. You can offer a mailing list that automatically sends E-mail to stockholders with timely information. These are online home-based business suggestions if you want to expand your resume-writing business. Products need to be upgraded and recalled at various times. E-mail is the quickest way to reach a lot of customers at low cost. Mailing printed notices are expensive. The usual direct marketing mail is through news releases. An electronic mailing list of updated customer's addresses can be sold to manufacturers if you start this type of small marketing update business on the Internet.

For marketing promotion, an electronic fan club works well, but if you're marketing someone's book, subscribing to the author's mailing list works better. Ask universities whether the particular book would interest them. Provide subscribers to similar mailing lists, or your list site in case there's an interest in the author's (or your) books. Start a mailing list for readers of your own books. Ask subscribers to mailing lists related to authors and their works, whether they think the market in which you're interested—such as mystery novels—is already saturated with that genre before you write or market a particular book.

Of the hundreds of ways to market a product or do market research on the Internet, the best way of marketing anything is to let customers share information using RSS content syndication or podcasting of MP3 audio files that any listener can download and save to play later.

Marketers a decade ago sent annual reports by automail servers. In order to save money on an answering service, an automail server also was able to answer key questions about your fees and services. Today, a variety of servers are available to marketers, including the popular RSS news feeds at Web sites, syndication online, pod casts of MP3 audio files, streaming video, and various news feeds to which anyone online can subscribe. Stockholders shouldn't be the only ones interested in your annual report.

Journalists also use reports to create visibility in trade magazines and the daily news, for job applicants, and customers. Create a gopher server so users can download pictures of your product, resort, home, or business. Content also is syndicated by RSS feeds and in audio with MP3 audio files in podcasting from Web sites. You, too, can also stream video on the Internet or send it on a DVD or other disc format. It's one more form of pushing the news at you and publicizing or promoting information to help people make choices—logical, visual, or emotional.

A decade ago, businesses on the Internet used to let users select groceries by Telnet. The groceries were selected and delivered. Other online businesses published pet care information, followed alumni for contributions, prepared tax returns, offered moving advice, provided antique information, recruited fitness club members, provided church information, critiqued resumes, posted restaurant menus, offered painting tips, provided home health care data, and offered a News Net of everything in trade journals all in the name of providing Web users with industry events.

Trade journals such as Modern Plastics, Commercial Mortgage Alert, and Medical devices Litigation Newsletter went online with NewsNet and its software, Baton. The online service monitored industry events by its NewsFlash feature for industrial and financial information. World-wide marketing research on patents is now at Questel Orbit Intellectual Property Group at: http://www.qpat.com/jsp/login.jsp.

MicroPatent is at http://www.micropat.com/, and Master-McNeil, Inc., product and naming service is at http://www.naming.com/naming.html. Many market researchers have opened a small home based business tracking scientific and technical or trade journals and delivering Internet information packages to consumers.

You get the information from journals, books, and proceedings or clinical trial publications and track the table of contents of many journals. One company, Research Direct Alert is online at http://www.isinet.com. Also checkout http://journals.at-home.com to find the tables of contents and abstracts of scientific and medical journals. These tracking businesses are useful tools for marketing researchers doing customized work for busy professionals and corporations.

Financial information for individual firms on the Internet is at http://www.tipnet.com. Federal news is at http://www.access.gpo.gov/

su_docs/. Only by creating your own online group of marketing researchers and Internet searchers working together, can you establish a marketing research service that monitors and selects pertinent material from the news groups for your clients. Check your Internet server's own home page for marketing material.

The Burwell Directory of Information Brokers contains more than 1,500 names of marketing researchers and other information brokers. An information broker offers services of finding and packaging information for profit, often on the Internet or on other databases. A marketing researcher is concerned with consumer feedback and tracking sales online and by other means, such as telephone interviewing.

One of the first places market researchers hit online are the companies that offer online or CD-ROM databases of trademarks. If you need to search the trademarks to see if anyone else shares the same name of your product, a trademark search is required before you find you have infringed on someone else's trademark. Thomson & Thompson's home page at http://www.thomson.com/thomthom.html, lists regulations, groups, laws, government agencies, and any other pertinent information about trademarks.

The U.S. Patent and Trademark Office is at http://www.uspto.gov. Learn from their pamphlets how the process works or find the libraries that have the trademark documents. At http://www.naming.com, find Master-McNeil, Berkeley, California, a creative and strategic naming services firm that offers on the Internet the complete international trademark class list.

Some marketing businesses on the Internet specialize in doing trademark searches. These service businesses make a living from searching files online. The Easy Online Trademark Research & Registration site is at http://law.net/sponsors/tm/.

DataStar is at http://www.rs.ch/www/rs/datastar.html. Also try ARIndustries at http://warrior.com/tmsearch. For Japanese trademark searches, try http://www.netaxs.com/~aengel/ista.html. ISTA's source is a Japanese CD-ROM.

For more trademark information, try http://www.uspto.gov/cgi-bin/goods-services.pl. It's an index of the Trademark acceptable Identification of Goods and Services Manual. Yahoo lists its own Guide to Trademark Information on the Internet at http://www.yahoo.com/Law/Intellectual_Property/Trademarks/.

If two products are similar and have similar names, there is more of a chance of trademark infringement than if two products are totally different, yet still have similar names. When doing market research on the Internet, success brings scrutiny.

If you know the business of the "intelligence broker" and the market researcher, you can combine the two skills profitably searching markets on the

Internet for whatever niche you create and customize for your clients. Keeping track and studying queries that come into your E-mail also can be lucrative.

Marketing research directors could sample E-Mail queries. Feedback provided by tracking and answering E-mail inquiries informs you what voids need to be filled by your marketing research or your new business direction. Helping a potential customer online by answering E-mail inquiries encourages people to return later to buy. Valuing the individual's E-mail importance also lends credibility and visibility to your service.

If you receive an overwhelming number of E-mail queries, answer the most important ones first. When you can no longer answer individual inquires, put universal answers on a Web page like a "Dear Abby" column or a "How-To" tips page. Track responses. Start with RSS feeds and MP3 podcasting audio files on your Web site.

You may soon find yourself marketing a valuable news column and niche mailing list, or using E-mail to respond to someone else's direct marketing E-mail in your box. Internet users don't like uninvited direct response marketing mail, but they do want a Website to retrieve marketing information about the evaluation and prices of products and corporations. The most direct marketing research is desktop videoconferencing on the Internet combining desktop publishing with Web phones. Add to that multicasting through personal broadcasting networks on-line. When you start an online business at home, it can branch far beyond offering to write resumes and business letters for clients.

✶   ✶   ✶

Tracking Progress for a Living

If you want to sell information about your business or your business information, write in the publications that show other writers how to write as well as in the trade publications and books. Track progress in others and write about progress. Only don't sound like a publicity press release. Dig in deeper and ask why the good fortune happened. Track the steps the person took to reach a success story or other experience.

The new media wants writing that shows what programs exist, who participated and benefit by which aspect of it. Write about what people are doing in terms they can understand. Know your reader. Write for the professional in the trade journal and for the beginner in the general magazines and e-zines.

New media focuses on trade journals. In your query letter, give a bare bones solution to a problem the editor needs to have. Ask first to find out what problem has to be solved. Then find the expert to interview who solves the problem step by step. Write about that. Focus on what's most cost-efficient.

Let your reader choose which solution they want to use as a marketing tool for their own new media business or interest. Write about the benefits and advantages of value to the readers. The editors of any new media publication have similar goals. They want articles or books that show that the writer can define the problem and then solve the problem. Define the problem for which you'll solve the problem. Research all your niches. If you're a generalist who can't solve any type of problem in the new media, then find experts to interview who have solved current problems or who can offer quotes that solve problems for readers.

Stick with the niches. Every new media writer needs a tag name. It's like a tag line in a romance novel. "She said, with a sneer of disdain," (how she said it—the body language—is your tag line). In a nonfiction article or book chapter, your tag line identifies how you manage risk within your paragraph. You define the arrangements rather than the body language. The arrangements include equipment, supplies, and customized services that your expert discusses and solves problems within your article.

New media writing can be hypermedia or hypertext fiction, interactive fiction, game scripts, or drama, or nonfiction, trade journal, and training or general advice writing, as in investment newsletters online. The genres are unlimited. You can write about office systems and equipment or how people react behaviorally to computer information overload.

To market new media writing, position yourself as a writer specializing in a niche within a niche. For example, suppose you used to be a nurse, medical records clerk, physician, lawyer, or teacher who now wants to write full time for the new media. You position yourself as a writer of books and e-zines, or interactive media specializing in writing about computer problems that law offices, medical offices, or schools have. You interview consultants with expertise. What you're marketing about your niche is that you have a name and a tag that always will work for you as you gain experience writing about a very narrow niche—at least at first.

Your goal is to get finely honed experience marketing new media pieces about a small specialty i.e., how medical offices can use specialty software. The former medical records clerk or technician now can write for two dozen hospital and medical trade journals from emergency medical care to running the medical office in terms of economics, solely by specializing in interviewing computer consultants who focus on telling doctors how to solve their computer software and hardware problems in running their office or department.

Read magazines such as Home Office Computing. These specialty niche magazines and trade publications help you build your reputation, if you can write for them. To find people to interview, seek referrals from former clients of computer consultants. Market yourself as a speechwriter, and develop speeches for computer and new media consultants. Approach their colleagues and clients and offer to write their speeches too, for presentations or publication.

Query the new media publications of national associations and organizations where the clients of consultants join and attend trade shows and conferences. You attend also. Your market research as a writer would be to analyze press releases from companies about whom you want to write. When you interview people for the new media, it's a little different than when you interview for the print media.

In the digital media, you listen and question with the goal of turning opportunities into business. In the new media you compose your interview questions with the goal of:

1. Diagnosing problems—one question at a time.

2. Ask your interviewee how that person designed the solution. Most people who solve problems for a living focus on thinking rather than feeling and they use the logic to design the solution. Most people who solve relationship problems use feeling, but they don't design the solution, they solve it through placing a quality of worth on the solution, as in "Is it worth it?" Degrees or values of how much it's worth in terms of well being or feelings solve problems.

Ask the person you're interviewing how the work was delivered. In the new media, anyone you interview will try to debrief you after you finish the interview. Be aware of this. What helps most is to keep a profile of people you interview. They are your clients.

Return to your interviewee profile now and then to ask the people who talked to you and saw your article in print to tell you who else they know who might be interested in having their problems solved by a new interview with the same person or other colleagues that person recommend you interview.

To market your new media writing, ask questions. Don't talk. Ask the person you interview if the individual is aware of the many magazines (name them) who might be interested in articles about their business with new angles.

If you don't like your editor's contract, use your own contract documents. It may work with a few, new media publications that are beginning to startup. Keep a journal about the new media.

Use buzzwords when writing for the new media. Only use NEW BUZZ-WORDS. Use "rocketpack" more often than "cyberspace." Editors are so tired of cyberspace. How about words such as "help desk?" Have your buzzwords in the first paragraph of your article, script, interactive introduction, or book chapter. Buzz words, like tag lines, define your writing and reveal the timeliness and freshness of your information.

If you're trying to market your writing to a new media publication, it's better to show up in person at the editor's office, even if it's only to hand a query letter with a sample article to the receptionist. In the world of email where you must send your article across the globe, showing up in person at a publisher's business still works better than faxing, emailing, or snail mailing. If you're relatively nearby, show up in person dressed appropriately, and hand your material to a live person. Always hand in both a paper and a disk copy of what you write. Nobody likes to retype your material to disk.

The new media writer is hired for his or her technical knowledge. You're paid for what problem you can solve, for how you can think. A problem to be solved for the writer is how to market information about the new media when you have a non-technical education, such as a broad liberal arts education with a degree in creative writing or fiction writing.

To solve this problem, get the name of the editor who has the power to buy your writing or assign you something to write. Call the receptionist and ask for the mailing address. The (role not the person) or job of a receptionist is "sensing-judging" (SJ)—to get the right messages to the right people at the right time. The secretary's job (the role, not the person) is to screen you out from reaching the editor and bothering the person. It's a protective, guardian role.

The job of the editorial assistant is also to screen out the slush pile and protect the editor-in-chief from having to wade through the masses coming over the transom. Therefore, after you have the mailing address and have asked the receptionist for the correct spelling of the editor's name, ask to leave a message in the editor's voice mail. "When may I come in person to interview you for my feature on the new media?"

It's important to note that the term "administrative assistant" or "receptionist" refers to the *role* in the job, not to the personality of the individual in the role or on the job. Any personality preference can work as an administrative assistant, general office clerk, or receptionist. What is meant is that the role of receptionist is to get the right message to the right party at the right time, and the role of the administrative assistant (what used to be called an executive secretary two decades ago) is as guardian and protector of the boss and conservator of the employer's time.

An administrative assistant today might also be an event planning assistant or a personal assistant in a corporate setting and sometimes perform public relations work with the media in addition to more traditional duties as letter writer, appointment setter, and records or case history manager. The screening out role played by the secretary of two decades ago is today still focused on how to allow his or her boss to make the most efficient use of time during the workday and to prioritize the boss's time and her/his own.

The best way to meet an editor in person is to interview that person for another publication or for a chapter in a book or pamphlet you're writing—even if you're self-publishing the pamphlet on the Internet on your own Web page. Every new media writer needs a personal Web page to feature articles and showcase editors of publications you want to write for as your goal. Interview new media book publishers for magazine articles online or in print.

Interview magazine publishers and editors-in-chief for books and pamphlets or trade newsletters. Interview a general magazine editor for an article you write for a niche specialty trade journal. Interview a trade journal editor for a chapter in a book or in a general readership magazine unrelated to the editor's publication.

For example, the editor of a new media magazine on fixing widgets is 80 years old and working 60 hours a week. Interview that person for a magazine such targeting people over age 50 on the joy of being in the digital media at 80, "Life Begins Online at 80" for this editor who loves her work.

If you write about digital media human resources instead of technology, write about turnover in the Internet Industry, or the problems ad agencies have of copywriters and Web designers working together and how they solved them.

Digital media writing markets well when you offer insight, support, and specifics wrapped up by showing how a problem was solved. Most new media problems are universal, even when unique, individual, and practical.

Get to the concrete through the universal and show the details. Read between the lines and give the big picture in the first paragraph and the trees rather than the forest in each descending paragraphs. Then sum up with applications to the digital, interactive, or new media and how the Internet, CD-ROM, telephony, or other industrial application fitted in to solve the problem.

CHAPTER 3

Combining Being a Job Coach with Writing Several Types of Resumes for Clients

According to the Wall Street Journal, "Career management coaches…can identify missing skills or style difficulties and offer pragmatic tips…" Learning how to present your client's competencies can lead to further training to become a job coach.

When you have learned to be a job coach, you can combine job coaching with writing resumes, business letters, and help your client find work rather than simply help your client get appointments for job interviews. Contact the Coach Training Alliance at: http://www.coachtrainingalliance.com/. You can combine resume-writing services with helping others succeed as a career coach. The function of a job or career coach is to help people reach a specific goal related to career issues.

According to the **Coach Training Alliance** Web site (at the time this book goes to press) the site reports that, "Within six months, you will be a Certified Coach with **paying clients in a growing practice.**" The Coach Training Alliance (CTA) is located at: 885 Arapahoe Avenue, Boulder, Colorado 80302 USA. Courses in career and other types of coaching are offered, including downloadable courseware and tele-courses, as well as courses in executive and corporate coaching.

What Other Services Can You Add to Career Coaching?

If you want to be a job or career coach, you'll have to put your skills in context and see what new skills you'll need to enhance the life experience skills you already have. Be aware of the various niches or specialties in coaching. These niches include the following and have room to expand personal services such as writing resumes, business letters, news releases, promotional material on your clients, public relations services, career-related ghostwriting, editing, screening, executive relocation services for career transfers, including families moving to new locations, retirement coaching, extreme telecommuting, and helping people classify skills to find new careers:

- Life Coaching
- Career Coaching
- Executive Coaching
- Personal Coaching
- Leadership Coaching
- Spiritual Coaching
- Mentor Coaching
- Relationship Coaching
- Corporate Coaching
- Support Group Coaching
- Facilitating
- Resume & Business Letter Writing Personal Service Business
- Event Planner

Whatever specialty you choose to combine if you want to be both a career coach and run a resume and business letter-writing service, understand what coaching is. It's a professional service that provides clients with foresight, insight and hindsight. You give your clients feedback and show them what pitfalls to avoid. You offer guidance as an outsider. Your life and business experience are used all the time along with your people skills.

You can be a coach online or face-to-face. If you're introverted and people drain you, yet you love to offer information to people, run your business entirely online or by correspondence. If you're an extrovert energized by constant contact with people face-to-face, you can be a mobile coach or have people visit you or run your business on the telephone.

Sometimes clients you meet when you open a job-coaching business online also can be beneficial for obtaining clients for your business letter writing and resume writing services. It's easiest to combine corporate and executive coaching with business letter writing services. And job or career coaching is more easily combined with operating a resume-writing service.

I. Employers Hire Your Clients to Increase their Corporation's Advantages and Benefits

Each year in the United States 10 million employees are terminated from their jobs. Another 10 million workers leave voluntarily. Every five years the entire work force turns over. Twenty million job seekers annually wonder how to repackage their competencies. Resumes are viewed as safety nets. Is your resume easy to understand?

Only three questions clarify goals in a resume:

1) Where have you been?

2) How long have you been there?

3) Where are you going?

These are the same three goal-clarifying questions asked of travelers by every border crossing guard in the world. Writing a resume is similar to crossing a boundary. Moving forward challenges you to seek a better future.

Employers hire you for reasons of their own. Many are concerned with the clarity of your goals.

List Your Client's Benefits

An employer looks for benefits such as familiar patterns in any resume that you write for your client. Look for patterns that are found in the company. The corporation or educational institution sees your resume as a predictor of the company's future. You're hired for very concrete, common sense reasons.

You're hired to solve problems. You're hired because you're the least possible risk to the company. An employer invests hundreds of thousands of dollars in your salary, insurance, on-the-job training, perks, and other benefits during the time you're working for the firm.

You're hired to increase profit and production and create new markets. You're hired because you made it your business to learn all you can about the company. You adopted the company and showed your enthusiasm concerning the company's goals.

Small business entrepreneurs see your resume as a future spin-off of their plans for expansion. In contrast, an employer might look at a carelessly written resume and see self-rejection. Or an employer might only observe whether your skills fit the exact needs of the company at a given time. You're hired for your excellence.

Emphasize Your Client's Key Benefits

Everyone in the computer industry is hired to organize. Yet the most common complaint of personnel departments is that the resumes coming in aren't organized to emphasize the applicant's most beneficial abilities.

A resume aimed at the sales department of a computer company should look very different from one targeting a job as a training manager. A resume for a job as a graphic artist or corporate animator will emphasize different benefits than one that is addressed to the director of research and development. Combine job/career coaching with resume design. Plan a resume.

What Are Your Client's Natural Abilities?

Designing a resume around your client's life purpose means emphasizing what your client does well and does easily or naturally. Before you begin to plan a resume, ask yourself the following five questions:

1. What kind of mental or physical work would you do as a labor of love without ever being paid?

2. What job would you choose if you knew you could not get fired for doing your best?

3. What work activities offer you enough mental and physical challenges for life long growth?

4. Does your resume show how you spend your time and money doing what you love to do?

5. When listing your successes, ask yourself: what was there about the situation that makes you consider it a success? Then express that on your resume. An employer wants to know why you consider your work successful.

Recognize Opportunities for Success

If the activities your clients enjoy most can't go on your resume because they aren't related to your career, it indicates an opportunity you have finally recognized. Change your career. If you don't want to change your career, then change the job description and duties within the same career.

For example, if you are a medical transcriber doing word processing on a computer all day and don't enjoy it, perhaps you would enjoy being a manufacturer's representative selling medical records software to hospitals as you travel. You might enjoy meeting new people and talking about the efficiency and benefits of software, instead of keyboarding data.

If you would rather have a more recreational career, you might enjoy working as a computer camp counselor or owner/manager of a computer camp.

Computer camps allow children or adults to learn about computers while vacationing in a recreational camp environment.

Another avenue is that of the computer playroom designer or play shop consultant. Learn the creation of joy by participation in use of all the senses. You can become a playographer, a person who studies play behavior around the globe, or a designer of playgrounds for older adults or children.

If your business is writing resumes, you still need to understand how to express creativity in practical ways by putting into words how your client applies imagination. Change the way you play at your work because it's very profitable to enjoy what you're doing. What goes into a resume reflects what your client enjoys doing most.

II. Understanding an Organization's Character & Nature
Each Organization Has Its Own Character

If you are going to be a job coach and a resume and business letter writer, you need to understand the characters of organizations. Are you familiar with the character of the organization for which your client wants to work?

A job coach and a resume writer need to understand the characters of corporations reflect the characters of their owners and sometimes of key employees. People have different personality styles. Companies are made up of people with often conflicting personality preferences. These personality differences approach solutions to problems in very different ways, but the outcome may be similar when results are studied. Differences lie in the step-by-step solutions that outsiders can follow. Different people may have used different steps or paths to arrive at the same result.

Like people, companies have different personalities that reflect the attitudes and preferences of whoever is in charge. Comparing your personality type to the character of an organization before you apply there is known as taking the personality-centered approach to job hunting.

By matching your personality type with the character of an organization, you can create optimum productivity in any situation where you have to work with others. When the work is satisfying, you will do your best.

When the people for whom you work cause too many conflicts, you'll be more interested in looking elsewhere for better opportunities. Employers want your personality type and preferences to fit the character of the organization. Each employer has developed patterns and habits, and may look for these same patterns in your resume.

Why Organizations Act As They Do

How do you find out a company's character? Why are companies so hard to change? Refer to the company's attitudes not the personal views of one interviewer. Ask an employer these two questions before mailing in your resume:
1) Where is the company going?
2) What is its mission or philosophy? (You want to know what the company is all about).

There are only two ways the company will answer. Either it will describe itself as a benchmarking or as a visioning organization. For information on benchmarking, visioning and the character of organizations, read <u>The Character of Organizations</u>, by William Bridges, Consulting Psychologists Press, Palo Alto, CA 1992.

These terms are fully discussed in his excellent book. Now, let's briefly take a look at **other** definitions of companies emphasizing tradition and what's worked before compared to companies emphasizing change and looking for something different.

Tradition-Seeking Companies

The corporate world often uses the word benchmarking. The term has appeared in several books on organizational behavior to describe companies emulating what's worked well before. Tradition-seeking organizations model themselves after other companies that make something very successfully as a way to determine how things ought to be made. Benchmarkers, or to use more familiar words to those not in the business world yet, tradition-seeking companies, emulate the best and most popular. An example is the company that tries to model itself after Intel today or IBM (a decade before the compatibles competed). The tradition-seeking corporation simply wants to model itself after the most successful company where everything worked right.

Intuitive Corporations

Change-seeking companies are idea-focused. These companies have often been described as 'visioning' or change-seeking. These future-oriented companies enjoy looking into the future for new possibilities and new ways of doing things. These new ways must satisfy a great need.

Visioning or change-oriented companies seek out new ideas, new ways to think, however wild, imaginative, creative, and fantastic as long as they work. The word 'visioning' is often used in technology to describe a kind of forward-looking, user-oriented, intuitive boss who enjoys hiring smart people with new or better ideas that can be turned into new products.

San Francisco is the official headquarters for the interactive multimedia industry, the ultimate in visioning. For further information on interactive communications, write to this group: San Francisco Multimedia Development, 2601 Mariposa St., San Francisco, CA 94110.

Examples of *visioning*-type of ideas a variety of industries are presently developing into actual projects and business ventures include the following:

- Virtual reality equipment or desktop animation software for public entertainment and training surgeons, pilots, architects, designers, and soldiers.
- Hypermedia and new media publications.
- Robots for education and military security.
- Artificial intelligence for financial database management and predicting growth stocks.
- Software for fashion designers.
- Video tape and computers in desktop animation.
- Satellite linked cable, computers, and wireless phones.
- Interactive CD for distance learning or entertainment.
- Fiber optics to link multimedia information highways and libraries.
- Electronic tracking.
- Media laboratories.
- Branching pathway fiction with alternate adventures.
- Computer game icon agents.
- Telecommunications, conferencing, and phone line-computer-satellite links.
- Electronic universal information libraries.
- University courses by computer-to-home linkups.
- Software for fashion designers.
- Camera and camcorder cell phones
- Satellite linked cable, computers, and wireless phones.
- Interactive multimedia compact disks for distance teaching or entertainment.

Know the Organization's Needs

A company's character defines how it communicates its needs. The organization shows you the hole that has to be filled. The character of your resume defines how you communicate what you are about and where you are going. Visioning people need to be matched with visioning organizations.

Before you send your resume blindly to any company, understand what kinds of help that organization needs. Getting hired has a lot to do with being in the right place at the right time. Benchmarking employees feel better when they are working with benchmarking companies.

Fitting In With the Group vs. Work Competency

Your online clients will be consulting you to write resumes or generate sales letters, reports, cover letters, or follow-ups, are not hired only for their skills and competencies. They are hired because they fit in with the group.

As an entrepreneur, how can you put words on paper so that an employer and a whole industry find a comfortable fit with your client? Comfortable fit works both ways. More people are terminated for personality conflicts than for incompetence or tardiness.

Every advertising agency on Madison Avenue knows "you don't get a second chance to make a first impression," as stated in the marketing classic, Positioning: The Battle For Your Mind.

Positioning works the same way for job hunters in the computer industry. You only get one chance to position your first impression. The company's first impression of you is your cover letter followed by your resume.

The first impression is like a mirror held up to a company's image. When an employer looks at your client's resume, that person wants to see similarities of skills, talents, and goals.

The resumes you write for other people reveal which part of a particular industry feels right for your client. What you write is an image of your client on paper or online. A resume is propaganda. It's a buzz piece—publicity. It's a newswire.

That resume is designed to manipulate the reader with visual images even though no image is on the paper. Using only words, you have to create a visual image. It's like writing the positive image-arousing words, "think of a pink elephant." Immediately, the reader will visualize a pink elephant in his mind's eye.

Impulsive vs. Compulsive Organizations

Like people, companies come in compulsive and impulsive types. It's important to match a compulsive routine-seeking job hunter who offers dependability, loyalty, service, and duty with the same type of employer.

The compulsive company emphasizes the security of and need to belong to a large, solvent firm offering steady work. Routine isn't seen as stressful while climbing the corporate ladder. (Example: hospitals, government, schools, and the military.)

Equally important for the impulsive applicant, is to be matched with an independent, change-oriented, and innovative employer. The impulsive company emphasizes time flexibility, creativity, achievements, analysis, communication, and a nonlinear fast track to the top. Advancement in an impulsive organization is based on ingenuity, inventiveness, and hot-track profits.

Examples of impulsive computer industry organizations include the following:

Cutting edge virtual reality companies, software firms dealing with the newest in CD-ROM interactive learning machines and software, educational software and video production firms, computer games manufacturers, artificial intelligence research firms, the most successful computer publications, the computer training management industry, computer human resources specialists, special effects/corporate animation/computer graphics, and simulation software design firms.

Other examples of compulsive companies include:

Banks, utilities companies, law enforcement and computer security, accounting firms, electronic systems suppliers, the electronic home response industry, home healthcare software suppliers, and the more traditional computer giants.

To match your resume, and ultimately you, to either impulsive or compulsive corporations, ask the employer who will be in charge of your career track if you are hired what magazines the company's president and your potential supervisor subscribe to? Does your future employer enjoy science fiction as inspiration?

Find out whether the publications your employer reads are impulsive like The Futurist, New Media, CD-ROM Professional, Desktop Communications, Publish, QuickTime Forum, Verbum, Computer Pictures, Wired, and scientifically oriented mass media magazines like Omni, and Discover, or compulsive like all the mainstream, traditional business and historically oriented magazines are, Forbes, Fortune, and The Saturday Evening Post. Even the computer industry has its own compulsive and impulsive publications.

The compulsive computer industry publications follow the computer giants more than the independent company spin-offs. These periodicals follow the smaller, one-person startup companies, the independents, and new technology that compete with the giants. How can you tell whether the firm you select is impulsive or compulsive?

Does the firm emphasize utility, the present moment, and the practical? Is the company making the computer equivalent of the safety pin? Does it look back in time to tradition in order to move forward new technology?

Does it run a tight ship? It could be compulsive.

Does the organization make its tremendous profit by selling imagination? Does it sell interactive escape, hypertext, hypermedia, learning as entertainment, or interactive multimedia and virtual reality?

Does the organization look at consumer needs and offer education as fun? Can the creative employees work flexible hours? It could be impulsive. Knowing whether you are compulsive or impulsive in work habits helps match your resume with a company that emphasizes your life purpose, values, and natural abilities.

Do Your Clients' Resumes Reflect Each Employer's Traditions?

When a change-oriented resume lands on the desk of an employer looking for tradition in the most rapidly changing of businesses, you have a battle between logistics and analysis.

Consumer need for user-friendly education as entertainment technology collides with the old notion of number-crunching computers based on the universal need to count and store. The employment result pits tradition against new media that changes the way people learn and play.

New technology emphasizes creating fantasy as reality in three steps:

1. Virtual reality and interactive media as entertainment.
2. Entertainment as learning.
3. The living room as the learning center of the home.

Every new job applicant in the computer industry is like the fiddler looking down from a rooftop in the play, "Fiddler On The Roof," which is about tradition versus change. Traditional resumes circulate electronically for newly emerging job titles that reflect change. Where else but in the computer industry can one job description combine computer security management with industrial anthropology research or hypermedia fiction writing with optical compact disk software design?

iii. Networking
Network or Use Recorded Phone Job Referral Lines

Most people enjoy networking with others employed in coveted positions. It's draining to job hunt alone. Professional associations use recorded telephone job referrals to increase membership and attendance at evening networking meetings. The purpose of networking is to help you feel more in control of your job search by making helpful contacts.

Incorporating Resumes to Help Your Client Network

If you're combining being a career coach with writing resumes, your client needs to organize a time budget because job hunting can be like a full-time job. Always carry copies of your resumes; distributing your resume face to face while networking frequently results in job offers.

According to numerous firms providing career services, sending resumes to blind advertisements in the classified section of a Sunday newspaper resulted in 90 percent fewer hiring than making face to face verbal contact with an employer under relaxed conditions. It's easier to call and ask for an informational interview to find out about a company than to cold-call and ask for a job.

Hand out resumes and business cards at trade shows, conventions, conferences, seminars, computer exhibits, or fairs. Employers no longer have the time to answer your follow-up questions. Decades ago it was the custom to have informational interviews whereby job applicants, students, and interns made follow-up calls and asked to interview employers for job-related information for files on companies and employers. With today's time constraints, a follow-up letter should be a brief thank-you letter for the interview.

Interviewing an employer in person used to be the best way to find out whether the character of an organization matches your personality type (and resume format or focus). Today, few employers have the time to spend with a flood of job applications seeking similar information.

Company tours sometimes replace the old informational interview. If you take the company tour, you will probably be remembered by any pertinent questions you ask that relates to your research on how you'd increase revenue, production, or efficiency of that company. Clip any news articles you write about the company's newest product when each is published. Keep these in a file to help you match your technical skills to possible new job openings.

Networking for Visibility

Pass resumes to the most important vendors in the exhibitor's booths at conventions. Reviewing books, videos, and software for publications, even the free trade publications, employee in-house newsletters, magazines, the bulletins of business, trade, or professional associations and newsletters give your clients visibility.

Excellent networking strategies include article writing, product reviewing, and informational interviews. These types of networking appeal to the marketing communications, sales, software, electronic publishing, technical communications, advertising, and public relations departments, or if you seek a job as a technical journalist.

Article writing is a good networking strategy if you have services to sell. How to articles publicize the abilities of computer repair technicians, technical trainers, animators, and software designers.

Public Speaking

The quickest way to get your client's resume in front of an employer is to invite several employers to volunteer to speak for an hour at a conference where your client is in attendance or participates in some way—as a volunteer, on a panel, or with a professional or trade association. Ask your local niche industry trade journal, newspaper, or a national group whether you can plan a product-users' seminar or conference for them at their expense to showcase their products and services. As a catalyst, you can bring people together as part of your career coaching service.

Volunteer to set up a panel of speakers or experts, a seminar, conference, event, product-users' group meeting, convention, exhibit, trade show, or workshop at the expense of the national and trade press, or at meetings and seminars of manufacturers and distributors. The majority of manufacturers or distributors of products related to your clients' interests would be glad to advertise what they have to sell to a captive audience full of potential clients, customers, or colleagues.

They might even suggest that you take a 10 percent commission as an event planner for organizing and publicizing the event. If they don't, do it anyway as a volunteer to create visibility for your own resume.

How good or bad the seminar is will reflect on you as its planner. Invite the business community members with interests related to event theme: computer graphics, desktop publishing, multimedia, educational software, management of information systems, artificial intelligence applied to stock markets, or whatever your chosen field of interest. Charge attendees a small fee to cover the cost of the room and supplies.

Open the conference to students and vendors. Let them talk, give a few demonstrations, and hand out their cards. Then give them your resume and business card. Every job applicant needs a business card printed professionally with name, address, phone, and primary skill.

Volunteer yourself to do some public speaking on panels at conventions. Even if you only speak five to ten minutes about your computer education, experiences, or internships, or introduce the other panelists, it's the most visible way at an event to make important friends with interests in common.

Providing the Competitive Edge for Your Clients

Think providing the competitive edge is what your clients should do without your participation? It will promote your client services business if you coach your client on what to do, but you can obtain clients by public speaking or training others in corporate settings.

Chances are if the employer enjoyed giving a speech and pitch to the audience you captured free of charge, your client's resume will be flagged for the next job opening. Be sure to instruct your client to make a follow-up call within a week and each month thereafter for 12 to 18 months. For a fee from the employer as a key people locator—and/or as a coach or consultant, you can make this call for your client.

Sometimes the employer will give you the follow-up call to see whether you can arrange future speaking engagements, recommend potential clients, or otherwise perform a service for the company. This is the time to let the company know you appreciated its involvement in your event.

Thank the speaker for the presentation, and ask for a job as soon as one opens with the firm. Organizing the event gave the company the benefit and advantage of demonstrating and exhibiting its products before a captive audience that you provided. Focus realistically on the choices that the employer offers.

Networking Resumes through Job Hot Lines

Professional and technical computer and technical communications associations now have job hotlines with tape recordings announcing job openings 24 hours a day to members, directing members to employers seeking specialized resumes. There is a hidden job market throughout the nation that where 80 percent of all jobs available are kept from the classified ads in daily newspapers, where most people look first for a job.

Nationwide, classified daily newspaper advertisements now only list 20 percent of all job openings in any one local area. The remaining 80 percent of the hidden job markets are never advertised to the public.

Eighty percent of the hidden jobs are advertised in trade magazines, in the publications of professional associations. Or jobs are placed on recorded telephone messages available only to association members. Many applicants are recruited from calls put in to hidden job market hotlines accessible to members of professional computer interest organizations or technical communication societies.

Jobs are advertised in business newspapers, in chamber of commerce newsletters, or posted on electronic bulletin boards accessed by persons using a computer and modem who know the number to call because they belong to specific software user groups with professional interests in the computer industry (or related industries such as corporate animation, graphic design, drafting, video, or technical writing).

Job referrals are passed around on the backs of business cards or on "hot sheets" at business mixers and socials sponsored by local chambers of commerce. Jobs are advertised in national employment publications.

Most job openings are posted on cork and electronic bulletin boards inside corporate and academic walls. There is less risk to hire from inside a company.

There is less risk to hire the known, the permanent staffer, the temporary clerk or contingency professional who has solved a problem, worked out well, and is now a familar face. Only when there is no one available and qualified to fill a position from inside do companies go outside the business to seek an employee.

When corporations must go outside to hire, they frequently offer a bonus to any employee who brings in a colleague and friend to fill a job opening. The hidden job market is a network of diverse people in different occupations serving and doing business with one another under the umbrella of the computer or any other industry.

What they all have in common is that they want to meet people who can solve their problems while posing the least risk to them. Employers will hire the person who is the least risk to the company's financial investment in salary, insurance, training, and other benefits.

Does your resume position and market you as the least possible financial risk to the company? Have you emphasized how you solved problems for your last employer?

Where And When Can Resumes Be Circulated?

Most job applicants give up a search too early. Several jobs open approximately every 12 to 18 months in the average computer firm. Industrial buying patterns also cycle in 12 to 18 month periods. Companies tend to hire in rhythmic cycles.

Therefore, coordinate resume mailings with industrial buying cycles. To find out the cycles, call the purchasing department. Then compare those dates to hiring patterns by calling the personnel department. Compare the company's patterns.

For example, corporate desktop animation hiring peaks every February. That is the same time animated toy commercials and new Saturday morning cartoons (made the preceding February) air on television.

Research Hiring Cycles

Resumes are sought in cycles and by categories during the computer industry's spring cleaning cycle. More resumes are requested by employers that job applicants meet by networking within professional and trade associations. You won't find the job you want by limiting your search to classified ads in daily general newspapers.

Communicate Your Interest in a Niche Area of Industry

Frequently resumes are requested in classified or display advertisements or articles in computer business, professional, and trade journals. Your resume can be tagged by those companies who ran the ads for the next job opening if you show the company how you can solve a problem it has or give the company some favorable free publicity.

One way for those applying for jobs as technical writers or public relations personnel can stand out from the crowd is to write company approved freelance how-to articles or software reviews for public relations directors of computer firms or trade journals. This works well if the job you want is in marketing communications, training, public relations, corporate advertising, or technical communications. It's useful if you aspire to those hidden creative expression jobs in the computer industry.

If you're aspiring to a technical communications position, or if your business depends on repairing computer equipment for clients, it's a mistake to think that writing articles on your experience with computers is a waste of your personal time. It gives you visibility and opens doors when you share your knowledge with the newspapers, magazines, and trade journals of the computer industry, or newsletters of computer user groups. If you're selling anything, especially your mechanical ability to repair, keep your name in the papers.

Adopt a Company

Writing about a company is great if your career aspirations are in corporate communications. Freelance writing for trade journals about how a company solves its problems may backfire if you don't have professional writing and interviewing skills. If writing and publicizing a company to make it notice your byline and favorable reviews is not your niche, then adopt a company and learn everything you can about it.

Letting a company know you have learned all about it (or adopted it) is something you communicate by phone, during your interview, and in your polite cover and followup letters. Even if you are interested in doing some free-lance writing for the trade magazines about a company, it pays to adopt the firm and learn all about it.

Keep a record of the changes within and success strategies of the company that you adopt, the financial impact the company has made on the computer industry, and the problems the company has solved. Read the trade journals.

IV. Identifying Resume Databases

Your resume has a good chance of ending up stored in a computer database, filed under the category of work you do or the skills and training you have. If you send your resume to a national outplacement agency or employment service that specializes in electronic resume transfer, your resume could make its way anywhere in the nation or even overseas if you specify that you would be willing to work anywhere.

As needed, the database of job applicants is searched, and the applicants are called for interviews. Some software firms have turned into electronic employment agencies. They refer applicants to jobs without the applicant coming in personally by sending the scanned resume by fax or modem across the country or internationally to an employer.

Resume Screening Services

Electronic personnel referral agencies specialize in putting resumes on computer disc for the purpose of screening them for employers too busy to interview in person. Outplacement and national computer employment recruiting agencies scan your resume onto their databases.

Your so-called confidential resume is at the mercy of the rapidly changing computer industry. It's probably going to be put into a database and possibly sold to a mailing list.

Employment referral, outplacement, screening, and resume consulting agencies may infrequently download your resume from databases directly to employers all over the country (or the world) through linkage with a computerized recruiting service (and more narrowly focused databases), or corporations on mailing lists.

Once on disc, your resume could end up in market research and advertising agencies or with employment trend forecasting businesses. Once mailed out, a resume is like a note in a bottle floating on the sea.

In a national chain of agencies and outplacement services, your resume could be accessed by any of the local branches of such services. It's important to realize that the purpose of most in-house corporate personnel departments is to screen resumes out.

You may get faster results if you send your resume directly to the supervisor of the department you want to work for in the company of your choice. Some colleges also keep a computerized database of teachers and technical trainers who specialize in certain types of software in use by the institution.

It's important to know that when you send out a resume, it could end up in anybody's computer, downloaded on a disk. You don't always know whether your resume is being handled as confidential or was scanned onto a disc and is accessible to anyone on an electronic mailing list. Most outplacement agencies will not let resumes out of their offices and do promise confidentiality. Always ask first what happens to your resume over time before you send it anywhere.

Resume-Producing Software

Inexpensive commercial or public domain software is easily obtainable to create resumes for you in a variety of formats. You key in the details of your previous employment and education. Out prints a completely organized resume in the style you select. The resume business itself is now computerized, but there are still consultants who write resumes for you by hand and then put the information on computer disc.

Resume Consultants, Career Coaches, and Government Job Search Specialists

Resume writing companies charge a fee to create resumes and cover letters on a computer—either online or face-to-face with clients. Civil service resumes are put on a special, detailed resume form called the Civil Service (SF 171). Retiring military personnel and others applying for government (civil service) jobs may use these official job applications.

Civil Service applications also may be used in place of personal resumes when applying for government jobs. You can specialize in writing government/civil service resumes for clients who are about to retire from military service or from government service jobs such as moving from state or city government employment to apply for federal government jobs.

Many resume-writing agencies double as job search specialists or consultants. They identify your unique capabilities and interests and put them into a resume package. Some of these job search specialists use job search organizer software to help you set your goals. The purpose of the software and the consultants is to get you to plan your career and organize the details on software or in a workbook.

There are numerous and successful national electronic resume networks linking thousands of companies nationwide. By casting your resume on the computerized waters, you hope a job can find you. The resume-writing and job search assistance services electronically notify these companies of your career interests and qualifications.

The Computerized Resume Industry

The resume industry itself has become computerized—all because employers want candidates matched to specific jobs. Employers are flooded with stylized, look-alike, formula-written resumes.

Each service is different and is designed to make your resume stand out from the crowd inside the electronic networking systems. Yet even as you stand out because of your talents, employers wish you stood for company profits.

V. Resume Writing: What to Do if You Want to Combine Resume Writing with Job Coaching

A. Control Your Client's Job Search

What all job seekers would like most is to take control of a job search. You want to know exactly what stands between you and a career. You want to know an employer's reasons for choosing an applicant to fill an opening. You need a tool to provide the competitive edge to show you mean business.

What you want most is to be in control. To give you more control over your job search, you prepare a resume that offers filtered information. Many employers confess they expect to see an image of themselves reflected in your resume. Employers are looking for patterns of success, familiar patterns of what worked well in the past. Employers really want you to know important details about their company before you apply. You have only a one-page resume representing a lifetime of training and experience.

One strategy can put you back in charge of your career destination: In the computer industry, making a career out of a hobby is the norm. Computer CEOs are famous for trying to find new ways to make high profits from hobbies.

Chances are that each company you apply to also has made a business out of a computer-related hobby that fell in line with the organization's character. The force driving the changing computer industry is the need to find alternatives that link unrelated technologies.

Customize Clients' Resumes to Target Different Needs

Job hunting in any one of the emerging niches requires a customized resume. Send your resumes only to employers who are looking for someone with your skills, training, experience, and habits.

Resumes are slanted (with honesty) to fit the "qualifications needed" description for each job. Act as if your qualifications will be checked and verified. You don't know when questions will come up requiring a reference or transcript check.

B. How to Slant Your Clients' Resumes

The systems analyst's resume will emphasize a track record of increasingly responsible problem-solving consultant work with contract requirements. The resume focus will be on moving company operations into "intelligent systems" that are easier to use in a change-oriented environment.

Systems analysts want to change the way the public shops, plays, and learns by teaming up with software and hardware engineers. They want to make these changes within the fastest growing industry.

Systems analysts who rise to the top of their niche as analysts are more like autonomous consultants. Their purpose is to troubleshoot and redesign, always hungering for change and breaking away from routine.

Work Preferences

Let's look at how work preferences guide you into a specific type of job. Some job titles (like online RSS content syndication editor) are so new that no one has more than a few years experience in them, so an employer must scan your resume to find out your work preferences.

An employer sees your resume as a business plan. Persons who state they are destined to gravitate to the top levels of computer firms as executives will have resumes that look different from systems analysts who want to solve research problems in software design by making software easier to use.

The difference between the resume of a research and development systems analyst who wants to solve problems and an executive who is certain of rising to the top is that the executive's resume will emphasize sales based on consumer needs.

The executive's goal is to profit by filling a void in the community with the best (or most popular) products. Those sales oriented administrators who rise to the top of computer firms may not be the most creative, but they will have managed the best marketing staff.

Responding to Online Podcasting, RSS Content, Blogs, and Communication Changes

Look at how content and news are disseminated online from news to resumes. Your clients' resumes show how you and your client respond to change. In the evolving work place, online resumes reflect how you and your clients respond to changes in spur-of-the-moment job scheduling. Your approach needs to deal with how everyone changes horses in midstream.

Your client's biggest asset on a resume is that your clients work well under pressure, which is common in the techno-stressed workplace. (Psychologists and physicians treating stress symptoms of online workers applied the word, 'techno-stressed' to computer industry workers in the early 1980s. In the late seventies, the word was used by engineers, systems analysts, and programmers to describe mainframe computers worn out by too much number crunching.)

Show that where employees must find spontaneous solutions to problems and challenges, you can do the totally unexpected with computers and thrive on it. Resumes in this field should show that change challenges your clients and that each client can grow on the job and continually learn new skills.

C. What To Include

Salary History

Regarding salary history, never list your past salaries on your resume, even if advertisements state that only those resumes listing past salaries will be read. The time to discuss salary history is at a job contract negotiation interview.

If you received high salaries in the past because of many years experience, there is a good chance you could be passed over for a younger applicant with far less experience who might work for less than you would. Your cover letter may state that you will be happy to negotiate salary details or job contracts in an interview.

Order of Details
Your Clients' Resumes Need to State Profit Making Abilities

Every company wants to know how much money you brought in for the former firm last year and how much you expect to bring in for the new employer this year.

The bottom line is profit. Leave qualifiers out of your resume. Only state the facts using dramatic, action verbs that emphasize achievements that brought a company profit.

The bottom line is everything in a resume.

Profit is a hidden factor in fields such as academia, research, and human resources. In academia, if a public college course is not popular, fewer students will pay to register for it, and profit for the institution will be lowered. As state governments cut budgets for public schools, state colleges, and non-profit organizations, profit increasingly rests on the shoulders of the public.

The bottom line goal of profit is hidden inside grant proposals that use direct marketing techniques to compete for what money is available from the government or from private organizations. Profit is hidden inside fundraising events and campaigns.

Profit results from getting the public to donate money in return for a benefit. Profit is obtained by creating visibility through public relations efforts for non-profit organizations. Public relations includes news story planting in the media to persuade people to spend money on an organization's technology, courses and conferences.

Currently, public relations has created new visibility for the computer industry by shifting articles about interactive multimedia (including optical media and fiber optics) from the trade press to weekly mass media news magazines and daily newspapers. More than a decade after the *interactive learning* 'evolution,' we are in the midst of the wireless communications revolution. On Newsweek's May 31, 1993 cover page, the word, *Interactive* was the headline. Interactive was defined on the cover page as:

1. "New technology that will change the way you shop, play, and learn."
2. "A zillion-dollar industry (maybe)."

For weeks preceding Newsweek's cover and story on interactive multimedia, the daily and business newspapers contained a multitude of articles about the emerging technology. In the last two years several successful national magazines opened devoted to the digital media, to CD, DVD, or to other interactive technologies from music to desktop video to hypertext, following on the heels of the new and successful desktop publishing and home office periodicals that opened in the 1980s. The real purpose of industrial news is to create profit through the use of action verbs. The real purpose of creating your resume is the same.

Beware Of Conveyor-Belt Resume Styles

It's ironic that many of today's resumes appear so similar, considering the variety of jobs that exist in the computer industry. A person applying for a job as a word processing secretary sends in a resume of the same size, appearance, and format as a person applying for a job as a software engineer.

The only difference is in the college major and degree listed under the education heading and in the related job experience section. After reading hundreds of resumes a week, they all begin to look alike to many interviewers. What makes your resume stand out from the crowd?

The Electronic Power Resume

Resumes are online, sent by mail as paper documents, put on video DVDs or CDs, sent as audio files or streaming video, podcasted as MP3 audio files on a Web site, and sent in the "old fashioned-way," by fax.

Your clients' resumes are maps of your presentation strategy. Find out what is important to the company your clients choose to receive your written presentations. You want to anticipate problems or questions.

You want your resume to be powerful; but a resume is an original product that is an authentic expression of your inner voice. The challenge is to fit your inner voice into a company's business plan. You would like to be at ease in a job that works for you and reap benefits from the multiplying number of computer industry niches.

How Resumes Find Jobs, Not Only Encourage Appointments for Interviews

Before you even sit down to organize details, sort facts, and begin to write your clients' resumes, you will have to do some detective work about the computer companies to which you plan to send your resumes. Adopt a company and learn all you can about the organization. Find out how applicants are chosen to fill jobs. Seven steps are required to find a job:

1. Show a company how you can solve problems. Identify employers with problems to solve within your abilities to solve them.

2. Show a company why you are the least possible risk if you are hired.

3. Motivate an employer. Computer firms always help you for their reasons.

4. List ten of the company's reasons why they might want to hire you—and note them on your resume.

5. Tell your prospective employer how you can serve the firm.

6. Sell your benefits as if your resume is a personal direct mail marketing campaign.

7. Use the rule of a dozen. Marketers have a rule of a dozen, by which they send out direct mail flyers twelve times a year to target the same potential customers. Treat your resume exactly as if it were a direct mail flyer and start a direct mail campaign.

How to Impress Readers in 20 Seconds

The resume is like a flash card vision of your achievements that must imprint itself on the brain of the person who's skimming the page. Your resume is similar to an advertisement. In advertising, a black background with white lettering imprints the brain of the reader permanently and is used in large display print advertising.

Never send out a resume printed on black paper with white lettering. The small, white letters blur. Reverse printed resumes are offensive to the reader's senses and may contribute to some people's migraines. Instead, use bold headings, plenty of white spaces between sections, and bullets to direct the reader's attention. The impression your resume makes determines where it is filed.

Changing Resume Formats

A resume format showing diversification is preferred by employers. Resume formats do change as technology evolves. Employers today are searching less for number crunchers and more for user-friendly types both in computers as well as in personnel.

A strong resume today emphasizes a search for job satisfaction through innovation and change. As you move vertically up the career ladder and deeper into your specialty, also grow laterally in breadth. Growing 'laterally' means learning wider applications for your specialty.

Itemize breadth and diversity in your client's last job. If your client doesn't have relevant experience, emphasize how the client can transfer all creative, technical, administrative, people, or general skills to the new job.

D. Assessing Your Client

Slow-Down as You Write Your Client's Resume

Writing a resume allows you to address your emotions and to reappraise your employment situation. As you outline your competencies (before you write your resume), it's helpful to write about your deepest feelings about being terminated or switching careers. Slow down as you write the final draft of your resume. Reflect on your past job satisfaction.

Negative emotions should be worked through at that moment not during a job interview.

Carefully writing a resume may prevent you from sabotaging yourself in an interview. By the time you finish writing your resume, you'll have less need to justify why you are changing jobs. You'll feel less impatient and more comfortable networking with colleagues.

Where is Your Client Headed?

Is your client acting like future-and-change-oriented companies or tradition-imitating-oriented firms when someone asks your client where he or she is headed or what mission is in the client's career? Resumes emphasize skills sought by either visioning or benchmarking experiences, skills, training, job preferences, and career goals. Your client's resume, like an organization, has a character of its own.

Identify Your Client's Qualifications

Writing a resume is a process of relearning about your abilities. Your future employer may see your resume as a history of your responsibilities.

During this decade, computer personnel will see the health care field growing and seeking more resumes from trainers and equipment designers. Technology has reached a critical point where fantasy or simulation may be played as reality because of vast leaps in the quality and quantity of data transmittal through fiber optics. This is the first generation of a new technology known as interactive multimedia in the computer industry.

Cross-training will increase. Promotion of re-entry programs will tap into previously untouched sources of future employees. Networking will increase the flow of resumes. Now let's take a look at how resumes, as navigators of self-exploration, can result in interviews and, ultimately, the right job.

IV. The Changing Computer Industry
Identifying Diversity

Today, new online and video technology offers hundreds more enterprising, instructional, creative, inventive, financial, marketing, and people-oriented careers within niches in the following fields:

Wireless communications, information dissemination online, Web audio/video, virtual reality, artificial intelligence, computer security, computer law, computer medicine, software talent management, preschool software product design, sales management, DVD interactive learning machines and software, desktop computer animation special effects for the corporate world, hypermedia (interactive communications and entertainment), multimedia communications, fiber optics design, optical disk design, computer presentation graphics, electronic publishing, wireless telecommunications, robotics, artificial intelligence, financial forecasting (using applied artificial intelligence software), neural networks and fuzzy logic, technical training, instructional technology and courseware design, documentation analysis, software manual writing and editing, the computer trade press: an entire computer newspaper, magazine, and the electronic and book publishing industry for journalists, computer-aided design and drafting for graphic designers, (engineering graphics or architectural drafting), computer-aided manufacturing, numeric control, beta testing of new software for errors, software review, and desktop video for satellite video and/or cable television, marketing research, branding, documentary video production, and a variety of creative and administrative jobs with advertising agencies.

Jobs exist for satellite and wireless technology workers, database managers, managers of information systems, local area networks (LAN) and wide area networks (WAN) technicians and managers, communications technicians in utilities firms, computerized accountants, systems analysts, software designers, computer video game designers, software engineers, repair technicians, telecommunications technicians, satellite technicians and wireless telecommunications technicians, teleconferencing personnel, telecommuters, support staff, such as word processors and supervisors, data entry clericals, and computer operators. The computer industry is growing more diversified each day.

A. Changing Job Titles

Each year, many more job titles are invented that didn't exist the year before. Resumes reflect the traits required to succeed profitably in each of these ever-changing job titles.

New upgraded software enters the market every six months, far ahead of annually upgraded hardware. New job titles and spin-offs from emerging jobs form every few months.

These jobs have titles such as the following: virtual reality designer, multimedia scriptwriter, corporate desktop animator-special effects, interactive hardware and software designer, computer security psychologist, fuzzy logic neural networks analyst, and applied artificial intelligence investments planner.

These are only a few examples of the hundreds of new job titles created to meet the needs of annually upgraded technology. Nevertheless, new and emerging jobs still require certain traditional traits such as objectivity, punctuality, and accountability to support production and profit.

Objective, dependable people whose skills offer an employer concrete benefits are most likely to rise to the top on the fast track. Computers are shedding weight, and so are resumes. They are becoming more focused.

B. Changing Needs

Two kinds of people work today's urban workplace: the number crunchers and the multimedia user-friendly. Two different resume formats are used for these opposite types of jobs.

Industry needs are changing rapidly from the number-crunching machines and the logistics people who operated them in the 1980s to multimedia, user-friendly, interactive people-oriented information catchers. Occupations that include training in corporate settings, teaching, communications, and entertainment compete for the same jobs with ingenious "courseware design" people who create more personal ways to share meaning (communicate).

Two decades ago, most workers in the computer industry were programmers, systems analysts, word processors, database managers, or computerized accountants who mailed out stylized, almost similar resumes. Today, resumes can show up online or sent as text, DVDs, video clips, RSS news feeds online, or Web-based podcasts.

C. What Would Your Clients Rather Be Doing?

Hundreds of different computer industry jobs exist. Some deal with service to people, some are highly technical and oriented to machines. Still other jobs are for full-time illustrators, animators, drafters, musicians, special effects persons, virtual reality designers, and video producers.

The computer press industry hires reporters, publicists, technical and manual writers, and software reviewers. The CD-ROM industry hires novelists and instructional designers.

Do you want the flexible time schedule of a video game designer? There are sales jobs and engineering jobs, careers for the artistic, ingenious, practical, or imaginative.

There is an ever-expanding need for computer-aided software engineers, systems analysts, database managers, accountants and financial analysts, local area networks managers, satellite technicians, multimedia producers, and computer specialists of every type. Programmers are less in demand now than software engineers, software designers, and systems analysts.

Would you rather be the person who designs virtual reality simulated models of the inside of the human body to train student surgeons? Perhaps you'd enjoy using your computer to design three dimensional architectural models of a city to present to architects so they can see how a neighborhood will look before building it.

Would you rather be a technical trainer? Do you teach courses in annually upgraded versions of the same word processing software program year after year in a community college?

Does your resume place you as an electronic publishing specialist? These examples are only a few of the hundreds of opportunities that the computer industry offers.

More than 650 small businesses exist for writers or artists using a computer full time. Such businesses include: technical journalism about virtual reality developments, infomercial writing and production, software user manual publishing, and color separation desktop publishing, or in hypermedia fiction writing, computer game design and illustration, desktop video scriptwriting, corporate animation, CD and audio book production, and interactive multimedia entertainment or training materials production, design, or writing.

Due to the variety of jobs in the computer industry, many employers scan resumes onto disks and store them in computer files of job applicants, which is then sorted into niches or job categories such as programmer, word processor, systems analyst, desktop publisher, or database manager. Sometimes, these files are given to professional screeners.

These screening businesses may interview and select job applicants for corporations that don't do interviewing. What you write on paper is important, especially when your resume is scanned onto disks and made permanent. In the next chapter, you will learn how to organize what goes into a resume and what to put on paper.

CHAPTER 4

What Goes Into Your Clients' Resumes?

Contents and Setup of Resumes

Resumes identify you and highlight your work history in one page and a cover letter. The contents of a one-page resume includes the following:

* Your name, address, home phone, work phone or message phone.

* A concrete, specific, targeted description of your work history highlights.

Leave out early job descriptions that would definitely not apply to the current job or the computer industry. (For example, skip the years you worked as a cook, hairdresser, factory assembler, babysitter, cashier, or retail sales clerk, unless it applies to the computer industry.

Include the volunteer work you did for the computer industry user groups, publications, training or tutoring, nursing, customer service, commission sales, writing, speaking, interviewing, editing, college computer and robot clubs, or anything relevant to the future job.)

*Include all software and hardware you can use.

If you have reviewed software free for throwaway newspapers in the trade, include that experience. Any computers and software, or machines related to spin-offs of the computer industry such as wireless telecommunications and video or multimedia you've worked on in the past should be included. Include computer camp counseling work, and any training or designing experience.

Currently computer presentation graphics, multimedia, video production, virtual reality, simulation, CD-ROM interactive software and hardware, applied artificial intelligence, neural networks/fuzzy logic, computer camps, vacations, and resorts, and computerized advertising design are burgeoning new fields with future potential. So include these related fields, now that video technologies, telephones, and computers can be linked by new spin-off equipment.

* Your education and training.

Include all degrees, diplomas, certificates, credentials, and special seminars which train you in the use of specific software and hardware. If you're self-trained, include what software you use and which training manuals you've used to learn the software or hardware.

If you're a self-trained computer repair technician, include how you learned your trade. It's important to mention job-related associations you belong to that present continuing education, correspondence courses, seminars, conferences, or workshops.

* Work related honors, awards, and other certificates of outstanding work evaluation.

*Professional associations you've joined for networking.

*Security clearance level.

*Civil service level, if relevant.

*Publications, articles, books authored, if relevant.

This information should fill a one-page resume. If you're a recent graduate, military retiree, midlife career switcher, or are changing occupations at any age, include optional information if space permits after the primary information is included. The optional information may include:

*Your career goal.

*Computer courses taken.

Your prior training might be in a non-related field such as the humanities, nursing, or design. Include life-long, continuous training, conferences, convention courses, seminars, workshops—any continuing education credits or certificates given by professional associations or schools.

*A brief summary of your transferable life skills or volunteer history.

Using action verbs to list transferable skills are especially recommended for military retirees entering an entirely new field and mature displaced homemakers without prior paid work experience outside the home. Action verbs include words like: designed, wrote, edited, sold, repaired, trained, managed, solved, created, illustrated, organized, publicized, researched, audited, interviewed, distributed, purchased, programmed, analyzed, presented, spoke, raised (funds), coordinated, marketed, published, and produced—to name a few.

Two examples of volunteer computer experience are:

"Designed and wrote the church newsletter using Ventura desktop publishing software on an IBM 486 with Ventura AdPro 1.1 for Windows and Word Perfect 5.1."

"Trained in adult continuing education in medical terminology and transcription and volunteered to process medical records at ABC Hospital's medical records deparment using medical transcription software and Word Perfect 5.1."

If you worked as a troubleshooter in any capacity, it shows you're interested in finding out what's broke and fixing it. If you trained anyone to use software, it shows an interest in sharing and communicating technical information to the public.

*Memberships in any organizations where networking with computer industry personnel is possible.

Include your professional organizations, computer user groups, student chapters of national computer-related organizations, intellectual organizations, and related industry organizations. Examples include associations of trainers in the computer field, computer press associations, and computer graphic artists' organizations, to suggest only a few. The Association for Computing Machinery is also an umbrella for many special interests groups.

Consult the *Enclyclopedia of Associations* in your public or university library. *The Enclyclopedia of Associations* lists thousands of associations and organizations you may join in every professional, trade, and social field imaginable.

Each one of these associations has its own publication and often a job referral service, resume databank, or recorded telephone job hotline for members.

*Foreign languages spoken, foreign software used. Bilingual skills are a plus in the computer industry. The fields of import and export of software and hardware, peripherals, and computer publishing are linked by global networking through modem, fax, and telecommunications equipment from satellites to phones.

*Diverse computer-related hobbies or hobbies work-related or especially creative, analytical, problem-solving, or ingenious.

*Military service, if any.

*Magazines you subscribe to that show your reading style.

Publications may be listed if job-related. Don't stop at subscribing. Offer articles on a freelance basis. It's a great way to obtain information interviews with people for whom you want to work.

Resumes as Marketing Tools for Clients

The first paragraph of your client's resume should be able to "close the sale" and get you the job in the first few seconds the employer reads it. The face-to-face interview that follows only is to verify the employer's decision.

How does that first paragraph close the sale? Begin by making it clear on your resume what you will offer and how you'll serve the company's needs in less than two sentences in the first paragraph. Use action verbs, and keep the sentences under ten words long. Next, tell the employer exactly what you're after.

Job applicants are turned down because their resumes fall apart in front of the powerful. Employers describe a resume that "falls apart" as one which looks like you don't know what you want. An unforgettable resume synchronizes you with a company. It allows you to find out the ambitions of the person you want to help you move up the career ladder. To make your resume unforgettable, send a follow-up letter to the person who interviewed you. Keep reminding the employer and interviewer of your interest.

What Not to Include in Your Client's Resume

*Leave out your client's age, marital status, children's ages and problems, babysitting arrangements, marital problems, divorce information, confidential information from medical files, or anything from your client's home life not related to the *duties of the job*. If the client can't lift anything heavier than 5, 10, or 20 pounds, that information must be revealed at the job interview only if the job description requires lifting.

You'd be surprised how many resumes include information that belongs in confidential medical files. Non-essential information frequently found in resumes includes children's ages, school information, and names of babysitters. Leave these notes off of your resume. This information belongs on another sheet of paper to be kept in your desk in case of an emergency.

*Leave out your physical challenges.

An employer will not hire your client solely out of sympathy that your client is 'handi-capable,' has multiple disabilities, is homeless, a victim, an ex-prisoner, a survivor, refugee, or needs telecommuting work because your client is home-based. "Telecommuting/home-based online work preferred" is all right to state. If your client has disabilities and needs to know whether the building at work is accessible or on a bus route, call ahead and discuss it with personnel before you send your resume.

*Leave out past salaries and present salary demands.

* Leave out any details that put you down.

Keep negative self-talk out of your client's resume. Employers are surprised by the number of resumes that start out with the statement "I dare you to hire me," or "I never worked for anyone before because I always ran my own business."

Salaries Don't Belong On Resumes

It's better to negotiate a job contract and salary requirement at the final interview or when hired. You'll have more bargaining power. Salaries don't belong on resumes because they either drag you down to your client's former pay or price your client out of the new employer's market. High salary requirements of older, experienced workers are partly what drive budget-cutting employers to seek younger, less-experienced workers at lower pay or overseas.

*Do not include your client's height, weight, or photo—unless asked.

If you are requested to send a photo, have it professionally taken and touched up to give a business appearance. It might end up printed in an employee in-house newspaper called a "house organ."

*Don't include names of family members.

*Leave out the reference letters or names of references.

If requested, you as a job coach or your client (if you're only writing the resume) can provide letters of reference later when your client is actually hired. Some employers put names of references into a database and automatically add them to their mailing lists. So be cautious about handing out phone numbers or email addresses of references in case the applicant is not hired.

*Don't mention how your client commutes. If driving is the primary requirement of the job, such as a delivery truck driver, state only what's legally required for commercial vehicle operation. It's not necessary to reveal your client is a non-driver and takes the bus if the job doesn't require driving to perform errands, and the job is located near a bus stop.

How Resumes Persuade: The Rule of the Dynamic Fourteen Traits

The most effective resume persuades employers that your client uses these action verbs and is:

- Accessible
- Accurate
- Adaptable

- Affordable
- Analytical,
- Committed
- Creative
- Decisive
- Dependable
- Efficient
- Energetic
- Prompt
- Responsible
- Re-trainable

Resume Style

There are four different resume styles. Choose the style that best becomes your client's work history. The four styles include:

- Chronological Work History
- Abilities
- Expanded
- Creative

If your clients have no paid work experience, the chronological style may not fill enough space. Or if you don't want to reveal your advanced or youthful age, an abilities or creative style works better.

The unpaid volunteer may wish to use an expanded, amplified resume to emphasize with action verbs the duties carried out in the volunteer work. A creative resume is right for the applicant who has created many imaginative projects, such as the following:

- Digital illustration and graphics
- Writing copy, training materials, books, or articles
- Freelance photography
- Editing
- Indexing
- Hourly tutoring, teaching, or corporate training.

Organizing Resumes

You could critique resumes by phone or online. An employer wants only the bare bones in your client's resume. There are three ways to create a terse resume: by arranging the order yourself, by hiring a resume writer, or by purchasing resume-organizing software. Resume-writing software arranges your facts chronologically and prints out a standardized resume based on the software's format.

Your goal is to write the most practical one-page resume from scratch for your client. Charge an affordable fee for the writing. If you want to add job coaching, you can charge by the hour. To find out what to charge, read the wonderful PDF file titled: **Who Are Résumé Writers? Results of 2003 Industry Survey** from the **Résumé Writer's Digest Volume V • Issue 3 November/December 2003** online at: http://www.rwdigest.com/sample.pdf. It's going to take you 2.5 to 3 hours to write a resume, but you need to take at least eight days to research and write each resume in order to check for errors and do some fact checking. Let's now discuss the four resume styles and their usefulness.

You also might want to look at the Web site titled: #1 Resume Writing Services & Resume Tips Resource Center: Resume Writing Services and Tips for 20 Career Fields at: http://www.free-resume-tips.com/resumecritq.html. Look at several resume-writing offerings and what they charge to get a feel for what the current rate is in various areas for writing resumes. You might want to add job coaching to your repertoire of skills offered to job seekers that you can offer online from your home base. Also search your Internet search engines with the key words "resume writing services."

The Chronological Work History Resume

You list your last job first. Information is presented in a sequence. It's practical and familiar if the job you're applying for requires sequential information processing as in programming, word processing, systems analysis, troubleshooting, accounting, training, research and development, and data entry. The chronological resume is based on facts presented in reverse chronological sequence.

The less experience you have in the computer industry, the more likely you will list your education first. The chronological work history resume begins with your name, address, and phone number listed at the top of the page. Omit the word 'resume' in the middle above your name. The personnel department's screener or an employer knows what it is and regards every piece of extraneous information as a time waster.

If you decide to list your education first under your address because of lack of solid computer industry experience, begin with your most advanced degree. Employers are skimming your resume in order to see whether your strengths fit company needs.

Work history, volunteer experience, and participation in trade and professional associations combine together unrelated fragments into your career profile or portfolio. If you're targeting a job in video art, computer graphics, animation, or multimedia, an actual portfolio is required in addition to a resume and cover letter. Each item on your resume represents a talent or skill which shows how you handle responsibility.

It's necessary that a resume look professionally printed using an up-to-date word processing program and a laser printer, 20 bond white paper or resume paper, and easy-to-read font, such as Times New Roman 12 with highlighted titles on the items you need to emphasize. Highly recommended is Microsoft Word as a word processing program because it's used by most employers for standard business letter writing.

The Chronological Resume Is an Umbrella

Chronological resumes emphasize smooth transitions—bridges, from one job to the next, or one period of time to the next. To an employer, your resume is a creative concept. It's a basic framework used like an umbrella to tie all your different facts and categories together.

Without a creative concept umbrella or a framework, all your strengths and skills would hang together like a string of beads with no facts in common, no bridge to relate the fact that came before with the fact that lies ahead.

The purpose of an umbrella or creative concept in a chronological resume is to hold the employer's attention. To find your umbrella, look for strengths—facts, skills, talents, experiences, or training which tell exactly what you can do for the future employer and what you did for past employers (or teachers if you are a recent graduate). These strengths are your smooth transitions. Employers hate gaps and jumps.

What are your benefits, advantages, and features? How will you meet the employer's needs? Tell your future employer exactly what you will do for that person or company. When writing a resume, always consider the audience. Ask yourself, what's in my resume for the employer?

Separate Your Client's Skills

Before you write the final draft of your client's resume, it's necessary to list each of your client's skills in its own category. If your client is writing a resume from the beginning by hand, and polishing the final draft by computer, begin by separating each of your client's skills that are related to the job description.

Take a pack of index cards and write down one factual strength or skill per index card so you can sort the facts in a logical order. Even computer wizards prefer to handle index cards so they can be tacked up on a cork bulletin board. Sort your facts and organize your notes into categories.

Color-Code Categories

Assign a different color code to each of the categories. Put a different colored dot next to each category of strengths, skills, experience, and education. As you color-code your notes, identify each fact or strength with its proper category. Weed out what doesn't belong in that segment. Save what you've weeded out for a different area of your client's resume.

Important information can be color-coded with different colored dots. Stick-on colored dots are all uniform in size and easiest to sort. If you're color-coding on a computer, highlight the text in different colors from your word processing program. Color-code similar items with similar colors. For example, you might color code all courses taken relevant to the job description by highlighting those courses in red. Choose font, choose color, and highlight the text right on your computer for your first resume draft. This helps you organize the resume and group similar items together.

If you're working without your computer for your first draft, write down the name of each category at the top of a page of a blank sheet of paper. If you have many scraps of paper with notes on them, cut the notes apart. Clip, staple, or cut and paste together all of the items in the same category.

The result is a pile of neat packets of notes organized in a chronological order showing your client's entire work-style, school, hobby, and volunteer experience. You can tell at a glance which activities relate most to the job in question. That's why it's best to work with hard copy at the beginning of resume organization rather than categorize your client's whole work life on a computer screen.

Working with color coding also organizes resumes of people with volunteer or home-making experience outside the paid work force. It helps to group all similar volunteer or household experience in one category so that the job skills can be transferred to paid work categories.

Orderly Resumes

To review what employers prefer on an applicant's resume: they're orderly, chronological facts lumped into related categories without gaps. The facts impress if the categories are tied together in a concrete manner with the most recent experience listed first, then the most recent training.

If your client is recently graduating, and doesn't have any experience, list degrees and relevant credentials first. If your client's work history hasn't followed a chronological order, you may either try the abilities resume instead of the chronological resume or use active verbs (in a chronological resume) to list unpaid activities, internships, or training practice, in a work-like setting.

Related job experience uses all active verbs whether you worked for pay or volunteered for work experience practice during training or internship. Let's take a look at a sample **chronological** resume format.

SAMPLE—   CHRONOLOGICAL RESUME FORMAT

NAME
Street Address
City, State, Zip
Phone Number with Area Code

JOB OBJECTIVE: Use exact job title or specific statement indicating the type of position you want and type of organization selected.

**HIGHLIGHTS OF
QUALIFICATIONS:**   Summarize your abilities, responsibilities, skills, qualifications, and achievements.

RELATED SKILLS   Begin each skill with an active verb. List skills and accomplishments. Relate and transfer skills to the position preferred. Draw from all volunteer and paid experience. Group skills under subheadings.

**WORK HISTORY
(DATES LISTED IN
CHRONOLOGICAL
ORDER)**   Begin with the most recent paid or unpaid work or activity, including computer-related hobbies where you offer people training, how-to advice, or share information within computer user special interest groups. Include any freelance

article writing—e.g. public relations press releases for trade journals, associations, or businesses.

EDUCATION LISTED IN CHRONOLOGICAL ORDER)	List the most recent training first, name of school, degree earned, major study, or relevant Include workshops, GPA average of 3.0 or better. List any relevant seminars or workshops or continuing education in a computer-related field. List any licenses or teaching credentials.

MEMBERSHIPS IN ASSOCIATIONS

List any memberships in business, educational, professional or occupational-related associations, such as organization newsletter editor, convention and events planner, speaker, membership, or job referral director.

REFERENCES   Furnished upon request.

*   *   *

The Abilities Resume

Names of employers, educational history, and dates are left out of an abilities resume which is designed to emphasize your qualifications. The abilities resume rejects any chronological order.

An abilities resume is excellent if you don't want to reveal your age or lack of corporate experience, are seeking work after retirement, if you worked as a consultant, or independent contractor, are a homemaker or a househusband, or if you want to switch from owning your own firm to working for others.

What If You Have Gaps?

The abilities resume is suited for persons with gaps in their work history. Perhaps you did job-unrelated military service, served time in prison, recuperated from health problems, became a perpetual student, took time out to stay home with children, volunteer, travel to gain insight on the meaning of life, seek spiritual education, paint, write plays, articles, poems, or books, decided to lead the life of a fine artist, photographer, tried your hand at drama, made documentary videos, became a professional traveler, and decided that another industry is right for you now.

Or maybe you owned your business for a time and decided to moonlight part time or pull out and look for a full-time job. You could have followed the mommy track for years after graduation. How do you account for large gaps in time when you weren't employed for someone else in a paying job?

The strategy for filling in time gaps is to use an abilities resume. At the start of creating an abilities resume, you'll find that your skills are fragmented into related categories of talents, skills, abilities, hobbies, or interests.

You do all day what interests you most or wish you could. The books you read are generally lumped in one category you prefer. Everyone has preferences for tasks they do and would like to continue doing. Everyone has a work temperament where some skills come more easily than others. In fact, it has been said in books that you do what you are. (Read the wonderful book titled: *Do What You Are: Discover the Perfect Career for You Through the Secrets of Personality Type—Revised and Updated Edition Featuring E-careers for the 21st Century* by Paul D. Tieger, Barbara Barron-Tieger, ISBN 0-31688065-5).

List Your Responsibilities

Your abilities to you are really responsibilities to your future employer. So it's your responsibilities that would be listed on an abilities resume. Responsibilities cross over to many different jobs. They're known as transferable skills. In an abilities resume, you don't list a sequential job history. Instead, you emphasize your abilities and responsibilities.

The reason why your employer's names and dates of employment are left off of an abilities resume is because you're emphasizing your expertise in a field. Expertise builds up during a lifetime of responsibilities. These responsibilities accumulate from many different jobs, interests, life experiences, training, service, volunteerism, freelancing, consulting, traveling, hobbies, and care-giving.

List Your Client's Job Objectives

An abilities resume is brief and limited to one page. It's concise and structured. You begin an abilities/responsibilities resume with your name, address, and phone at the top.

Below, you state your specific job objective or concrete employment goal. There should be no vagueness about your job objective stated briefly.

Expertise

Under the job objectives, write the body of the resume. The abilities resume is only five paragraphs long. Each paragraph has a bold heading which stands out to group one area of expertise.

If you think you don't have expertise in any one area, then list any involvement. To an employer involvement is expertise. Involvement suggests future expertise and present interest or preference. Most computer personnel find one area of the industry appealing.

What's Your Client's Payoff?

Ask yourself what's your payoff for your interest? If you have the involvement, you'll soon become an expert if you are motivated to practice your skills. Is it a labor of love or a love of the labor? Is your motivation the money you earn or the ego satisfaction? List any skills. Think of the possibilities of what you're involved in now for what you'll be an expert in with continued experience.

If you have expertise in anything that can be applied to any facet of the computer industry, list it. Expertise in fashion design software sales or accounting systems database management are interests far apart, but relevant to the computer industry.

No Experience

If you have no experience in any field related to the chosen industry, but would like volunteer experience in writing about your selected specialty, try writing reviews of new advances, studies, or software and sending these brief articles to weekly and monthly industry newspapers and magazines. Thousands of new innovations and programs in every category imaginable flood the market monthly.

Niche publications may print your reviews or articles. Some pay only in copies. Information on new software is available from manufacturers.

Accumulate a batch of news clips reviews with your byline. It's impressive to an employer if the job for which you're applying requires or public relations. For persons seeking programming experience, try volunteering to work on computers at public or private schools or tutoring at business and technical schools. The easiest place to get a foot in the door is by reviewing books, DVDs, videos, and software for free publications that earn income from advertisers and are in need of content. You also can syndicate your client's content or your own writing on the Web through RSS feeds or MP3 audio files as Web site podcasts.

Abilities Resume

The function of an abilities resume is to outline how you turn your interests into involvement; how you turn involvement into responsibilities; and how you shape responsibilities into expertise. Job coaches can combine writing abilities resume by focusing on working with clients who want to channel abilities into hidden and niche market industries such as new age markets for publishing or biomedical technology—DNA-driven genealogy, informatics, and forensic DNA testing jobs.

Skills and Competencies

Under your expertise paragraphs, group your skills by category in the order of the importance of each of your skills. List as your first skill the one which you use primarily in your present job or the skill you wish to use in your next career objective.

Typical headings for your "skills paragraphs" might be Documentary Video Production/Visual Anthropology, Professional Traveler, Desktop Video Editing, Biomedical Publishing, Proofreading, Indexing, Organization and Editing of Software User and Training Manuals, Support, Coordination of Documents, Documentation Analysis, and Word Processing. All of these skills show you have expertise with specific software that required training—either on the job, self-taught, or in a classroom.

Responsibilities

By grouping your client's skills as expertise, you tell an employer what responsibilities you handled on your past job and what you are capable of handling in the next job. What you're aiming for is a smooth bridge or transition between the skills used as a word processing secretary, for example, and the skills you'll need as you step up the ladder in a higher-paid job as a technical writer or editor.

When an employer's eyes travel down the page to your education and training, the fact that you finished a two-year community college degree in technical writing while working as a secretary for a computer firm will wield enough power so you can move up without having experience in exactly the same job.

Your client will be competing against dozens if not hundreds of applicants who have many years of experience in similar fields, four-year college graduates, two-year college graduates with technical skills, retired military job applicants, and public relations majors with no corporate work experience as well as novelists and freelance writers, home-makers, retirees seeking part-time work, and re-entry career changers .

For example, say the job your client want calls for someone to write software user manuals so they're easy to understand. Who will the employer hire as the right person for the job? The former secretary who stopped working to raise a family a decade or two ago and who now longs to be a technical writer? Or the experienced technical writer with a programming and electronics background? Most often the person hired would be an individual who can make complex manuals easy to understand for beginners using the software for the first time. The person hired for the average job usually is the individual who costs the company the least amount of money to insure or pay in salary and offers the most benefits and revenue to the corporation.

What Stands Between Your Client And The Job?

Responsibility stands between your client and the job your client wants. The only wall which stands between your client and a new job is the concrete, brief summary of your client's achievements that illustrate responsibility and productivity.

The brief summary of your responsibilities is one paragraph. It's the paragraph which lists your skills. The brief summary is listed under each category which groups your similar skills together.

Use the abilities resume only as a last resort if you absolutely must leave out dates, names of employers, and educational material that would prejudice an employer at first glance. Most employers overwhelmingly prefer the chronological resume.

The abilities resume is excellent for freelancers, artists, consultants, temporary workers, and independent contractors of all types looking to switch from freelance to corporate or educational employment. Sometimes it accompanies a portfolio or list of publications.

What Employers Dislike About The Abilities Resume

For most full-time in-house jobs, the abilities resume arouses suspicion that the person writing this type of resume may be better off as an entrepreneur or independent contractor.

Suspicious staff managers complain the abilities resume is frequently used to cover up job hoppers who've had many jobs for short periods of time.

Temporary work should be listed as such. Make sure you're seen as a steady or long-term, loyal employee of a temporary employment agency and not as a constant job changer. Many temporary employment agencies offer benefits to long-term workers who are sent out on many assignments over the years.

A dramatic increase in temporary desktop publishing and word processing jobs have made 'temping' an acceptable way of networking and presenting your computer skills until a company offers you a full-time or permanent job.

Drastic Career Change

If you feel that an abilities resume might throw suspicion on your work history, use the chronological resume instead. However, when you make a drastic career change, the abilities resume is excellent for transferring old skills to new job areas.

An abilities resume is used only when you are making a drastic career change and want to show how your experience in an unrelated field is relevant to the computer industry. You'll be fighting the stereotype that resumes lose their effectiveness when employer names and dates are withheld.

Modified Abilities Resume

The modified abilities resume adds a concise historical listing of job titles, employers, dates, and job descriptions. This abbreviated history follows your description by ability or function with the latest employment date listed first (called reverse chronological order).

Military retirees switching to a totally different career field, former entrepreneurs, and mature homemakers re-entering the workplace after a long absence are comfortable with modified abilities resumes. They can show their entire work histories summarized in one page of work peaks and highlights. Let's look at a sample abilities resume format.

*   *   *

Sample—Abilities Resume Format

Name
Street Address
City, State, Zip
Phone, Email, Web site

OVERVIEW

(Job title) utilizing (name specific) software or hardware

HIGHLIGHTS OF QUALIFICATIONS

* Knowledgeable in various applications of
* Hardworking, dedicated, and dependable;
  can be counted on to get the job done.
* Easily develop good relationships with
  co-workers, staff, and students.
* Adjust well to new learning environments.

EDUCATION & SPECIALIZED TRAINING

A.S., Office Information Systems
Microcomputer Professional Certificate
San Diego City College, San Diego, CA

Access	Microsoft Word	Database Management	
Excel	Desktop Publishing	Spreadsheets	
In Design	Microcomputer	Disk Operating Systems	Presentations
Graphics	CorelDraw!	Adobe Illustrator	Adobe PhotoShop

RELATED EXPERIENCE AND ABILITIES

* Organized _____
* Coordinated _____
* Revised _____
* Proofed _____
* Determined _____
* Recorded _____
* Entered information from_____into_____

* Processed _____
* Drafted _____
* Prepared _____
* Maintained _____
* Performed _____
* Tracked _____
* Inventoried _____
* Answered _____

REFERENCES FURNISHED UPON REQUEST

*   *   *

The Expanded Resume

On those rare occasions when you and your client use the expanded resume, include important information related to skills required on the job description. For example, your client is a computer scientist working on highly classified material in a government job. Your client applies for a university teaching position or a research and development job in the corporate world using scientific knowledge to develop special software. You can't fit important material in a one-page resume.

Your client may be a writer who wants to work in a niche field such as medical copywriting. Your client may want to attach a list of published articles done as a freelance journalist when applying for a job as a documentation analyst or technical editor. A video game artist's portfolio also would also use an expanded resume/portfolio package.

Detail and Simplify With Action Verbs

The purpose of an expanded resume is to use detail to stretch and simplify. The first page of an expanded resume contains your name, address, telephone number, and a brief summary of your work history. This includes all the software and hardware you're familiar with, and your job objective.

Names of employers and dates are included on the first page along with job titles starting with the most recent job. You'd also list your training, education, degrees, and certificates with the most recent dates listed first.

The second page expands the job record in reverse chronological order, summarizing descriptions of duties performed using action verbs. Start your sentences with action verbs such as 'programmed,' 'designed,' 'illustrated,' 'animated,' 'edited,' 'wrote,' 'coordinated,' 'analyzed,' 'managed,' 'operated,' and so forth, stating whatever action you took on the project. Use the correct verb which best describes the duties you want to emphasize for each job.

The sentences should be brief—fewer than ten words each. Action verbs should be strong, dramatic, and show exactly what you did.

Instead of writing, "Participated in the revision of a software manual," simply state the following:

Dates: 2005–2006
Job title: Documentation Analyst:
ABC Corporation
123 Rex Drive
City, State   (phone, fax, and email)

Duties:

1. "Revised (name of software) manuals and classified reports on fire control according to military specifications.

2. Re-wrote, edited, and proofread manuals, reports, training materials, and documents.

Narration

A short narration expands your job titles into job descriptions on the second page of an expanded resume. The responsibilities always encompass more than the job describes. The work history is very long in an expanded resume. The experience is diversified. Sometimes each succeeding job is unrelated to the one that came before.

One example would be working with the resume of a mature person re-entering the work force after retirement seeking part time work online at home. One example would be writing a resume for someone applying for a computer graphic designer's job or internship. The person applying could be a 65-year old woman with a 41-year work history of diverse, unrelated jobs such as private school dance instructor, nurses' aide, real estate sales person, career counselor, computer operator, photographer, newsletter designer, oral history tape transcriber, literacy tutor, and software manufacturer's representative.

Such an applicant could have earned a Masters degree in career counseling in the sixties, followed by an associate degree in graphic design in the eighties and a second A.S. degree in computer-aided design and animation in the late nineties. A two-page resume in this case would serve to emphasize how more than 40 years of *diverse skills* as an independent contractor or freelancer can be drawn together and applied to the new job objective.

Disadvantages

The main disadvantage of a two-page resume is that employers won't take the time to read it. More than one page may get lost. Many employers don't like an expansion of self-importance on a resume. Once employed, however, employers insist workers toot their own horn to show they have the self-esteem to turn hard work into advancement. The following view shows a sample resume of the expanded format.

*   *   *

SAMPLE—EXPANDED RESUME FORMAT
NAME
Street Address
City, State, Zip
Phone number with area code

OBJECTIVE—To be responsible for_____ (use appropriate action verbs such as analyzing, solving problems, illustrating, designing, coordinating a specific department, writing/editing, researching, programming, troubleshooting, etc.)_____
To work with challenging projects with a leading provider of _____(insert the specific type of industry such as "a leading provider of clinical laboratory services").
To have an outstanding growth opportunity with an organization providing _____(e.g.—data processing)_____services to _____(e.g.—the federal government)_____.

SUMMARY: More than _____years experience in _____.
Expertise in_____. (Use action verb such as designer or coordinator) of_____ for_____(type of problem solved). In one, brief sentence state whether you've authored related articles, books, or illustrated any published computer art or designed animation.

SOFTWARE EXPERIENCE IN:

List all the software your client knows how to use and has had experience using. Indicate whether your client installed the software and designed or modified it.

HARDWARE EXPERIENCE IN:

List the models of computers your client used, the hardware equipment, whether your client is knowledgeable in networking, whether the computers are PCs or mainframe, Cray supercomputers, or any other relevant hardware information. Indicate whether your client will troubleshoot and repair the hardware.

PROFESSIONAL EXPERIENCE:

List the most recent date of work and list your client's job title.
Under "job title" list what your client did.
Which division, team, or department did your client work?
Use action verbs similar to the samples listed below:
*Analyzed_____problems.
*Operated _____programs.
*Solved_____ problems.
*Reduced costs by $_____in_(year)_____
*Increased gross sales by $_____annually for Corp.
*Made mathematical approximations.
*Interpreted
*Established
*Translated
*Interfaced/interacted
*Produced documentation for_____.
*Met deadlines for_____.
*Published_____.
*Produced_____.
*Presented_____.
*Wrote_____.

TEACHING OR CORPORATE TRAINING EXPERIENCE:
(Most recent dates first)

Date   **NAME OF SCHOOL OR COMPANY WHERE YOUR CLIENT WAS TEACHING OR TRAINING EMPLOYEES**

Job title (such as graduate assistant)
* Taught_____to community college students.

Date   NAME OF SCHOOL
* Taught_____to high-school students as a substitute and part-time hourly instructor.

Date   NAME OF SCHOOL
* Taught—————-to senior citizens at an intergenerational computer camp.

Date   *Lectured on_____assystems on_____lic speaker.

MILITARY SERVICE:

Dates   *BRANCH OF SERVICE, Job title.
                (job duties if related to your field now)
                state whether you were honorably discharged.

EDUCATION: Names of universities or technical schools.
                Dates attended with latest listed first, and degrees with the
                most recent listed first.

LANGUAGES: List any foreign languages your client reads and speaks.

RECOGNITION IN PUBLICATIONS:
                Use a brief space to itemize a partial list of your client's pub-
                lished articles, books, or produced videos. If your client has
                written books or professional articles, attach a separate page
                entitled: "List of Books And Articles Published"

REFERENCES AVAILABLE UPON REQUEST

                        *   *   *

The Creative Resume

If you have clients applying for highly creative jobs, then use a creative
resume to show how your client applies imagination to promote the prospective company's character. For the majority of creative people in the computer
industry who adapt imagination to reality, the creative resume reflects the old
adage, "It's what we do, not what we have that matters."

Computer industry employers receiving creative resumes include the following niches:

Web design, documentary video production, multimedia, content syndication
online, presentation graphics, entertainment software and video game design,
virtual reality, midi-synthesizer/computer music software design, special
effects, corporate animation/desktop animation, desktop video, desktop publishing (electronic publishing), graphic design (commercial art), hardware

architecture design, neural networks research, telecommunications, instructional software design, interactive fiction software production, corporate and entertainment scriptwriting, technical writing, fashion and textile design, interior, or building architecture design with software, computer-aided drafting, healthcare personnel training video production, robotics, children's programming, and applied artificial intelligence design, to mention only a few.

Some of these niches, such as interior, textile, and fashion design, regularly use software to create their patterns and designs. The software is manufactured by computer firms, but purchased by employers in the garment, textile, or interior decor industry. That's why portfolios are often part of a creative resume package.

Portfolio with Resume

If your job objective is creative, use a one-page resume and attach a laser color photocopy portfolio of your work for art job objectives, a gift video DVD, for desktop video and virtual reality jobs; and slides for technical illustration. For writing jobs, attach photocopied, published writing samples or clips and include a list of publications.

A creative resume can be used for job objectives which emphasize imagination and analysis—especially for jobs with ad agencies or software design firms. In addition to art and writing, creative resumes can be used to show originality in programming or systems analysis, entertainment games design, and computer hardware architecture.

Artwork doesn't belong in the resume itself. It should always be attached as a sample or portfolio. Keep the size of the resume limited to an 8 1/2" by 11" sheet of 20 pound bond typing or laser copy paper. Printed resumes are excellent as are quality photocopies on what "copy shops" call 'resume' paper.

Cute resumes with teddy bears, scrolls, and resumes on computer disk and audio tape are all going to end up in the round file after the staff has a good laugh. If you use a creative resume, keep it brief, traditional, and business-like. Most employers now advertise for faxed resumes. Therefore, it's acceptable, and even preferred to fax your resume. A mailed resume can take from one to three days to get to a destination. An emailed or faxed resume takes only minutes to travel from your computer to an employer's fax machine or email. Faxes as long as they are only one-page in length are taken more seriously than email due to the large amount of spam email that may be discarded without being read.

Employers prefer computer artists to attach to the back of their resumes a non-returnable portfolio of labeled artwork or slides accompanied by a table of contents. For interactive software and technical writers, employers ask to see a list of publications or published books and manuals and two writing samples or news clips of your published articles.

Your best work shows your creativity, imagination, and originality. In twenty seconds an employer will scan your resume and samples for a quick, first impression.

Persuasion

The creative resume has everything to do with persuasion. Its purpose is to convince an employer to make a purchase and hire you. Creative resumes are fashioned after the most persuasive direct marketing mail.

The most creative industrial direct marketing letters are tracked to see whether they bring in sales. They're brief, but professional sales tools designed to convince companies not to toss them away.

A creative resume is like a highly focused marketing letter. It's written to be so interesting that a company buys the product—in this case, you. Track your resume to see where it goes. Who is your audience?

Training Shortages

Effective resumes sustain interest in a workplace atmosphere. Design your creative resume to coincide with the current training shortage in your field. The economy announces that manufacturing employment in general is decreasing and downsizing in the United States. Ironically, training shortages exist in the field of computerized manufacturing in many cities. When it comes to computerized manufacturing, minimal awareness of this career field overlooks the burgeoning jobs in numeric control (CNC) technology.

Understaffed Fields

A creative resume can emphasize how your client fits into the expanding and understaffed fields. Detail briefly how your client will create and expand visibility for companies using numeric control technology, for example. On such a resume you could show all the benefits of computerizing manufacturing and how your client will fit in to the organization.

Create Your Client's Personalized Job Description

Create your client's individual, customized job description. In this way, a creative resume is used to create a new own niche or job for your clients in a new industry your client could be introducing to several types of companies. The firms may not know how to create jobs for your clients that doesn't yet exist—until a resume reveals a pitch in one sentence explaining what your client can actually do in concrete terms.

Your client's cover letter could include terms such as the following: "increased accuracy, greater repeatability, and faster production." For example, there is an explosive growth of numeric control machines in the marketplace, but American companies have fallen short of attracting new workers into the changing manufacturing industry.

A creative cover letter would show how you would attract new workers. You'd convince management that by hiring you, you'd show them how numeric control would make the changes needed for the company's benefit, production increase, and profit. These facts explained in your cover letter also would be summarized or detailed briefly on your resume by use of action verbs because such verbs show motion and are direct.

Create Bridges by Researching a Company's Needs

If you're switching careers, this type of creative resume could act as your bridge between the trades and the professions. Your client's resume appeals to a worldwide market. Explain briefly how your client will accommodate the more creative resume which shows an employer the potential of a company's investment in you.

A creative resume lets an employer know that your clients don't intend to be used in rudimentary ways. In a capsule, an imaginative resume can show a company how to stop using computerized equipment in rudimentary ways. Creative resumes show that you've done your homework—that you researched a company and know its needs before your clients are hired.

On-The-Job Training

Creative resumes focus on training objectives. If you're competing for a training manager's job, training materials designer, or a trainer's slot, the winning resume explains that buying software and machinery won't be enough. Briefly state how and why specific employers would benefit by investing in your client.

On-the-job training looks great on a resume because you have the pressure on you to produce and the focus on learning at the same time. Classroom training outside of the work environment doesn't have the interruptions of the workplace.

You can learn in a shorter period at work. For example, if you're a machinist who wants to enter the computer industry, perhaps as a robotics technician, this creative type of resume can act as a bridge or umbrella to change careers and get an employer to retrain you at company expense.

Respond To Changes Competitively

A correctly written creative resume makes you more competitive. Computerized manufacturers are no longer competing with one another in a closed market. Your creative resume reveals how an employer can hire you as a supplier to a worldwide market.

A creative resume responds to changes. The computerized medical products industry, artificial intelligence, robotics, and computerized manufacturing are receptive to creative resumes.

A creative resume is practical, but also has a vision for the future that compels the employer to call you back. It's fine if you want to upgrade your skills. The only point to remember is to keep the one-page resume business-like: no cute stuff.

Response Is All That Matters

Your creative resume is an honest ad, not a slick ad. A resume, like a direct mail ad, is probably the only type of writing where the quality of the words can be measured—precisely, accurately, and scientifically.

The measurement is based on how many interviews each resume generated before your client is eventually hired. A resume is measured by how much money it lost.

You can test your client's resume against one written by another person with the same qualifications. The best resume is the one which produced the most solid job offers.

In resume writing, response is everything. Changes are occurring in the places least conspicuous. For example, as urban daily newspapers merge and decrease in number, the computer press grows in terms of job openings for creative people.

There are many more computer industry newspapers hiring creative personnel such as reporters and desktop publishing designers than there are urban daily newspapers absorbing journalism school graduates. (The bad news is that smaller periodicals often pay less.)

Creative people in most newly emerging industries today such as wireless communications and satellite video frequently find higher-paying jobs with publishers of books and manuals for courses training others in leadership for the same emerging industries. Now let's look at a sample *"creative resume"* format which emphasizes the *benefits and advantages* your clients are offering to organizations.

*   *   *

SAMPLE—CREATIVE RESUME FORMAT

NAME
Street Address
City, State, Zip
Telephone number with area code

OBJECTIVE

INFORMATION PACKAGER

SUMMARY OF QUALIFICATIONS

* Gather information.
* Reshape information.
* Sell information in a variety of formats.
* Design information to meet different needs.
* Information is my most valuable resource.

EDUCATION/TRAINING

DEGREE, Major, Minor
College, University, or School
Certificates or Specialized Training

RELATED SKILLS

(Action verbs)   **BENEFITS TO ORGANIZATION**

Created_____   _____
Produced_____   _____

Planned_____   _____
Selected_____   _____
Announced_____   _____
Illustrated_____   _____
Designed_____   _____
Wrote_____   _____
Edited_____   _____
Proofread_____   _____
Researched_____   _____
Analyzed_____   _____
Prepared_____   _____
Delivered_____   _____
        Coordinated_____   _____
        Managed_____   _____
        Trained_____   _____
        Volunteered_____   _____

WORK HISTORY

Dates   * Most recent job first

REFERENCES ON REQUEST

BEST PERSONALITY QUALITY   Easily develop rapport

        *   *   *

Focus On Presenting and Supporting Your Objectives

Most resumes today are electronic or hard copy paper hybrids. They're combinations of many components taken from chronological and abilities (formerly called functional) formats which most powerfully present your abilities.

A resume emphasizes your ability to do the job. Whichever format you choose, you'll highlight those qualifications which best support your objective.

The benefits you'll get out of preparing an unforgettable, professional-looking resume is that it will get you interviews. The exercise in organizing your resume will help you focus your knowledge, skills, and experience. You're hired for your attitude.

Writing a resume puts you in touch with where you are and where you want to go in your career. Resume critiquing practice also prepares your client for the interview.

Help Companies Gain Recognition

The best tip anyone can give you about your resume is to use it when you join associations. Use it when you become an active member. Get to know people with the authority to hire you. Have your client sponsor awards or contests or scholarships to give others recognition and to help them grow in their jobs. This is the quickest way to gain recognition in the computer industry, even if you have no experience.

Someday when your client is hired, such activities will help your job coaching or resume writing company or personal service enterprise to gain recognition. As you further your image, your client or you as a corporate coach could be hired to continue similar activities for the company that selects you to further its image. The first step in furthering your image is not only writing your client's resume. It's writing a convincing cover letter.

Summarize Success

A resume is a summary of success (work history plus training). Resume styles differ in the order of concrete work life details. The chronological work style is what most employers prefer because of its effectiveness and efficiency.

Each resume positions a different client. The personal interview(s) that finally follows match your client's abilities and personality with the character of each organization receiving the resume.

Always Be First In an Employer's Mind

The quickest way to get into an employer's mind is to be first. American businesses process 1.4 trillion sheets of paper annually. One sheet is your resume. Many computer companies average 400 resumes for each 'good' job opening. Your resume could be buried under towers of paper or software.

Reposition Clients Using Visual Appeal on Cover Letters

If a visionary, future-centric client seeks frequent change at work, it's better to be a big fish in a microscopic pond and increase the size of the pond. If your client can't be first in an employer's mind, then reposition your client by finding a niche or void and filling it. Change the position your client could occupy in an employer's plans.

Not every job applicant wants to increase the size of the pond. Instead, job applicants may wish to increase their own visual appeal on paper. In the next chapter, we'll explore how to create the visual appeal of cover and follow-up letters. We'll also discuss the four types of cover letters.

CHAPTER 5

PAPERWORK

Cover Letter Format

A cover letter personalizes your client's resume for each, separate company. Before you sit down to organize a resume, first write a cover letter. Your mind and your client's recall will be fresher before you begin to sort the many details that will form a resume.

Your client's three-to-six-paragraph (one-page) cover letter introduces a resume and communicates a specific message about your client's value to a company. It gives an overview of what's coming in the resume.

The reason for including a cover letter is because it lends a powerful force to anything else included in the envelope. After you've proofread for typos, make sure your specific message is offered in the first sentence of the first paragraph in less than 15 words. A cover letter is like a one-line sales pitch to a movie producer for introducing the impact of a new film or like a short headline describing a news article. For example, ponder this one-line pitch: "Star Trek is Wagon Train in space." Every cover letter is judged as a sample of your client's written and oral communication skills. When you write resumes and cover letters for a client, it will be the client who is judged, not your writing skills because you never sign a resume or cover letter with "written by Your Name." You are like a ghostwriter. You'll have to publicize your own job coaching or resume writing service business by keeping a portfolio on disc and in hard copy to show prospective clients your work. If you also write direct mail sales letters or other business correspondence, your work portfolio also will be seen by the corporate world.

Your most important sales tool is the direct marketing letter known as the cover letter. Without it, an employer will have to wade through an entire resume to find out where you'll fit into the company. Without the cover letter, the resume looks unfocused.

A cover letter is the focus of your expertise. It narrows your focus. The cover letter is a mini-infomercial, a capsule of the resume which summarizes what abilities you'll give to the company.

Pitching

What makes a great four-paragraph, one-page cover letter? It's pitching in the first 10-15 word sentence of the first paragraph exactly what position you want to own in a company. That's right, own. Your cover letter establishes a unique position for your clients as specialists or generalists. The job market today belongs to the generalist who also has experience and training as a specialist with continuously updated skills.

The generalist who also has a specialist niche must be able to switch tasks when required. For example, let's look at one job description: Medical Writer. As a writer, your client, is a generalist. As a writer specializing in medical communications and pharmaceutical ad copywriting, your client also is a specialist who can switch job tasks when required to write articles on health or nutrition for popular magazines or continue to write ad copy for drug companies.

Your client may have an undergraduate degree in biology or any of the life sciences, but your client also has a Masters degree in medical journalism with a minor in technical writing. Your client belongs to a professional organization such as the American Medical Writers Association and as a member, receives newsletters with job openings listed.

A cover letter positions and defines your clients. It's the sales tool that explains why the interviewer needs to read your client's enclosed resume. It carves out a niche. A cover letter is like a growth company aimed at tomorrow. It's the horse your client's resume rides.

It's like a business friend you and your client makes outside of your present company or your client's work place, a friend who recommends you or your client for the biggest break of you and your client's career lives. In that letter, sum up your position in a single concept. Less is more.

Emphasize Reality

A cover letter is advertising news about the resume that follows, and advertising is seduction. If your resume looks for a hole and fills it, then a cover letter is a hard-sell concept that returns you to reality. To be successful today, you must aim for the (personal) reality in an employer's mind. It's the only reality that counts in a job interview.

Cover Letters are Convincing Arguments

To move a new idea, cover letter, resume, or product into an employer's mind, move an old idea, letter, resume, or product out. You move the old reality out when your cover letter convinces or prove a point.

Your cover letter becomes your convincing argument. The simplest of arguments is to give the employers an observation they can verify themselves. Computer companies are always searching for new ideas to plug holes and fill needs in the industry. Position your cover letter and resume as a plug.

An imaginative cover letter "closes a sale" by making your client stand out from the crowd. A creative resume may undercut any existing concept in a company.

Cover Letters Create Reputations

Your cover letter creates your client's reputation long before that individual is called in for an interview. Everybody (in a specific industry) is "eager to watch the bubble burst," according to Al Ries and Jack Trout's book, Positioning: The Battle For Your Mind.

For further information, read the classic, Positioning: The Battle For Your Mind, by Al Ries and Jack Trout, Warner Books, NY, 1986. The paperback is one of the most important communication books about how to stand out from the crowd and win.

In human resource management, less is always more. It's often necessary to use Madison Avenue techniques to find an entry point into a job. The purpose of your cover letter is to convince and position you first in the employer's mind. The purpose of your resume is to sell you. Getting you an interview is only half the fun. Getting hired is the goal.

The One-Page Corset

As your computer skills and experience expand, you'll have to squeeze yourself into increasingly tighter one-page girdles. Think of the entire computer industry as high-profile niches, areas of specialty. Your cover letter is a brief, but detailed road map taking an employer (in exact steps) to where he or she wishes to be.

Cover Letter Steps

Each time your client's resume goes to an employer, it should be topped by a cover letter. The courtesy of a cover letter is held in such high esteem by employers, that resumes coming in without them frequently are discarded.

Response to a resume without a cover letter sometimes is a reply of complaint letting you know what you already know—that there was no cover letter accompanying a resume. Most often, though, resumes without cover letters are ignored because they take too much time to decipher in order to find the objective or overview of what the applicant specifically wants summarized in one brief, concrete sentence.

Use a cover letter to personalize your communication. It satisfies your need for rapport. Your client's hidden goal is to make friends with someone on the inside with the authority to hire. After all, most people find jobs because friends recommended them. A resume without a cover letter is too impersonal. Employers hire people they know personally.

Your Client's Sales Pitch

The cover letter comes across as your enthusiasm and energy. Sparks fly. It's your unique style, strength, and personality type which shines through and moves a stranger to think of ways in which your client could be profitable.

A cover letter is your client's sales pitch, your storyline and premise. It's your closing statement. A resume doesn't reflect the more action-oriented parts of your personality. It only states facts.

The cover letter and the follow-up letter after an interview, close the sale by positioning your client first in the employer's mind. The cover letter is where the employer can "read between the lines" of the resume and get the big picture about you. If a resume is a sign of your skills, your cover letter is a symbol of you, the whole person, on a deeper level.

Spam and Junk Mail Mentality

Thousands of resumes a year may pile up on employers', interviewers' or human resource managers' desks. All these resumes create a mass mailing attitude, a junk mail mentality.

These piles are given painful names like "the slush pile" in electronic publishing, "the stable" with information processing and technical communications firms, and "portfolio puss" in the corporate animation industry. Only an action-oriented cover letter saves a resume from the heap. How do you stand out in that kind of a mass-mail crowd?

Your cover letter can emphasize that you're an award-winning computer illustrator or have recently completed an internship in data analysis or programming. Maybe your volunteer work has won you recognition, or your sales record is outstanding.

If nothing outstanding has happened to you in your work or school life (due to excellence or dependability), then join a professional or trade association and learn all about several company's newest products. Act as a volunteer contributor to a local or national computer industry publication, or volunteer to do research or help out on a professional association's special task force or speaker's panel in the area of your interest at the next convention.

Ask for information rather than a job. Interview a department manager to make informed career decisions. That keeps you in touch with the company on a friendly, fact-seeking basis.

Address your information-seeking letter to the person in charge of hiring in the department in which you want to work. Never send your letter to anyone in general without first phoning and getting the correct spelling of the individual's name.

Letters sent to the personnel or human resources department tend to get screened out. Everybody knows a personnel department's purpose is to weed out the unqualified in the most impersonal way possible.

It's the department head you want to target for rapport. Only the division specialist has the expertise in your area of interest, not the generalist in personnel. Unless the job opening is in the personnel department, address your fact-finding letters with the name the person with the authority to hire you in the department where the job opening exists. Use a specific title such as: Mr. Gene Wright, Manager of Information Systems, Day Computer Corporation, Inc.

It's up to you as an individual how you respond to a blind newspaper ad. Some people never respond to blind ads. In a highly competitive industry, you may want to know exactly in whose hands your resume will fall, since it contains confidential information and your home address.

To be fair, thousands of companies use blind ads because they have economic reasons to remain confidential. Only you can decide individually whether you want to discount potentially great opportunities.

The first paragraph of your cover letter determines whether the reader will finish the letter. Here's where you make your sales pitch, selling yourself in the first, brief sentence.

You need a positive hook in your cover letter. Introduce who you are, your skills, or service. You're selling yourself. Describe specifically how your skills will be used in the company.

If your cover letter is timely, it's hot. In the first paragraph of your cover letter, state how timely your facts are to the company.

Use Hook Questions in Your Cover Letter

Make your first paragraph personal and universal to the firm. Use a 'hook' question such as, "What's your most powerful resource?" The answer should be specific, detailed, and concrete—-never vague, idealized, or abstract.

Then ask yourself this question: "How many times have you settled for something less than your dreams? Do you think you sold out on your goals?" Before you put the answer in your cover letter, think of what personal question hook you'll use in the first paragraph of your cover letter. You need to 'hook' the reader right away so the person will read the rest of your letter.

First ask yourself and then the reader of your cover letter, this hook question: "If you could perform one act of power in this decade that could change your life forever, what would it be?"

The purpose of creating a question hook in the first paragraph of your cover letter is to create an audience in the shortest period of time. A cover letter that looks business-like or professional will publicize you and create the visibility you need to stand out from the heap of resumes as quickly as possible.

Your resume lists examples that employers can tune into. The resume and cover letter act together. The purpose of these cover and follow-up letters is to bring in the widest number of people in the shortest amount of time. A cover letter sharpens the focus on your resume.

Use Exclamatory Hooks In Your Second Paragraph

There are three exclamatory hooks you can use in the second paragraph of your cover letter. 1) A fear hook—when you list a series of corporate fears and then tell how you'll solve the problems. 2) A story hook—when you briefly explain how you'll benefit the company. Mention any media contacts or any chance to give the company a little free publicity during your volunteer activities. 3) An exclamatory hook or startling statistics—when you mention surprising numbers or statistics that shock the employer to attention in a positive way.

Take The Reader To A Positive Place In Your Last Paragraph.

Your client's last paragraph closes the sales pitch by taking the reader to a positive moment. You can finish the letter with something like: "Have you ever had a day when everything was going smoothly?"

Everyone likes cover letters to end on a positive note. People enjoy going back in time in their imagination to when everything was positive. Look at the success of "Back to the Future."

Show the employer how to have more of these positive moments (benefits) by applying your skills to the company's needs. Sell your service. The final, positive moment of your cover letter closes your sale. Describe how your service or skills are used and end.

Why Cover Letters Are Important

You'd be surprised at the number of employers who spend money on classified newspaper advertisements requesting cover letters to accompany resumes. The format of your letter is important. The following is a cover letter format:

Use Cover Letters for Branding When Presenting Your Client to Corporations

As a career coach, create a high-imagery name for your client starting with the resume and working through to a memorable "brand name." What is your client about—precision? Then create a *memorable* brand name for your client that sounds like precision. Don't create brand names that are hard to remember for most people, such as those names with Greek or Latin roots (unless the client is Greek or from a Latin nation.) Names with more than two-syllable roots are not easy to remember. Use one-syllable names of people or objects that produce vivid mental imagery and recall. For example: "Apple computer" or "Mrs. Field."

Choose a powerful name for your client that combines wonderfully with visual treatment. A resume is a visual treatment because you're balancing contrasting letters smoothed on white space with equal margins. Create a memorable brand icon for each client and for your own business as a career coach and resume-business correspondence editor. You know you have an innovative idea when clients call you. Clients visit a coach because they want to feel dignified.

If you are adding job coaching skills to your resume writing enterprise, use branding to present, promote, and sell your client's skills, experience, and personality to corporations. Human brains always have been hardwired to notice anything that's different or stands out in a pleasing, attractive way. By branding a client, that is presenting the resume and cover letter as a brand name, you are showing approval and displaying feedback for a proposed concept.

Use social networks to spread messages in cover letters that come with resumes. This is part of branding as a social issue. Co-branding is used to send information by email to link exchanges online or off line through the use of word-of-mouth advertising and publicity about the client's skills, personality, and expertise or experience.

A resume is a short story. It tells where a job applicant is moving in a corporation and shows the aspirations of an individual. The resume and cover letter drive future growth of your client's career.

Resumes need to offer competitive advantages to organizations. The resume and cover letter create and drive a charismatic brand. Use an MP3 audio file to build a brand with auditory associations. Use a song similar to Hewlett-Packard's use of the song "Pictures of You" that the corporation used in their Photosmart advertising.

You need to create for your client a resume and cover letter that also can be transformed into a news release that forms a charismatic aura of authenticity. What you're selling is the quality of being genuine. The idea that the skills your client offers are genuine then becomes a powerful brand attribute.

Next, the cover letter creates a story behind the brand that includes the brand's origin, the meaning of your client's skills, and the underpinnings of why your client is authentic and offers charisma. The whole idea of using branding as a job coach is to show how your client can focus a corporation. Resumes and cover letters are about customer-driven branding and marketing.

Resumes have strategic value. To understand how to use branding on any product, read The Branding Gap, a book by Mary Neumeir, New Riders, Berkeley, CA, 2005.

The excellent branding glossary in the book explains the definitions of how branding is applied to any product. The book is highly recommended if you're going to train to be a job coach. The reason is that your client is your personal service product. You need to test your concepts before you open an online, home-based business writing resumes and cover letters and also running a career coaching service online or in-person. Let's now look at cover letter formats. Use visual language and action verbs.

The Cover Letter

Your cover letter shouldn't look like a sales letter. Instead, it should detail with concrete facts how well you fit into a company or family. Sales letters get tossed as spam, especially online. What your cover letter is supposed to do is position you first. The first step in positioning you first in the reader's mind is to show with active verbs how well you fit into the company or family. How do you show with active verbs instead of telling in a cover letter? You create an action verbs resource sheet in alphabetical order and draw on those verbs to show what you can do or what you did that brought profit into the company or harmony into a relationship.

Use words in a cover letter for a resume or a book proposal such as "detailed, activated, accomplished, adapted, advised, demonstrated, designed, detailed, encouraged, entertained, established, edited, enhanced, fixed, generated, identified, inspired, maintained, motivated, operated, persuaded, orchestrated, organized, produced, protected, provided, streamlined, succeeded, supervised, systematized, tested, troubleshot, upgraded, used, validated, visualized, won, or wrote. A list of active verbs appears in one of the appendices at the back of this book.

Select the active verbs that apply to your situation. The point is the active verb needs to show results—the bottom line of how you will bring profit to the company or relationship. Be very concrete and detailed in explaining how you will do this. A cover letter, a book proposal, or a marriage proposal all use active verbs to show how you will bring in something the other part is seeking—either profit for a company, harmony for a relationship, love for a marriage, and solid explanations of how you will bring in what you promise.

The cover letter personalizes your resume for each company. Before you sit down to organize your resume, first write your cover letter. Your mind will be focused on the position as you begin to sort the many details that will form your resume.

Your cover letter is really a sales pitch letter. Only to position yourself first, you have to work the words like you would work a room at a convention or party, without letting the letter appear like a sales pitch. Think of your cover letter as a springboard or letter of introduction that brings people together. Without a cover letter on a resume, an employer will have to wade through your entire resume to find out how you will fit into the company. Your one-page cover letter introduces your resume and communicates a specific message about your value to a company.

A great one-page cover letter begins by pitching (in the first sentence) exactly what position you want in a company. Define yourself as a specialist; today's job market belongs to the specialist rather than a generalist. A cover letter also serves as a powerful introduction to (or umbrella for) anything else included in the envelope and is a sample of your communication skills.

Magnet Questions in Your Cover Letter

The first paragraph of your cover letter determines whether the reader will finish the letter. For your springboard, don't let it sound like a spam-filled sales pitch. In the first brief sentence you need a positive magnet. Introduce who you are, your skills, or services. Describe specifically how your skills will be used in the company. Draw the employer toward you by stating how timely your services or skills are to the company. Or use a magnet question such as, "What's the most profitable and powerful resource you have?" You are going to have to position yourself first as the company's most powerful and profitable resource.

Figure out how you can do it on the scale you are able to do. Then detail this kind of magnet question because it acts as a hook to capture your audience. Use this kind of catalyst magnet for employers, publishers, or clients. It goes beyond the sales pitch letter even if what you are selling are your skills. The other side sees your skills or services as a potential gauge of profit, results, troubleshooting, solving problems, or increase in production. That's what a cover letter is about: making your proposal irresistible. Your proposal can be your resume or an actual proposal.

You have a cover letter as your springboard. Your proposal or resume is your treatment. The offer made by the other side for you to negotiate is your contract. So what's your pitch? It's your first sentence and it should summarize everything you want to say in one sentence. For example, "Star Trek is Wagon Train in space."

Your pitch is not to be viewed as a sales pitch. It's explaining what you are offering in your first sentence. Define and compare what you are offering to something familiar and universal. If the employer, client, or relative can recognize what you mean, you've explained yourself. That's what a cover letter pitches in the first sentence: summarizing and explaining what you're there to do for the person who reads your first sentence. That first few seconds seals the first impression. So pitch in the first sentence of your cover letter without letting the words hint of a sales letter.

Next, convince the employer to hire you. The simplest way is to give employers an observation they can verify themselves. The observation can be about their needs, or your skills. Computer companies are always searching for new ideas to plug holes or fill needs in the industry. Position your cover letter and resume as a plug to fill a need.

Try using exclamatory magnets like 'Velcro' in the second paragraph of your cover letter. There are three types:

1. a fear magnet—where you list a series of corporate or business fears and then tell how you'll solve the problems.

2. a story magnet—where you briefly explain how you will provide benefits to the company, using professional expertise or media contacts.

3. an exclamatory magnet or surprising statistics—where you mention surprising numbers or statistics associated with your career that startle the employer in a positive way. Use statistics to grab attention and motivate the reader to think about you.

Finally, a persuasive cover letter closes by making you stand out from the crowd and get hired. (A resume doesn't reflect the more action-oriented parts of your personality—it only states facts.) End the letter on a positive point. Show the employer how hiring you to apply your skills to the company's needs will bring positive results. What are positive results for an employer?

Positive results include more profit, increased production, problem solving, less employee turnover, lower costs of hiring employees, improvement of reputation, credibility, and image in the media, and bottom-line results—increased revenues. Positive results for you include happiness and security with the results you obtain from a cover letter, resume, or proposal.

Does your fate really depend upon positioning yourself first on a pile of resumes and cover letters or proposals? It does in the mind of a reader with the authority to bring you in as part of a team. For further information on positioning yourself, read Al Ries and Jack Trout's book, *Positioning: The Battle for Your Mind*, Warner Books, NY, 1986. It provides advice about how to stand out from the crowd and win.

Cover Letter Tips

• Each time your resume goes to an employer, it should be topped by a cover letter. The courtesy of a cover letter is held in such high esteem by employers that resumes coming in without them frequently are discarded.

• As your computer skills and experience expand, you will have to work hard to condense them in a one-page resume or cover letter. Think of the entire computer industry as niches or areas of specialty. Your cover letter must be brief, but detailed enough to show your specialty or your unique qualities.

• Use your cover letter to personalize your communication and to establish a rapport with potential employers. Your goal is to build a relationship with someone who has the authority to hire you. A resume without a cover letter is too impersonal.

• The cover letter should express your enthusiasm and energy. It's your unique style, strength, and personality type that should shine through and move an employer to think of ways in which you could benefit the company.

Junk Mail or an Attention Grabber?

In the computer industry, thousands of resumes a year may pile up on someone's desk. These resumes begin to overwhelm an employer, and some may begin to see them as junk mail. These piles are given derogatory names like "the slush pile" in electronic publishing, "the stable" in information processing and technical communications firms, and "portfolio puss" in the corporate animation industry. How can you stand out? Only an action-oriented cover letter saves a resume from the heap.

Your cover letter can emphasize that you're an award-winning freelance writer, Web designer, or teacher or have recently completed an internship in journalism, counseling, new media, healthcare, design, marketing, genetics, government service, customer service, public relations, or programming. Maybe your volunteer work has won you recognition, or your sales record is outstanding.

If nothing outstanding has happened to you in your work or educational life, or you are a re-entry parent who had spent the past decade or two rearing children at home and volunteering for projects or causes, then join an occupational, special interest, professional, training, national association, or trade association and learn all about the newest products of several companies. Join projects or libraries and museums as "friends of" or members.

Volunteer to be on various boards or teams that focus on projects linking community and business. Genealogists can work with DNA-driven genealogy projects and surname groups. Act as a volunteer contributor to a local computer industry publication, or volunteer to do research or help out on a professional association's special task force or speakers' panel in your area of interest at the next convention.

Most employers who place classified newspaper advertisements request cover letters to accompany resumes. Most jobs come from information given through friends and contacts at work or through courses and special interest groups, associations, and projects. The format of your letter is important. Your first step is to find out when to use cover letters in what kind of situations.

Focusing on resumes only at first, or when seeking work, a job, or more customers and clients if you're an independent contractor, you send a cover letter with a resume on ten different types of occasions. Notice that a cover letter is a noun, an object, sent in response to an active verb. The cover letter is active rather than passive. It accompanies the action taking place—the sending of a resume or proposal of any kind. The proposal can be for almost anything—a book proposal for a publisher or agent or a marriage proposal. The cover letter acts as a link to seal a relationship or ask for a contract.

A cover letter also can be turned into a greeting card, and you'll find in this book, samples of greeting card cover letters. So the cover letter is a kind of 'seal' or request for a legal contract. When accompanied by a resume, book proposal, or other springboard, the cover letter in one page tells the reader at a glance what will be in the resume or book proposal or even a marriage proposal. It works with almost any kind of proposal, resume, treatment, or report accompanying it. When you send a cover letter, you also send a follow-up letter.

TEN KINDS OF COVER LETTERS

You send a resume and cover letter when:

1. answering an advertisement.
2. writing to a specific employer—the informational cover letter.
3. asking a friend for job-related information.
4. consulting an employment or outplacement agency.
5. networking with members of a professional or trade organization.
6. attending a trade show, exhibit, convention, or conference.
7. interviewing people for information, photos, or video projects.
8. asking bookstores or distributors to carry your self-published book.
9. launching your project in the media or on the World Wide Web.
10. traveling to do research.

Answering an Advertisement

Clip ads from trade journals, national employment newspapers, professional organizations' newsletters, computer magazines, and the publications of computer user special interest groups. Write down phone numbers from the tape recorded phone messages of job hotlines for members of trade and professional organizations. Clip ads from your daily newspaper's Sunday help wanted section.

The hidden (not advertised) job market appears mainly in trade journals, those magazines and newspapers directed to readers interested in a particular industry. Most jobs advertise qualifications for the ideal candidate. If the ideal job applicant doesn't respond, often the employer will take what's available.

Send your cover letters and resumes to the widest variety of ads possible, even if you only have some of the qualifications. One reason for this is that company paid training is sometimes available after employment. On-the-job training is offered when the technology is so new that little training is available outside the company.

When new software is designed, technical trainers are trained on the job so they can go out to other corporations and train the new software users. In a classified or display help wanted ad, ob requirements are listed according to their rank of importance, with the most important skills listed first. If you don't have all of the requirements, list the capabilities you have and specify which requirements they meet.

State how you will be an asset to the company. Take out all extra words; only list strengths in your cover letter. Let's look at an advertisement and analyze how to compose a cover letter.

Software Systems Specialist

You will install user devices, diagnose hardware problems, load software maintenance releases, monitor system and subcontractor performance, maintain communications systems, assist customer end users, and perform other duties as assigned. Requirements include: a demonstrated knowledge of VAX/VMS or DSM operations, maintenance is a plus; a high school diploma/GED and five years directly related experience, or an AA in a related field and three years directly related experience. We offer a competitive compensation and benefits package. Please send your resume and cover letter indicating department code for position of interest.

The actual ad appeared as a display in the Sunday section of a major urban daily newspaper. The company name and address were listed. Your first step would be to call the company and find out the name of the person to whom you would direct your letter. You can also ask about new company information, such as new products. In your cover letter, this information can allow you to tell the employer how you could help the company reach its goals.

Some interviewers hold resumes a long time before getting back to you. To offset this waiting period, send a mailgram cover letter. Be assertive and courteous. Call the staff manager first, before you are called, and ask to set up an appointment for an interview. The cover letter on page 53 is a sample of an answering-an-advertisement cover letter.

Blind Ads

How you respond to a blind newspaper ad is up to you. Some people never respond to blind ads (ads in which the hiring company is not identified). In a highly competitive industry, you may want to know in whose hands your resume will fall, since it contains confidential information and your home address.

Thousands of companies use blind ads because they have economic reasons to remain anonymous. They may be placed by executive search firms on behalf of corporations. You must decide whether you want to discount potentially great opportunities by not responding to such ads.

Writing To A Specific Employer—The Informational Cover Letter

A different approach to your career search is to ask for information in your cover letter, rather than a job. Interview a department manager to make informed career decisions. This keeps you in touch with the company on a friendly, fact-seeking basis. Read the biographies of executives of major or fast-moving companies, which can usually be found in public libraries.

The department head for the area in which you want to work is the person who should receive your cover letter and with whom you should establish a rapport. Only the division specialist has the expertise in your area of interest, not the generalist in personnel. Address your fact-finding letters to the person who has the authority to hire you. Use a specific title such as Mr. First Name Last Name, Manager of Information Systems, XYZ Computer Corporation, Inc.

Never send your letter to anyone without first calling and getting the correct spelling of the individual's name and title. Letters sent to the personnel or human resources department tend to get screened out. Often a personnel department's purpose is to weed out the unqualified.

You will have the best chance of getting hired if you send a mail-gram cover letter and resume with your business card. All job applicants should have business cards listing their three best skills and any degrees or technical school diplomas. Such a business card may look like this example.

Technical Writer/Software User
Your Client's Name, M.A.
Public Relations, Training Materials,
Courseware Design
Street Address or Post Office Box Number
City, State, Zip
Phone
Email Address
Web Site, If Any

If you're looking for a job as a technical writer or editor and you have little or no experience, your database of employers may be gleaned from professional and computer journals, business publications, trade and professional associations, computer user groups, industrial directories, and the Yellow Pages.

Most of your research will be in finding out what type of software and hardware or applications systems are used in each company. Call the companies before you send them any letters or resumes and ask what systems they are currently using. Never waste your cover letters on companies that you didn't research.

You can also ask for a list of their suppliers and research those firms for possible job leads. For example, one salesperson didn't land a job at the company first applied to but found a great job with one of the company's material suppliers.

In addition to companies that supply computer corporations, there are other businesses that provide technical staff training with all of these companies. Networking expands the possibilities of finding jobs that match your skills. Employment agencies use this same kind of research to drum up job orders.

Most corporations outside the computer industry still use computers as tools. Even the one-person home-based office uses online services, libraries, media, and computer-based research tools. Larger companies also may have information systems departments where data entry, word processing, database design, online retrieval, content production, Web design, desktop publishing, and educational or corporate training video production are developed.

Also, corporate video production studios have computers connected to VCR machines and video cameras to create multimedia presentations, usually for training videos or product demonstrations called desktop video (DV) studios. Large corporations have management information systems (MIS) departments and computer operations divisions. Smaller companies have Web development, database management departments or data processing (DP) departments. Electronic publishing companies have desktop publishing departments and technical illustration or computer-aided design departments. Computer-aided manufacturing companies may use computer-controlled robots.

When you first telephone a company, ask for the director of computer operations or the manager of information systems. Either person can usually tell you which types of hardware and software are used by the firm. What you are seeking in your research are facts about a company's hardware and software, people, and job openings. Send out a dozen letters at a time to carefully targeted firms where you have already made verbal contact by phone or have interviewed directors of departments for company or product information.

Personalize all cover letters. Never send a form letter or a letter with a photocopied signature. End the letter with a question that makes it easy for the person to call you back with a product related or technical answer.

By asking a technical question rather than asking for a job at first contact, you're seen as a potential customer. Emphasize how you can be of value to the business. Direct mail campaigns emphasize showing companies the specific advantages and benefits of your abilities. See the sample cover letter to a specific employer. You don't want to sound like a direct-mail campaign. However, you need to use the technique used by direct-mail campaigns that is, showing the benefits and advantages of bringing you into the 'family' in a relationship cover letter on the team in a resume or business cover letter.

Asking a Friend for Job-Related Information

This type of cover letter is used to gather job leads. Use it so that a copy of your resume may be passed to people your friend meets at work or during meetings. You are not asking for a job in this letter. You only want information. Use the information to develop a profile of employers, companies, or job requirements.

Let your friend know you're looking for a certain type of job—maybe even with clients of your friend's company. Write an informal, friendly letter instead of a formal business cover letter, and have your friend pass the resume only to personal friends and clients with authority to hire you. Sending three copies of your resume with the letter is acceptable.

Ask for suggestions in the letter. Mention any plans for, or openness to, relocation. Let your friend know whether your correspondence is confidential. Leave out salary references. Human resources information is harder to obtain than product information. Some companies promote from within or pay a recruitment fee of several hundred dollars to any employee bringing in a qualified friend who fills a new job opening. Many new jobs aren't advertised to people outside the company until all employees are given a chance to apply. It pays to have a friend on the inside to pass around your resume.

Consulting an Employment or Outplacement Agency

Target only those agencies that specialize in your field. For example, write to those agencies that specialize in placing military retirees, displaced homemakers, programmers, word processors and desktop publishers, Web designers, DVD designers, database managers and systems analysts, accountants, software engineers, technical writers and editors, clerical workers, counselors, persons over age 55, recent college graduates, graphic designers, animators, drafters, technical writers or illustrators, temporary technical contract workers; or write to outplacement services for displaced computer personnel or other specialized jobs.

You can also write to executive search and recruiting firms and job consultants who work within placement agencies. Address your letter to the director. The purpose of a cover letter sent to an employment agency is to set up a personal interview. Ask to have your resume kept in the active file. Include in your cover letter when you'll call to set up an interview.

Keep the cover letter to an employment agency brief. Most executive recruiters will rewrite your resume according to their own formats. Ask to see your resume before they send it out. If you don't, you'll lose control of how they present you on paper.

Find out whether your resume will be downloaded onto a disk and sent electronically to companies across the nation or added to mailing lists. Look at the sample cover letters as they apply to your needs and use them as inspirational templates to motivate you to develop your own cover letters specifically targeted to your needs.

Networking With Members of a Professional or Trade Organization

You can use a professional organization three ways:

1. Use their letterhead when you write your cover letter to an employer.

2. Send your cover letter and resume to the director of a trade organization for job referral or use of the job bank.

3. A cover letter and resume directed to the job-referral officer or job hotline coordinator of a professional organization can be helpful if you do some homework. Work on the job bank for the trade organization, where you can develop a portfolio or database of details about the companies you solicit for job openings to go in the organization's job referral databank.

Volunteer to work with a professional, special interest, or trade association. There are regional or national organizations of people interested in specific areas of what you do or want to do—from technical writing to genealogy. Select an area of your interest and explore. Once you are in a professional, trade, or special-interest organization, seek increased responsibility to establish contacts and relationships with other members and to show your talents. Volunteer to speak on panels at conventions.

Most of these professional or special interest societies have task forces or committees, user groups, or networks of people employed in the same or related areas of computing. There are public relations task forces, newsletters, fundraising committees, membership drives, speaker special interest groups (SIGs), and job bank listings. If you are looking for a job, try the professional or vocational-oriented groups and trade organizations first and then the hobby groups such as sellers and speakers marketing scrap booking supplies. You pick the field and the association or group. It can be educational, cultural, artistic, musical, technical, commercial, creative, paraprofessional, legal, medical, or social.

Target the job bank SIG. If you are part of this SIG, focus on calling employers to get job listings for the recorded telephone job hotline for your members. Your job bank task force might work alongside a committee that arranges internships for students, or recent graduates or retirees reentering the workforce (often the student membership committee).

After you have established telephone rapport with a recruiter or department manager at several of the corporations, you can call for the hotline jobs and then send your cover letter and resume to recruiters with whom you've talked. Keep it brief, and mention your affiliation with the trade or professional organization.

You might ask your contacts to provide you with old job performance evaluations from former employees with jobs similar to yours. These evaluations will give you an idea of what people in the company thought of employees' skill levels. That way, you'll know what's expected of your performance on the job.

If your qualifications are appropriate for the job you want, include some of the job evaluation terminology in your cover letter to a prospective employer. At least knowing the details will help you fit in with the company on the same level of terminology.

Joining a professional or trade association demonstrates to employers two important facts about you:

1. What you can do as a volunteer.

2. How you handle responsibility.

Always include in your cover letter your volunteer association experience and the details of how you handle responsibility for your trade or professional association.

Analyze the template or sample cover letter used to network with members of a professional, cultural, special interest, or trade association. Then write your own cover letter directed to members or directors of an association related to your own interests.

Attending Trade Shows, Exhibits, Conventions, or Conferences

When you attend a convention or conference, visit the exhibit booths of each company. Ask the person at the booth the name of the department head, president, or person in charge of hiring for the department of your interest.

Write that person's name down on a sealed envelope containing your cover letter and resume. Your cover letter would be addressed generically, for example, "Dear Exhibitor." Hand the envelope to the booth clerk.

If the person in charge of the booth or exhibit is the company president or employer, hand it over and start a conversation about the company's products, services, and personnel needs. Smile, chat, and leave a positive impression of yourself with whomever is representing the company at the exhibit booth.

If you know about a convention or trade show well in advance, volunteer to be on a panel or announce a workshop, even if you only introduce others or speak for five minutes. If you have experience, send your proposals to read a research paper, speak on a workshop panel, or give a seminar.

Many conventions have exhibitions of your state's task force in a specific field. Send your cover letter and resume to your state advisory board on training and practice in your computer specialty. You might volunteer to join your state advisory committee board for drafting, or whatever your computer specialty is. For example, the Minnesota State Drafting Advisory Committee (MSDAC) is a task force located at the Department of Vocational and Technical Education of the University of Minnesota.

Consider handing out samples of your work with your cover letter and resume at conventions and trade shows. If your job interest is in computer illustration or drafting, hand out non-returnable samples in a mini-portfolio to key representatives at trade shows.

If you are a writer, include a list of publications and a published (or self-published) writing sample or news clipping with your cover letter and resume. Similarly, if you are in a creative field or teaching, include anything you wrote related to what you want to do. Hand your cover letter (with your resume) to prominent speakers and company representatives at trade show exhibits, job expos, conferences, or conventions.

✳   ✳   ✳

Interviews

Rarely will companies give first interviews at trade shows or conventions—unless the expo or trade show also is a job fair sponsored by several companies who are set up to recruit personnel at the gathering. Job fairs are usually sponsored by colleges or by professional and trade associations.

After you make contact with someone at a trade show such as a vendor or exhibitor, write a follow-up letter based on what you spoke about at the first meeting before you send a resume with a cover letter. Then write a follow-up letter after you've had a formal interview based on the interview.

✳   ✳   ✳

1. Template—Generic Cover Letter Template Format—For Resumes:

Your Client's Name
Street Address

City, State, Zip
Phone number
Email address
Web site URL, if any

Date of Letter

Name
Title
Name of department
Company name
Street address
City, State, Zip

Dear Mr./Ms._____:

Opening Paragraph—State the position you want. Tell why you want to work for that company. Make your sales pitch.

Middle Paragraph(s)—Mention your two best qualifications (related to the job in question). Explain how your skills and/or experience would benefit the company.

Point out any specialized training or skills that relate to company plans. Sell your abilities. Document your sales pitch with startling statistics or statements showing evidence of your talents. Don't repeat yourself by listing what's on the resume.

Closing Paragraph—Readers need to know at first glance that what's attached is your resume or resume and portfolio, list of publications, samples, or other itemized achievements. In the last sentence, let the employer know when you will call to follow up. (Don't wait for them to call you.) Your closing sentence should ask for a specific action from the company. Reread the letter to make sure nothing is vague. Make every word concrete and practical enough to be remembered. Anything vague is quickly forgotten. There may be hundreds of competing cover letters on someone's desk.

Sincerely,
Your Name Typed
Enclosure

*Note: Your handwritten signature needs to be in black ink, never another color.	Book printing is done in black for contrast and clarity.

Cover Letter Templates and Samples

2. Sample Cover Letter: Generic Template—Resume Cover Letters:

> Your Client's Name
> Street Address
> City, State, Zip
> Phone number
> Email address
> Web site URL, if any

Month, day, and year

Mr. or Ms. Person's Name
Director of Employment
Company
Street Address
City, State, Zip

Dear Mr. or Ms. Person's Name:

Here's why you would want me to serve Name of Corporation. I create exciting, high profile online Web and DVD games, working for the past year in the most fascinating industry possible of streaming digital video. Your advertisement in the June 30 issue of the Name of Publication for a video-game artist matches perfectly your needs to my skills.

What I can offer to obtain results, troubleshoot, and solve problems with your software are interviews from clients that have switched to your brand of software and have positive steps to detail that can help most of your other clients. These interviews showing how-to techniques form case history success stories for your marketing communications division.

(Detail three examples of exactly how you will fit into the group, get results, solve problems, or troubleshoot technology that will increase revenue, production, and decrease turnover.) Name of Corporation is a fast-expanding Name of City company offering the challenge, environment, and opportunity I'm seeking as an experienced artist specializing in computer graphics, video game design, and corporate animation.

I also have the ability to draw and paint cartoons and comic book-like characters or back-ground using Name of Software on a PC. Using illustration, computer animation, desktop publishing, Web authoring, and streaming video production on PC and Macintosh computers, I can build your marketing communications efforts with PowerPoint, PageMaker, Microsoft Publisher, and Director.

As detailed in my resume, my experience centers on writing freelance articles on video game design and illustration. As an award-winning team member, I gained an appreciation of the cooperation it takes in a large computer video game company to coordinate the art function with all the other areas.

My Special Studies A.S. degree in Computer Sciences and Fine Art from XYZ College in El Cajon, California, included specific coursework in computer graphics design, presentation graphics, video production, animation, and fine art.

Thank you for your consideration. Enclosed is my resume and photocopied samples in a portfolio. You may keep the portfolio. My salary requirements are negotiable. I look forward to meeting with you. I'll call you next Friday at 9:30 a.m. Or if you prefer, you may reach me at (insert telephone number) after 3 p.m. weekdays to schedule an interview.
Sincerely,
Your Name
Enclosure

3. Sample Cover Letter: Employment Agency—Resume Cover Letters:

                    Your Name
                    Your Street Address
                    City, State, Zip
                    Phone
                    Email
                    Web Url, if any, and if relevant
Month, Day, Year

Name of Person
Careers For Women Over Sixty-Five, Inc.
Street Address
City, State, Zip

Dear Name of Person:
Thank you for your exciting panel presentation on computer careers for workforce reentry women over 50 at the Displaced Homemakers' Center. As I mentioned in Monday's phone conversation, I feel my strengths are in computer sales and software retailing. A copy of my resume is enclosed detailing my software sales experience.

I have recently completed a course in sales given by the Broadview Chamber of Commerce. I am a full-time volunteer at the Mature Adults in Multimedia Network and president of the Computer Users' Special Interest Group at the Oaks Senior Center.

For the past decade I sold shareware and presented exhibits of software to computer user and hobbyist association members. Here are some ways I can serve your database search companies, software libraries, and software location services.

I am enthusiastic about selling your software as a manufacturer's representative. Here is how my lectures may be applied to the marketing communications goals of your company. I'm presently lecturing on Best Software for Screenwriters to the scriptwriting class of the Clarion Senior's Center. As a part-time software manufacturer's representative I could promote your software as a sideline when I volunteer as a public speaker, which is my avocation.

For this reason I feel I could be very successful you're your software sales and promotion job as a case history manager, interviewing people who use your software and writing success stories I can make available to selected members of the press through your public relations or marketing communications departments. I am eager to travel the country selling software, wholesale or retail.

As you review my background and areas of interest, you'll see benefits I can offer a manufacturer as a software representative. I am open to relocation anywhere.

I'll call you next week to set an appointment at your convenience in order to discuss an interview.

> Sincerely,
> Your Client's Name

*   *   *

4. Sample Cover Letter: Advertisement—Resume Cover Letters:

Your Client's Name
Street Address
City, State, Zip
Phone

Month, Day, Year

Name of Person
Company
Street Address
City, State, Zip

Dear Name of Person:

In response to your advertisement in the *San Francisco Chronicle* of April 10, (year) for a desktop publisher and desktop video producer, I'm enclosing my resume. I am deeply dedicated to both desktop publishing and desktop video. For the past two years I have been producing how-to computer videos as well as writing and publishing software user manuals for Windows software. I work at home as a freelance producer and writer using a PC with a variety of multimedia software for a variety of software designers.

For the field of desktop publishing, I create software user manuals using Microsoft Word, Corel WordPerfect, Microsoft Front Page, and Microsoft Publisher. My self-published software manuals accompany my how-to videotape entitled "Everything You Want to Know About DVD Design."

Using my industrial broadcast quality and digital Hi-8 Sony camcorders, Firewire 1394 cables, DVD burners, and other audio and video equipment to interface my computer with my camcorder, and a full range of videotape editing equipment and software such as Ulead systems and Power DVD, I can create DVDs or Web sites for your presentations and post streaming video on your company Web site or my own site.

By producing minor special effects and animation in my desktop video productions with Macromedia Director Eight, I can serve your company's marketing communications and training departments by teaching online courses in DVD design. The book I use with my students online and which I highly recommend because it contains the best DVD authoring techniques, resources, and instruction is titled, *DVD Design Workshop*, Robin Williams et al, Peachpit Press, 2004. I use this popular book with my students when I teach DVD authoring online.

With software such as PowerPoint and Macromedia Director, my presentations bring in motivated customers at conventions, expos, and trade shows. In fact, I like to inspire my students with new ideas on how basic design principles can improve usability. Speaking of usability, you can use my abilities to handle all the requirements of your position in both DVD design and desktop publishing.

My background includes an undergraduate degree in English literature and certificates in desktop publishing and desktop video/DVD design. I will call the morning of April 14 at 10:00 to answer any questions and to set up an appointment at your leisure. Thank you for considering me for the position.

Sincerely,

Your Name

Enclosure

*   *   *

5. Sample Cover Letter: Specific Employer—Resume Cover Letters:

Name of Person

Street Address

City, State, Zip

Email address
Web Site URL

Month, Day, Year

Name of Person
Company
Street Address
City, State, Zip

Dear Name of Person

I know what to do with your clients who want a $1,000 project delivered on a $500 |budget. I'm enclosing my resume and portfolio samples to demonstrate how my award-winning computer designs serve all aspects of your current marketing program. The reason I'm applying for a position as a computer graphics designer at Cosgrove Computer Corporation is because I know you're looking for computer artists who can design on a tight budget. One of the most powerful marketing tools any company can wield is a cohesive design program.

As a computer artist and graphic designer specializing in editorial illustration, I am eager to serve your company by customizing design strategies at very low-cost because I know exactly what to exclude from the design process to produce high-quality work your board is welcome to examine before an interview is scheduled. If I'm hired, I can promise memorable, award-winning, interactive 3-D designs.

Your marketing department wants Cosgrove Computer Corporation to be noticed. I see an excellent fit between my computer art qualifications and your department's needs. I would appreciate the opportunity to discuss how I may contribute to your company's success. Please keep my portfolio samples on file to show your clients. I will call in two weeks on April 15th (year) to set up an appointment.

Sincerely,

Your Name

(2) Enclosures

*   *   *

6. Sample Cover Letter: Asking an Acquaintance for a Job—Resume Cover Letters:

Your Name
Street Address
City, State, Zip
Phone
Email
Url Web site, if any

Month, Day, Year

Dear Name of Person:

I met (Name of Person) last summer while attending the Comdex convention in Las Vegas. She told me that you're using virtual reality technology at Laser Art Technologies to create special effects for the new television series, "The Ransomers in Togas Time Travelers." She suggested that I contact you.

I'll be finishing my DVD design and desktop video/publishing/digital media/Web authoring internship in the public relations and marketing communications division at Blocks Cable Television in Las Vegas on December 23. (I wrote infomercial scripts and created press kits on a PC there.) On January 2, 1 will relocate to Los Angeles and job hunt there for about four weeks.

Since I saw you last, I've been writing freelance for MIS magazine and other computer trade journals and networking with friends in several computer industry professional associations as a volunteer newsletter editor. Would you know of a way to get into an emerging technology like virtual reality and still make use of my degree in English?

I'd really appreciate any information or job leads you can pass on to me that could be helpful in my job hunting in technical writing or DVD or Web design. I've had a minor in educational technology and have a portfolio of instructional materials that I designed.

In exchange for any job leads or referrals, I'd be happy to write freelance articles and publicize any aspect of your work or any aspects of Laser Art Technologies that would welcome visibility. I've enclosed three copies of my resume.

I am circulating them freely in the virtual reality industry and among virtual reality client and supplier businesses. Since I have not made housing arrangements yet, if you know anyone who needs a house sitter while on vacation for at least a month or who needs to sublet or rent a room, I'm also available with references and am a non-smoker. I'm looking forward to seeing you.

Sincerely,

Your Name

*   *   *

7. Sample Cover Letter: Networking with Member of Association—Resume Cover Letters: One-Page Letter.

Your Client's Name
Street Address
City, State, Zip
Phone
Email and Url, if any

Month, Day, Year

M. (Name of Current President)
Management of Special Interest Group
Association
Street Address or PO Box Number
Station
City, State, Zip

Dear M. (Insert name of current president here):

As a new member of your association, I'd like to introduce myself and also announce my retirement from the U.S. Air Force on (Month, Day Year). A fellow member who sponsored me for membership, (Insert name of member used as reference here) who also is a member of your Management of Data Special Interest group, recently informed me of an opening in your organization for a volunteer position as director of membership recruitment.

I'd like to apply for that position as I enjoy net-working with colleagues interested in data management. I have enclosed seven copies of my resume. I am seeking information and job leads in order to make a career transition from military to civilian life. My goal is to find a new career in data management, and while I'm looking for a paid position, I'm available to volunteer for your association two days a week for about four hours per day to handle that opening for a newsletter editor.

For the past thirty years, my career in the Air Force as a recruiter centered on interviewing people and placing them in the right job. Now that I'm retiring from military service, I would like to devote the next twenty years or more of my work life to working with students interested in careers in data management. Last month I received my BS degree in Computer Information Systems (with an emphasis in data management) from (name of University), City, State, and became a member of (name of association).

Please feel free to email my resume to any member or to download it to disk. I've already submitted it to your association's electronic job referral databank system in the field of information processing. I look forward to hearing from you in person.

Sincerely,

Your Client's Name

*   *   *

8. Sample Cover Letter—Trade Show, Expo, Convention, or Conference Meeting:

Your Client's Name
Street Address.
City, State, Zip
Phone
Email, and URL (Web site) if any

Date: Month, Day, Year

Exhibitors and Key Speakers
Year, Name of Convention
City Convention Center
City, State, Zip

Dear Exhibitor or Key Speaker (Ask for Name of Person):

I enjoyed networking with you at this year's Comdex Convention and electronic products trade show in Las Vegas. In January 1998, I will receive my BS degree in Computer Science (with a minor in accounting and finance) from the University of (Name). I am interested in obtaining a programming position with a financial services corporation in February.

When you mentioned you needed some troubleshooting done on your software, recently I solved the same problem for a colleague. Let me know how I can be of service since I have recent experience programming in FoxPro for CPA Associates in Chicago.

During my five years at the University of Illinois, I worked part time during school and full time during the summers at CPA Associates. My experience is in a personal computer environment utilizing Novell Netware. I have knowledge of hardware and software (Lotus, WordPerfect, and Excel). I am willing to relocate to any area of major growth.

You mentioned your strongest needs are in areas of Novell Netware and Ethernet, 10 Base-T, and DBase. I have excellent recent experience in network administration, PC installation, software installation, PC maintenance, network trouble shooting, and network performance analysis. May I speak with you next week about some benefits and advantages to your company of putting my skills to work? I'll call you on Wednesday at noon, which you mentioned was a convenient time.

Sincerely,

Your Client's Name

The Follow-Up Letter Format

What Stands Between Your Client and That Job?

A follow-up letter may be used at two different stages in the job hunt or to find clients and customers if your client is an independent contractor:

1. Right after every interview, send a follow-up letter of thanks to the interviewer. Use this method also if you've met someone and chatted at a trade show or convention.

2. You have sent your resume with a cover letter. A few days later you made a follow-up phone call and still you were not called in for an interview. Now is the time to send a follow-up letter to seek the answer to the question "What stands between me and this job?"

The follow-up letter is more than a thank-you note or common courtesy. It's a reminder of your qualifications and continued interest in the company. The follow-up emphasizes to an employer that you want to work for the company, even if the job advertised isn't right for you this time around. If you didn't land the job for which you applied, another one will open.

Like the cover letter, the follow-up letter should be one page, usually three to six paragraphs. Practice developing the formats of follow-up letters. Practice writing cover letters. Look at the sample letter templates and adapt them to your own interests and skills.

Some companies give only one interview. Others put you before several individuals from the personnel department. You then interview with the department manager. At a later date, you may be given a final group interview, before a board of subject experts who will decide whether to hire you.

When each interview is over, send a different follow-up letter. Send a follow-up letter after speaking to someone at a trade show, expo, conference, meeting, seminar or convention. Then enclose a cover letter with a resume when asked for a resume. Follow interviews with a follow-up letter. The idea of a follow-up letter after an interview is to clear up one question: "What stands between you and the job—an invisible barrier, actual person, or a budgetary situation?"

✳   ✳   ✳

9. Template—Follow-Up Letter Format:

Your Client's Name
Street Address
City, State, Zip
Phone Number
Email and Url (Web site, if any)

Date of Letter

Interviewer's Name
Title
Company Name
Street Address
City, State, Zip

Dear Mr./Ms.____

Opening Paragraph—Express sincere thanks for being given the opportunity of the interview. Mention the courtesies extended to you by anyone present. Indicate the job title, where and when the interview was given, and the date. Refresh the interviewer's mind with the most important part of the interview.

Middle Paragraph—Restate your reasons for wanting to join the organization. Use your best one sentence sales pitch to close the sale. In one sentence state that you want the job because you will offer the following benefits and advantages to the company. If you left anything important out of the personal interview, include it now. Finish the middle paragraph with any sentence that enhances your abilities. State any specific qualifications that fulfill an important company need.

Closing Paragraph—Offer to provide any information the company may want, such as reference letters, security clearance, or transcripts. Indicate when you're available for further interviewing at the company's convenience.
Sincerely,
(Your handwritten signature in black ink)
Your Client's Name Typed

       ✶   ✶   ✶

10. Template and Sample—Follow-Up Letter—After the Interview:

Your Name
Street Address
City, State, Zip
Phone number
Email address
Web site URL, if any

Month, Day, Year

Person's Name
Company Name
Street Address
City, State, Zip

Dear Mr. or Ms. Person's Name:

Thank you for the opportunity you provided. Interviewing for the position of computer video games artist was exciting. I look forward to joining Web and Video Game Corporation and working with a dynamic manager like His or Her Name.

As I mentioned during the special effects tour with Ms. or Mr. His or Her Name, I am familiar with all of the duties and responsibilities of the job. I spent the last year as an intern working in the special effects department of the XYZ Web, Video, and Print-on-Demand Production and Publishing Corporation.

There I quickly learned the value of timely and original illustrations for the electronic publishing, Web authoring, content production, print-on-demand publishing for the game design industry. My excellent work evaluations and reference letters from my internship are available on request.

In addition to my internship experience in print-on-demand publishing for the video game design industry, the knowledge I gained through courses in animation production and online desktop video editing and Web design in my associate degree program will serve me well in fulfilling the requirements of the position. I can contribute significantly to your corporation with my school's award-winning illustrations and game designs by tailoring my details in editing and design to the expression of your online print-on-demand publishing or game design clients.

Thank you again for the opportunity to interview with your company and for the fascinating tour. I enjoyed our informative discussion, and the new animation was breathtaking. May I publicize your forthcoming video game by writing an article about it for the local weekly computer newspaper, The Web-Byter?

I volunteer each month to send the editor a column reviewing and recommending new software and computer video games. Also, I am available to write success stories from case histories by interviewing clients who switched to your software brand and would be willing to tell me why they switched and the positive results they had such as solving problems and achieving results from the software you manufacture. If interested, please make my email address or phone number available to your marketing communications representative. I look forward to hearing from you at your convenience.

Sincerely,

Your Client's Name

*   *   *

11. Sample Follow-Up Letter for Group or Individual Company Tours:

Your Client's Name (or client's letterhead)
Street Address
City, State, Zip
Phone
Email, Url, if any

Date: Month, Day, Year

Person's Name
Title or Department
Corporation
Street Address
City, State, Zip

Dear Name of Person:

Thank you for the opportunity you provided. Interviewing for the position of computer video games artist was exciting. I look forward to joining (name of corporation) and working with a dynamic manager like (name of manager you've researched).

As I mentioned during the special effects tour with (name of manager), I am familiar with all of the duties and responsibilities of the job. I spent the last year working in the special effects department of a video game design corporation and quickly learned the value of timely and original illustrations for the electronic game industry.

In addition to my experience in video game design, the knowledge I gained through courses in animation production and desktop video in my associate degree program will serve me well in fulfilling the requirements of the position. I can contribute significantly to your corporation with my award-winning illustrations and game designs.

Thank you again for the opportunity to interview with your company and for the informative studio tour. The new animation was breathtaking. May I publicize your forthcoming video game when you announce the product to the public by writing an article about it for the local weekly computer newspaper, The Visual Byter? Each month I volunteer to send them a column reviewing and recommending new software and computer video games. I look forward to hearing from you at your convenience.

Sincerely,

Your Client's Name

*   *   *

COVER LETTER FORMAT

Your Client's Name

City, State, Zip

Phone number

Email address

Web site address

Date of Letter

Name of person with the authority to hire you

Title

Name of department in which you want to work

Company name

Street Address

City, State, Zip

Dear Mr. Ms._____:

Opening Paragraph—State the position you want. Tell why you want to work for that company. Give your specific message.

Middle Paragraph(s)—Mention your two best qualifications (related to the job in question). Explain how your skills and/or experience would benefit the company. Point out any specialized training or skills that relate to company plans. Sell your benefits. Sell your abilities. Document your sales pitch with startling statistics or statements showing evidence of your talents. Don't repeat yourself. Don't repeat what's on the resume. Don't repeat what you'll say in the interview.

Closing Paragraph—Let the reader know that what's attached is your resume or resume and portfolio, list of published works, or other itemized achievements. In the last sentence, let the employer know when you will phone to set up an interview. (Don't wait for interviewers to call you.)

Also list your telephone number in the letter in case the employer is traveling and prefers to call you from out of town or is frequently tied up in meetings. Your closing sentence should ask for a specific action from the company. Re-read the letter to make sure nothing is vague. Make every word concrete and practical enough to be remembered. Anything vague is quickly forgotten. There may be hundreds of competing cover letters on someone's desk. That's why you need to position your client first by making sure the reader notices what is different and positive.

Best Regards,

(Your handwritten signature in black ink, not blue)

Your Name Typed

Enclosure

*   *   *

Sample Cover Letter

Your Client's Name
Street Address
City, State
Phone

July 1, 2005

Name
Director of Employment
Company
Street Address
City, State, Zip Code

Dear (Name of Director of Employment):

How may I serve Video Game Corporation? I create exciting, high profile Nintendo and Genesis games, working for the past year in the most fascinating industry possible. Your advertisement in the June 30th issue of the <u>San Diego Union-Tribune</u> for a video game artist is the perfect match between my skills and your needs.

I understand Video Game Corporation is a fast-expanding San Justa company offering the challenge, environment and opportunity I'm seeking as an experienced artist specializing in computer graphics, video game design, and corporate animation. I have the ability to draw and paint cartoons and comic book-like characters or background using CorelDraw! software on an IBM-compatible 486 model computer.

I also have illustration, desktop publishing, and desktop video production experience with IBM, MAC, and Amiga computers. I'm experienced with Ventura Publisher, PageMaker, and Word Perfect Presentations software.

As _____(insert job title) my experience centers on video game design and illustration. As an award-winning team member, I gained an appreciation of the cooperation it takes in a large computer video game company to coordinate the art function with all the other areas.

My "Special Studies" A.S. degree in Computer Sciences and Fine Art from XYZ College in El Cajon, CA included specific coursework in computer graphics design, presentation graphics, video production, animation, and fine art.

Thank you for your consideration. Enclosed is my resume and photocopied samples portfolio. You may keep the portfolio. My salary requirements are open to negotiation. I look forward to meeting with you. I'll call you next

Friday at 9:30 a.m. Or if you prefer, you may reach me at (619) 555-1234 after 3:00 p.m. weekdays to schedule an interview.

Best Regards,

Name

Enclosure

*   *   *

The Six Kinds of Cover Letters

You send your client's resume and cover letter when doing the following tasks:

- Answering an advertisement.
- Writing to a specific employer.
- Asking a friend for job-related information.
- Consulting an employment or outplacement agency.
- Networking with members of a professional or trade organization.
- Attending a trade show, exhibit, convention, or conference.

1) **Answering an Advertisement**

Clip ads from trade journals, national employment newspapers, professional organization's newsletters, computer magazines, and the publications of computer user special interest groups. Write down phone numbers from the tape recorded phone messages of job hotlines directed at members of trade and professional organizations. Clip ads from your daily newspaper's Sunday help wanted section.

The hidden job market appears mainly in trade journals, those magazines and newspapers directed to readers interested in a particular industry. Most jobs advertise qualifications for the best candidate for the job applicant. When applicants with skills preferred do not appear, often the employer will take what's available.

Company paid training is possible after employment. On-the-job training is offered when the technology is so new that little training is available outside the company. When new software is designed, technical trainers are trained on-the-job so they can go out to other corporations and train the new software users on staff. Send your cover letters and resumes to the widest variety of ads possible, even if you only have some of the qualifications.

In a classified or display ad asking for help wanted, job requirements are listed according to their rank of importance with the most important skills listed first.

If you don't have all of the requirements, list what other capabilities you do have and how those can relate to the requirements in new ways. List how you'll make an asset to the company. Take out all extra words. In a cover letter, list only strengths. Let's look at an advertisement and analyze how to compose a cover letter. Note the use of powerful action verbs as job descriptions.

SYSTEMS SPECIALIST

- You will install user devices
- Diagnose hardware problems
- Load software maintenance releases
- Monitor system and subcontractor performance
- Maintain communications systems,
- Assist customer end users
- Perform other duties as assigned.
  - Requirements include: a demonstrated knowledge of _____
  - Maintenance of _____
  - A high school diploma/GED
  - Five years directly related experience
  - Or an AA in a related field
  - Directly-related experience of at least three years
  - We offer a competitive compensation and benefits package
  - Please send your resume and cover letter for the position of interest.

The actual ad appeared as a display in the Sunday section of a major urban daily newspaper. The company name and address were listed.

Your first step would be to call the company and find out the name of an actual person to whom you'd direct your letter. Include new company information you found out from the first phone call.

This would include new products. Tell the employer how you could help the company reach its goals. Some interviewers hold resumes a long time before getting back to you. To offset this waiting period, send a mailgram cover letter.

Be assertive and courteous. Call the staff manager by name first, before they call your client, and ask to set an appointment for an interview. The following cover letter is a sample of an "answering an advertisement cover letter."

*   *   *

1) SAMPLE COVER LETTER: ANSWERING AN ADVERTISEMENT

Your Client's Name
Street Address
City, State
Phone

September 1, 2005

Name of Interviewer/Employer
Street Address
City, State

Dear (insert name of interviewer):

In response to your advertisement in the <u>San Francisco Chronicle</u> of July 1, 2005, for a desktop publisher and desktop video producer, I'm enclosing my resume.

I am deeply dedicated to both desktop publishing and desktop video. For the past two years I have been producing how-to computer videos as well as writing and publishing software user manuals for the latest version of Windows software. I work at home for a variety of software designers as a freelance producer and writer using an IBM-compatible computer and a variety of multimedia software.

I create software user manuals using Microsoft Word software as well as software that enables me to develop innovative security and surveillance solutions for a global marketplace. My self-published software manuals accompany my how-to video tape entitled "Everything You Want To Know About Windows XP Professional."

My industrial broadcast quality camcorder and equipment is available daily to interface my computer with any video camera, and a full range of video tape editing and DVD recording equipment. The enclosed DVD shows how I produce minor special effects and animation in over twenty recently produced desktop video productions.

I have the ability to handle all the requirements of your position in both desktop publishing and desktop video as well as multimedia presentations. I am interested in a staff job with Crest Computers handling all your desktop publishing and desktop video needs.

If you're looking for a good desktop publisher and video producer who can make technical subjects easy and entertaining to learn, that's my goal and yours. My background includes a master's degree in English literature and an associate degree in desktop publishing and desktop video. I will call on July 14th at 10:00 a.m. to answer any questions and to set up an appointment at your leisure. Thank you for considering me for the position.

Cordially,

Name/Signature

Enclosure

*   *   *

2) Writing to a Specific Employer

You'll have the best chance of helping your client obtain an appointment for an interview if you target specific employers by name and send a mailgram cover letter and resume to them with your business card. Every employee should have a business card listing three best skills and any degrees or technical school diplomas. For example, a job applicant's business card may look like the following example:

Your Client's Name
Street Address
City, State
Phone

June 4, 2005

Name of Employer
Street Address
City, State

Dear (insert title and name of interviewer or prospective employer)

I know what to do with your clients who want a thousand-dollar project delivered on a two-hundred dollar budget. I'm enclosing my resume and portfolio to demonstrate how my award-winning computer designs impact all aspects of your current marketing program. The reason I'm applying for a position as a computer graphics designer at Cosgrove Computer Corporation is because I know you're looking for computer artists who can design on a tight budget. One of the most powerful marketing tools any company can wield is a cohesive, across-the-board design program.

I'm a computer artist and graphic designer specializing in editorial illustration. My design tricks keep very low-cost designs looking great because I know exactly what to exclude from the design process. If I'm hired, I can promise memorable, interactive 3D designs that will break all barriers.

Your marketing department wants Cosgrove Computer Corporation to stand up and be noticed. I see an excellent fit between my computer art qualifications and your department's needs. I would appreciate the opportunity to call you for an appointment to discuss how I may contribute. Please keep my portfolio on file to show your clients. I will call in two weeks to set up and appointment.

Best Regards,

Name

(2) Enclosures

*   *   *

3) Asking a Friend for Job-Related Information
This type of cover letter attached to a resume is used to gather job leads. A copy of your resume is often passed to people your friend meets at work or during meetings. Use this type of letter for branching out.

Attach an informal note so that employers will know you're looking for a certain type of job—maybe even with clients of your friend's company.

It's a warmer gesture to write an informal, friendly letter instead of a formal business cover letter, and let your friend pass only the resume to personal friends and clients with authority to hire you. Sending three copies of your resume is acceptable.

Ask for suggestions. Mention any plans for relocation. Let your friend know whether your correspondence is confidential. Leave out salary references.

You're not asking for a job in this letter. You only want information. Use the information to develop a profile of employers, companies, or job requirements.

If you are interested in technical writing, speaking, public relations, document analysis, or technical marketing communications, ask for an interview to publicize or write an article about the company's newest products.

Your article may be sent freelance (on speculation) to trade, small business, or professional publications, daily newspapers, airline magazines, in-house employee newspapers, or professional association newsletters.

Human resources information is harder to obtain than product information. Some companies promote from within or pay a recruitment fee of several hundred dollars to any employee bringing in a qualified friend who fills a new job opening.

Many new jobs aren't advertised to people outside the company until all employees are given a chance to apply. It pays to have a friend on the inside to pass around your resume. Now let's look at a sample personal cover letter asking a friend for job-related information—or for an interview to obtain further information only.

    *   *   *

2) Sample Cover Letter—Asking A Friend For Job-Related Information

> Client's Name
> Client's Address
> City, State
> Phone, Email address

Date
Company's Address

Dear (name of friend):

I met (insert name of other contact/friend) last summer while attending the Comdex convention in Las Vegas. She told me that you're using virtual reality technology at Laser Art Technologies to create special effects for the new television series, "The Time Hackers." Karen explained all about the cutting edge technology special effects you're creating. She suggested that I get in touch with you.

I'll be finishing my desktop video internship in public relations at Blocks Cable Television in Las Vegas on December 23rd. (I wrote infomercial scripts and created press kits on an IBM 486 compatible.) On January 2nd, I will relocate to Los Angeles to do my job hunting there for the following four weeks.

Since I saw you last, I've been writing freelance for MIS magazine and other computer trade journals and networking with friends in several computer industry professional associations as a volunteer newsletter editor.

Would you know of a way to get into an emerging technology like virtual reality and still make use of my B.A. in English? I'd really appreciate any information or job leads you can pass on to me which could be helpful in my job hunting.

I'd be happy to write a freelance article and publicize any aspect of your work or any aspects of Laser Art Technologies that would welcome visibility. I've enclosed three copies of my resume. They can be circulated freely in the virtual reality industry or among virtual reality client and supplier businesses.

I'm house sitting your mother's condo while she's in Europe. I'm looking forward to seeing you.

> Sincerely,

> Name

CHAPTER 6

Organizing Your Skills

Looking at the variety of cover or follow-up letters and resume styles in the previous chapters showed you the formats employers select. Now it's time to organize for simplicity. This chapter will give you the umbrella or framework to write your simple resume briefly and concisely. It will help you organize your resume by using a simple plan.

The Simple-To-Grasp Resume

Interviewers use resumes to hastily screen out applicants. So resume reading is repeated frequently as a negative process. Often only the chosen few are referred to an employer for a decision. Many resumes never get past the interviewer to the employer because the resume isn't simple to grasp at first glance.

To keep your brief resume simple, organize a simple plan of work-related information. Employers will spend time on simple resumes. 'Simple' actually means being concise.

The Organized Plan

You know an effective resume unlocks doors, but how do you filter all that information? You need an organized plan to refer back to when you create a first draft of your resume.

Organizing a plan or outline for writing a resume involves asking yourself to itemize what's important. You can tell by looking at what organizations you belong to and what type of books you like to read. Organize your plan for writing a resume by filling in your own information in the space provided that follows.

Resume Plan Work Area

Identification Worksheet:
Have your client pencil in the following information on this plan.
Name_____

Address_____

City_____State_____Zip_____

Home Phone_____

Business or Message Phone_____Confidential? Yes___No___

Skills Worksheet:

Listing skills are required if you're changing careers, re-entering the civilian workforce after military retirement, re-entering the job market after being on the mommy track, or switching horses in midstream.

Employment Qualifications_____

_____

_____

_____

_____

Are you changing careers? If yes, explain concisely and briefly, why:_____

_____

_____

BEST ABILITIES WORKSHEET:

_____

_____

TRAINING_____

List your training like your employment record, in reverse chronological order: your most advanced traininsystems on_____ course, workshop, seminar, internship, apprenticeship, or on-the-job training is listed first. Be specific and concrete about details. Include all dates, certificates earned, schools attended, or pertinent training-related information.

Training Worksheet:

Job-Related Training:

Dates:

From (Year)_____To Year)_____

On-the job training_____Dates_____

Job-related continuing education_____ Dates_____

_____ Where trained_____

Apprenticeships_____Where served_____

_____Dates_____

Training Internships_____Dates_____

_____Address of Internship_____

_____Computer training and coursework____
_____Hardware_____
_____Software_____
_____ Repair_____
_____ Troubleshooting_____

General Education

List your formal educational history in reverse chronological order with your most advanced degree first. This section is for persons who have formal education beyond high school rather than job training. If you didn't attend an accredited university, four-year college, or two-year community college, it's appropriate to list your post-high school continuing education and technical school courses under **Training.**

General educational history includes all college degrees, dates, majors, and minors studied, and any licenses or teaching credentials. Show you're learning for the sheer joy of accomplishment.

General Education Worksheet:

Dates:
Advanced Degree(s): From (Year)_____To (Year)_____
     Name of University_____
     Address of University_____

_____

               From (Year)_____To (Year)_____
     Name of University_____
            Address of University_____

_____

Undergraduate Degree(s)_____From (Year)_____To_____
     Name of University
     Address of University_____

_____

Two-year college degree(s)___From (Year)_____To_____
     Name of two-year or community college
     Address of college or school

Diplomas or Certificates_____From (Year)_____To_____
      Name of School or Training Course
      Address of School_____

_____

                 Computer-related courses:_____

                 _____

                 _____

                 _____

                 _____

                 _____

College-level internships served_____

Job Objective

List the most important job-related objectives. Simplicity rules here. Keep your client's objectives brief and concise, remembering that employers will toss resumes with complex job objectives because they're too time-consuming to ponder. In the computer industry, you're familiar with the "access denied" software code. Too many resumes don't fit. They simply aren't the right match.

Your job objective is a mini-life plan of responsibilities. It's a tool for navigation over the obstacles thrown in your way by time constraints and competition.

Use the job objective segment of your resume plan as a terse, personal, and powerful ad. Dramatize your clients' resumes' selling messages with excitement. Your clients' resumes need flair. Pretend you're running your client's objectives in the daily newspaper classifieds and have to state your client's job objective in less than 20 words. Work with your client to pare the words.

_____

_____

_____

Hardware and Software Worksheet:
Computer Models:_____
Telecommunications Equipment:_____
Local Area Networks:_____
Operating Systems:_____
Modems and Faxes:_____

Computer Languages:_____
_____
_____

Monitors and Access:_____
Databases:_____
Utility Packages:_____
Peripherals:_____
Telecommunications and Multimedia:_____
_____

on_____

Subject Expertise Worksheet:_____
Emphasis:_____

Mathematics Background_____
Scientific Background_____
Engineering Background_____
Writing_____
Public Relations_____
Art, animation, and special effects_____

"The Day in the Life Page"

Pay attention to each feature of the systems or skills and job duties that your client has worked with in a selected specialty or industry. Write down your client's job roles in chronological steps. Include each job description—summarized concretely, with details.

Interview yourself in the mirror and write "a day in the life" page of yourself on an hour-by-hour basis at work during any typical day. To get your specifics flowing, you might record your typical hour-by-hour activities on a tape recorder and transcribe them.

Day in the Work Life of (Your Client's Name):_____Worksheet

9:00 a.m.   Arrive at work and begin (action verb)_____
10:00 a.m.   Program_____
11:00 a.m.   Analyze_____
12 noon-1:00 p.m. _____Lunch break
1:00 p.m.   Consult_____

2:00 p.m.   Sell_____

3:00 p.m.   Troubleshoot_____

4:00 p.m.   Demonstrate_____

5:00 p.m.   End of workday, or whether your client also worked evenings
                 doing which activities.

6:00-8:00 a.m. _____

Saturdays: _____

8:00 a.m.-1:00 p.m. Taught/trained/instructed_____

2:00 p.m.-4:00 p.m. Worked as a _____ at XYZ community college_____

You're ready to itemize and detail your client's *chronological* employment history. Keep in mind that at the live interview, your client will be asked to discuss the features of the systems and programs you worked on in each job in your field of expertise or experience. The questions will be taken right out of your client's chronological employment history, if you use a chronological resume.

Chronological Employment History:

If you're going to be a *job coach* and also write resumes, show the client why it's necessary not to make the employer search for specific information and dates. Don't leave unaccounted for gaps in your client's history. Show how your client's chronological work history relates to your client's career plan. Employers hire people who specifically choose a company because it's part of their plan.

Your client's employment history also summarizes your qualifications. It shows at a glance how many years of experience you've had with further specifics. The employment history tells the reader at a glance what you can do and how many years you've done it.

List the job title, company location, and years employed. Also list your responsibilities as accomplishments using active verbs and telling how much money you saved the company. (Example: Implemented audience tracking system which saved company $50,000.)

Focus on skills and accomplishments in your work history. Use an employment history worksheet to explain the nature of your career briefly and concretely. Start with your most recent job first. Include every job you've had since high school, if those jobs are related to the new job or show transferable skills.

Leave no gaps unfilled. Instead of leaving gaps in those years you didn't work, fill them in with volunteer duties you handled, so that all t for by job-related responsibility. Use separate pages to detail all your jobs if you had several jobs within the same firm.

Never include your client's salary information and your reasons for leaving on a resume. You can put them on your worksheet to help you discover what you really like to do most and what made you leave.

Only part of the material on your worksheets will actually appear on the final draft of your resume. However, these details will ease you through an oral interview. Think about these details and practice answering questions about yourself in front of a mirror. List your work history in reverse chronological order.

Chronological Work History Worksheet:

Name of Company:_____

Address of Company:_____

_____

_____

Job Title:_____

From_____To_____

_____ _____

                                            _____

                                            _____

                                            _____

                                            _____

                                            _____

                                            _____

                                            _____

Name of Company:_____

Address of Company:_____

_____

_____

Job Title:_____

Dates: Responsibilities:_____

From_____To_____   _____

                                            _____

                                            _____

                                            _____

                                            _____

                                            _____

_____

_____

Name of Company:_____

Address of Company:_____

_____

_____

Job Title:_____

Dates: Responsibilities:_____

From_____To_____   _____

_____

_____

_____

_____

_____

_____

_____

Personal Requirements Worksheet:

Willing to Relocate:_____

Relocation Areas Desired:_____

Willing to Travel:_____

Travel Areas Preferred:_____

Interests, Hobbies, Avocations:_____

Subjects or Types of Books Read:_____

Types of Magazines and Newspapers Preferred_____

Personality Type, if known on popular personality tests, such as the MBTI, etc._____

Prefer to work alone or with constant activity and people?_____

Introvert or Extravert?_____

Prefer Usefulness/Practical Skills or Imagination and learning only for learning's sake?_____

Like lots of free time, less schedules, or every working minute scheduled?_____

Highly organized person? _____

Prefer own space, not pressured by schedules, rules, and close supervision:_____

Creative?_____

What conditions preferred at workspace?_____

Professional and Trade Association Membership or Volunteer Work:

_____
_____
_____
_____

Publications, Achievements, Awards, Productions, Compositions, Presentations, Fellowships, Scholarships, and Kudos:_____

_____
_____
_____

Foreign Languages Spoken Or Reading Ability:_____

_____
_____
_____

Special Skills:

_____
_____

Military Service_____
From_____To_____Arm and Branch of Service_____

Highest Rank:_____

Service-Related Training or Schools Attended:_____

_____

                                    ✶   ✶   ✶

References

Never print the names, home phone numbers, and home addresses of your client's references directly on your client's resume. It's common courtesy to protect the privacy of references. When you do give out addresses, when asked for your references, get your reference's permission first and then use only your reference's current business address and business phone number.

For your own records, keep the names of your references and write to them asking for current letters of references, if your reference letters were written long ago. Employers want to see references dated within the current year.

Many people hold on to old reference letters because the people who wrote the letters are no longer available or cannot be located. On an employment application, your client probably will be asked to supply references from three people who know your client professionally. At this time, the accepted business etiquette practice is to supply the names and business addresses and phone numbers of the references.

*   *   *

References Worksheet:

Name of Reference:_____

Job Title:_____

Organization:_____

Business Address:_____

Business   Phone   Number_____Extension_____

Name of Reference:_____

Job Title:_____

Organization:_____

Business Address:_____

Business Phone Number_____Extension_____

Name of Reference:_____

Job Title:_____

Organization:_____

Business Address:_____

Business Phone Number_____Extension_____

Name of Reference:_____

Job Title:_____

Organization:_____

Business Address:_____

Business Phone Number_____Extension_____

Name of Reference:_____

Job Title:_____

Organization:_____

Business Address:_____

Business Phone Number_____Extension_____

*   *   *

Brief Worksheet:

Now that you have organized all of your client's personal information on these worksheets, it's time to create a brief outline. From this outline, you will choose specific information to highlight and include in your final, brief worksheet. This short outline is actually the first draft of your resume.

Show exactly why your client is qualified for the job in question. Include only the most important specifics to highlight your client's work-life story. Choose only the job-relevant benefits, advantages, and practical information. Now let's organize your outline further.

Clarity is your goal. The brief resume worksheet will cut your client's work life personal journal to resume size. Pencil right in book the brief resume worksheet that follows.

Brief Resume Worksheet:
Name_____
Street Address_____
City, State, Zip_____
Home Phone_____Business Phone_____
Email:_____Web Site Address_____

Objectives:

- _____
- _____
- _____
- _____
- _____

Summary of Qualifications: (Highlight Your Client's Best Skills And Experience Here.)

- _____
- _____
- _____
- _____
- _____

Education And Training:

- Institution:
- City,_____State:_____
- Degree/Certificate:_____
- OR
- Relevant Computer Coursework_____
- Workshops/Seminars/Internships_____
- _____

- Institution:
- City,_____State:_____
- Degree/Certificate:_____

- Or
- Relevant Computer Coursework_____
- Workshops/Seminars/Internships_____

Work Experience:_____

Job Title:_____
Company Name_____
City_____**State**_____
Employed From_____To_____

Major Job Responsibilities:_____
_____
_____
_____

_____

_____

_____

_____

_____

_____

_____

Special Awards, Assignments, Achievements in This Job_____

_____

_____

_____

Work Experience:

Job Title:_____

Company Name_____

City_____State_____

Employed from_____To_____

Major job responsibilities:_____

_____

_____

_____

_____

_____

_____

_____

_____

Special Awards, Assignments, Achievements in This Job_____

_____

_____

_____

Work Experience:

Job Title:_____

Company Name_____

City_____State_____

Employed From_____To_____

Major Job Responsibilities:_____

_____

_____

_____

_____

_____

_____

_____

_____

_____

_____

Special Awards, Assignments, Achievements in This Job_____

_____

_____

_____

_____

Work Experience:

Job Title:_____

Company Name_____

City_____State_____

Employed from_____To_____

Major job responsibilities:_____

_____

_____

_____

_____

_____

_____

_____
_____
_____
_____

Special Awards, Assignments, Achievements In This Job_____
_____
_____
_____
_____

Work Experience:

Job Title:_____
Company Name_____
City_____State_____
Employed From_____To_____

Your Major Job Responsibilities:_____
_____
_____
_____
_____
_____
_____
_____
_____
_____

Special Awards, Assignments, Achievements In This Job_____
_____
_____
_____
_____

Work Experience:

Job Title:_____
Company Name_____
City_____State_____

Employed From_____To_____

Your Major Job Responsibilities:_____

_____

_____

_____

_____

_____

_____

_____

_____

_____

_____

Special Awards, Assignments, Achievements in This Job_____

_____

_____

_____

_____

*   *   *

Special Skills:

Include your client's knowledge of specific skills, languages, software and hardware.

List skills such as the following:

- Web design
- Internet or digital content production
- Digital video editing/production,
- Digital journalism, word processing
- Desktop video editing, desktop publishing
- Software operation and knowledge of electronic publishing software, database operation, spreadsheets, programming, systems analysis, local area networks
- Computerized accounting skills, scientific programming, computer-aid design and drafting
- Healthcare paraprofessional or professional licenses and records administration
- Informatics, genomics technology and testing skills

- Technical illustration,
- Technical writing, courseware design
- Instructional technology
- Computer troubleshooting, repair

- Teaching or training skills
- Graphic design, animation, or any related computer
- Repair technology
- Scriptwriting, applied creative writing

- Include any office information systems equipment and software your client used daily in any capacity—from data entry to management of information systems

_____
_____
_____
_____
_____

Licenses and Teaching Credentials: List Your Certification.

_____
_____

Memberships In Organizations: List all associations in which you are involved that relate to the specific job, such as computer associations, training organizations, creative organizations, or scholarly research groups.

_____
_____
_____
_____

Awards, Honors, Scholarships, Fellowships: Include any special recognition you earned._____
_____

Publications and Productions: Include any books you wrote, articles published, videos produced, artwork exhibited or published.

_____
Computer Language Knowledge:_____
_____

Foreign Languages Spoken:_____

References: (Furnished upon request.)_____

Creative Skills_____

_____

_____

_____

_____

_____

CHAPTER 7

Achievements Are Action Verbs, and Action Verbs Are a Form of Branding

Your client needs branding, and action verbs contribute to branding by producing a moving forward action or a flow towards a conclusion about your client. Branding is about creating notability. Again, the eye is programmed to notice what is different—what stands out in a group. In a positive way, show how your clients will stand out on a resume, cover letter, or other information sent to a prospective employer or powerful audience that can influence the career future of your clients.

Now that you've outlined the first draft of your client's resume on this brief worksheet, you need to practice translating major job responsibilities into powerful phrases of achievement. The process of writing your resume gives you lots of practice in translating work history into action verbs.

Look at the list of action verbs in this book. Practice using action verbs in your client's resume. Describe work achievements with those action verbs. Refer to job responsibilities.

Instead of listing your client's accomplishments as duties, use action verbs to make these accomplishments powerful, memorable, exciting, appealing, and just as politely forceful as direct marketing advertisements designed to give pleasant *visibility* to your client's qualifications.

The following examples demonstrate how action verbs are used to describe a job applicant's powerful achievements:

*Redecorated the entire computer room, changing the work flow of the office to meet ergonomic health standards, increasing output by 85% and saving XYZ Corp. $200,000.

* Supervised the word processing department's computers valued at $9 million. Rerouted paperwork onto microfiches, saving the company $16,000 in 2005 and 3,000 cubic feet of storage space.

* Sold 3 million ABC software programs for XXY Corp., earning the company $10 million in gross sales in 2005; winning the best sales staffer of the year award. Trained 50 salespersons at 5 sites across the nation in sales operation in 2005.
* Created 3 new system upgrades for (insert brand) software.

Now it's your client's turn to use personalized action verbs to describe the highlights of your client's achievements. Briefly and tersely describe your own accomplishments using the verbs provided below.

When your client is finished, have the individual use action verbs to make a customized, personal list of achievements. Create action-oriented phrases to sell your client's skills to an employer with a specific job in mind. Action verbs often inspire people to recall important achievements done in the past. Peruse and make selections from the following action verbs:

Achievements Are Action Verbs Worksheet:

Organized_____

Planned_____

Established_____

Trained_____

Developed_____

Coordinated_____

Improved_____

Supervised_____

Created_____

Wrote_____

Presented_____

Illustrated_____

Designed_____

Analyzed_____

Managed_____

Instigated_____

Revised_____

Planned_____

Decided_____

Sold_____

Budgeted_____

Communicated_____

Evaluated_____

                              *   *   *

Action Verbs Resource Sheet

1,005 Action Verbs

1. Abated
2. Abbreviated
3. Abstracted
4. Abided
5. Abjured
6. Abnegated
7. Abraded
8. Abridged
9. Abrogated
10. Abseiled
11. Absolved
12. Abstained
13. Absorbed
14. Abstracted
15. Abutted
16. Accepted
17. Accelerated
18. Acclaimed
19. Accented
20. Accepted
21. Acclimatized
22. Accommodated
23. Accompanied
24. Accomplished
25. Accorded
26. Accounted
27. Accredited
28. Accrued
29. Accumulated
30. Accustomed
31. Achieved
32. Acknowledged
33. Acquainted
34. Acquiesced
35. Acquired
36. Acquitted
37. Acted
38. Activated
39. Actualized
40. Actuated
41. Adapted
42. Added
43. Addressed
44. Adduced
45. Adhered
46. Adjudged
47. Adjudicated
48. Adjoined
49. Adjourned
50. Adjured
51. Adjusted
52. Ad-libbed
53. Administered
54. Admired
55. Admitted
56. Adopted

57. Adored
58. Adorned
59. Adumbrated
60. Advanced
61. Advertised
62. Advised
63. Advocated
64. Aerated
65. Affected
66. Affiliated
67. Affirmed
68. Affixed
69. Afforded
70. Agglutinated
71. Aggrandized
72. Agreed
73. Aided
74. Aligned
75. Allied
76. Allocated
77. Allotted
78. Alternated
79. Amazed
80. Amended
81. Amplified
82. Amused
83. Analyzed
84. Anesthetized
85. Animated
86. Annotated
87. Announced
88. Answered
89. Anticipated
90. Appealed
91. Appeared
92. Appended
93. Appertained (to)
94. Applauded
95. Applied
96. Appliquéd
97. Appointed
98. Appraised
99. Apprised
100. Approached
101. Approved
102. Approximated
103. Arbitrated
104. Archived
105. Argued
106. Arose (from)
107. Arranged
108. Arrived
109. Articulated
110. Ascertained
111. Ascribed
112. Aspired
113. Assayed
114. Assembled
115. Asserted
116. Assessed
117. Assigned
118. Assimilated

119. Assisted
120. Associated
121. Assumed
122. Assured
123. Astonished
124. Astounded
125. Attached
126. Attained
127. Attempted
128. Attended
129. Attitudinized
130. Attributed
131. Attuned
132. Audited
133. Audiodidacted
134. Audio taped
135. Augmented
136. Authored
137. Authorize
138. Automated
139. Availed
140. Awarded
141. Became
142. Backed
143. Banked
144. Banded
145. Bartered
146. Beaded
147. Begot
148. Benchmarked
149. Benefited

150. Booked
151. Bought
152. Braided
153. Brailed
154. Branched
155. Brandished
156. Branded
157. Bred
158. Breaded
159. Broadcasted
160. Brought
161. Budgeted
162. Built
163. Calculated
164. Calmed
165. Campaigned
166. Camped
167. Captivated
168. Carded
169. Cared
170. Carried
171. Carted
172. Carved
173. Catalogued
174. Catapulted
175. Centered
176. Chaired
177. Changed
178. Channeled
179. Characterized
180. Charged

181. Charted
182. Chartered
183. Cheered
184. Cherished
185. Chiseled
186. Chronicled
187. Cited
188. Civilized
189. Claimed
190. Clarified
191. Cleaned
192. Cleared
193. Clocked
194. Closed
195. Clued
196. Coached
197. Coded
198. Codified
199. Coifed
200. Collaborated
201. Collected
202. Colored
203. Comforted
204. Commanded
205. Commemorated
206. Commercialized
207. Commissioned
208. Communicated
209. Compared
210. Compensated
211. Competed
212. Compiled
213. Complimented
214. Completed
215. Composed
216. Computed
217. Computerized
218. Conceived
219. Concentrated
220. Conceptualized
221. Conciliated
222. Concluded
223. Conducted
224. Configured
225. Congratulated
226. Congregated
227. Connected
228. Connoted
229. Conquered
230. Conserved
231. Considered
232. Constructed
233. Construed
234. Consulted
235. Consumed
236. Contracted
237. Continued
238. Contributed
239. Controlled
240. Converged
241. Conversed
242. Cooperated

243. Co-opted
244. Coordinated
245. Copyrighted
246. Corded
247. Corrected
248. Correlated
249. Counseled
250. Counted
251. Countered
252. Courted
253. Created
254. Credited
255. Crewed
256. Critiqued
257. Crusaded
258. Cued
259. Cultured
260. Curtailed
261. Customized
262. Cut
263. Cycled
264. Dated
265. Dealt
266. Debited
267. Debriefed
268. Debugged
269. Detailed
270. Decentralized
271. Decided
272. Deciphered
273. Declaimed

274. Declared
275. Decoded
276. Decorated
277. Decreased
278. Dedicated
279. Deferred
280. Defined
281. Deflected
282. Delegated
283. Deleted
284. Delighted (in)
285. Delineated
286. Delivered
287. Demonstrated
288. Demystified
289. Denominate
290. Denoted
291. Depicted
292. Deprogrammed
293. Deregulated
294. Derived
295. Described
296. Designed
297. Detailed
298. Detected
299. Determined
300. Detoured
301. Developed
302. Devised
303. Devolved
304. Dined

305. Disclosed

306. Divided

307. Divulged

308. Delighted

309. Derived

310. Devised

311. Devoted

312. Diagnosed

313. Dialogued

314. Diced

315. Dichotomized

316. Dictated

317. Differed

318. Digested

319. Digitized

320. Diluted

321. Directed

322. Digitized

323. Disagreed

324. Disclosed

325. Discovered

326. Discussed

327. Dispatched

328. Dispersed

329. Displayed

330. Dissolved

331. Distributed

332. Diversified

333. Divided

334. Divined

335. Documented

336. Docked

337. Donated

338. Doused

339. Drafted

340. Drew

341. Drove

342. Earned

343. Edited

344. Editorialized

345. Educated

346. Effected

347. Effloresced

348. Eked out

349. Elaborated

350. Elasticized

351. Elbowed

352. Elected

353. Elegized

354. Elevated

355. Eliminated

356. Embroidered

357. Emended

358. Emphasized

359. Employed

360. Empowered

361. Encased

362. Encountered

363. Encouraged

364. Energized

365. Engaged

366. Engineered

367. Engraved

368. Enhanced

369. Enlarged

370. Enlightened

371. Enlisted

372. Enlivened

373. Enriched

374. Ensured

375. Entered

376. Entertained

377. Envisioned

378. Epigrammatized

379. Epitomized

380. Equalized

381. Erected

382. Eructed

383. Escorted

384. Established

385. Estimated

386. Etched

387. Etiolated

388. Eulogized

389. Euphemized

390. Evaluated

391. Evanesced

392. Evangelized

393. Evidenced

394. Evoked

395. Evolved

396. Exacerbated

397. Exacted

398. Exalted

399. Examined

400. Excavated

401. Excelled

402. Exchanged

403. Exclaimed

404. Excoriated

405. Exculpated

406. Executed

407. Exemplified

408. Exercised

409. Exhorted

410. Exfoliated

411. Exhibited

412. Exonerated

413. Exorcized

414. Expanded

415. Expatiated

416. Expedited

417. Experienced

418. Explained

419. Explored

420. Exported

421. Exposed

422. Expressed

423. Extended

424. Extolled

425. Extrapolated

426. Facilitated

427. Farmed

428. Fascinated

429. Fastened
430. Faxed
431. Fed
432. Federalized
433. Felicitated
434. Ferreted
435. Fertilized
436. Fetched
437. Fictionalized
438. Filed
439. Filled
440. Filmed
441. Financed
442. Fired
443. Fitted
444. Fixed
445. Flattered
446. Flew
447. Flaunted
448. Flourished
449. Fluctuated
450. Flummoxed
451. Followed
452. Forecasted
453. Formalized
454. Formatted
455. Formed
456. Formulated
457. Fortified
458. Forwarded
459. Found

460. Founded
461. Franchised
462. Fraternized
463. Freed
464. Froze
465. Fulfilled
466. Functioned
467. Furnished
468. Gained
469. Garnished
470. Gathered
471. Gave
472. Generated
473. Genealogized
474. Geneticized
475. Genuflected
476. Gestured
477. Gesticulated
478. Girded
479. Glorified
480. Gnosticized
481. Governed
482. Graded
483. Grafted
484. Granted
485. Graphed
486. Gratified
487. Greeted
488. Grew
489. Guaranteed
490. Guarded

491. Guided
492. Hafted
493. Hailed
494. Halted
495. Handled
496. Harbored
497. Harmonized
498. Hastened
499. Harvested
500. Headed
501. Healed
502. Heaped
503. Heard
504. Heated
505. Helped
506. Hewed
507. Hired
508. Honored
509. Hoped
510. Hosted
511. Hugged
512. Humanized
513. Humored
514. Hustled
515. Hypnotized
516. Hypothesized
517. Identified
518. Ignited
519. Illustrated
520. Immigrated
521. Implanted

522. Implemented
523. Implied
524. Imported
525. Imposed
526. Impressed
527. Improved
528. Incited
529. Included
530. Incorporated
531. Increased
532. Indexed
533. Indicated
534. Indicted
535. Indulged
536. Industrialized
537. Influenced
538. Informed
539. Initialized
540. Initiated
541. Inked
542. Inquired
543. Inspected
544. Inspired
545. Installed
546. Instituted
547. Instructed
548. Insured
549. Integrated
550. Interested
551. Interfaced
552. Internalized

553. Internationalized
554. Interpreted
555. Interviewed
556. Introduced
557. Intuited
558. Invested
559. Investigated
560. Invented
561. Inventoried
562. Inverted
563. Invested
564. Invigorated
565. Involved
566. Issued
567. Joined
568. Journalized
569. Journeyed
570. Judged
571. Juried
572. Justified
573. Juxtaposed
574. Keyboarded
575. Lamented
576. Laminated
577. Landed (in)
578. Landscaped
579. Leased
580. Launched
581. Lectured
582. Legalized
583. Legitimized
584. Legislated
585. Lessened
586. Led
587. Left
588. Lighted
589. Linked
590. Listened
591. Litigated
592. Loaded
593. Loaned
594. Lobbied
595. Localized
596. Looked
597. Lyricized
598. Magnetized
599. Mailed
600. Maintained
601. Managed
602. Manipulated
603. Manufactured
604. Marked
605. Marketed
606. Mastered
607. Measured
608. Mediated
609. Memorized
610. Mentored
611. Merchandised
612. Merged
613. Met
614. Micrographed

615. Migrated

616. Ministered

617. Moderated

618. Modified

619. Modeled

620. Molded

621. Monitored

622. Morphed

623. Mortgaged

624. Motivated

625. Moved

626. Multiplied

627. Multitasked

628. Narrated

629. Navigated

630. Negotiated

631. Networked

632. Neutered

633. Neutralized

634. Normalized

635. Normed

636. Notated

637. Noted

638. Notified

639. Notarized

640. Nourished

641. Nursed

642. Obtained

643. Officiated

644. Opened

645. Orated

646. Operated

647. Opined

648. Orchestrated

649. Ordered

650. Organized

651. Oriented

652. Originated

653. Outlaid

654. Outlined

655. Outnumbered

656. Outpaced

657. Outperformed

658. Outplayed

659. Outran

660. Outshone

661. Outranked

662. Outvoted

663. Outwitted

664. Overawed

665. Overcame

666. Overdid

667. Overheard

668. Oversaw

669. Overstepped

670. Overstretched

671. Overwhelmed

672. Overworked

673. Overwrote

674. Owed

675. Owned

676. Oxygenated

677. Oxidized

678. Paced

679. Packaged

680. Packed

681. Parented

682. Participated

683. Partnered (with)

684. Patented

685. Patterned

686. Perceived

687. Perfected

688. Performed

689. Persevered

690. Persisted

691. Personalized

692. Persuaded

693. Perused

694. Petitioned

695. Photocopied

696. Photographed

697. Piloted

698. Pinpointed

699. Pitched

700. Placed

701. Planned

702. Planted

703. Played

704. Plotted

705. Pooled

706. Posed

707. Posted

708. Positioned

709. Practiced

710. Praised

711. Prayed

712. Predicted

713. Preempted

714. Prefaced

715. Preferred

716. Prepared

717. Presented

718. Presided

719. Pressed

720. Prevented

721. Probed

722. Proceeded (to)

723. Processed

724. Procreated

725. Procured

726. Produced

727. Professionalized

728. Programmed

729. Projected

730. Promulgated

731. Promoted

732. Proposed

733. Proscribed

734. Proofread

735. Prospered

736. Protected

737. Protested

738. Protracted

739. Proved
740. Provided
741. Publicized
742. Published
743. Purchased
744. Pursued
745. Qualified
746. Quantified
747. Quickened
748. Questioned
749. Queued
750. Quilted
751. Raised
752. Ran
753. Ranged
754. Rated
755. Razed
756. Reached
757. Realized
758. Reaped
759. Rearranged
760. Reared
761. Reasoned
762. Recalled
763. Recited
764. Received
765. Recited
766. Reclaimed
767. Recognized
768. Recommended
769. Reconciled
770. Reconstructed
771. Recorded
772. Recouped
773. Recovered
774. Recreated
775. Recruited
776. Rectified
777. Recycled
778. Redesigned
779. Redecorated
780. Redistricted
781. Reduced
782. Reenacted
783. Reentered
784. Referenced
785. Refreshed
786. Registered
787. Regulated
788. Rehearsed
789. Rehired
790. Reimbursed
791. Reinforced
792. Rejoiced
793. Related
794. Released
795. Relinquished
796. Relocated
797. Remedied
798. Reminisced
799. Remembered
800. Remodeled

801. Renewed
802. Rented
803. Reoriented
804. Repaired
805. Replenished
806. Replied
807. Reported
808. Reposed
809. Represented
810. Requested
811. Required
812. Requisitioned
813. Researched
814. Resized
815. Reshaped
816. Resolved
817. Responded to
818. Restored
819. Resourced
820. Resulted
821. Retailed
822. Retained
823. Retrained
824. Retired
825. Retooled
826. Retorted
827. Retrained
828. Retrieved
829. Returned
830. Reunited
831. Revamped

832. Reveled
833. Reviewed
834. Revised
835. Revived
836. Rewired
837. Roboticized
838. Rolled
839. Rose
840. Rotated
841. Routed
842. Rushed
843. Sailed
844. Sampled
845. Sanitized
846. Saved
847. Scanned
848. Scheduled
849. Scored
850. Screened
851. Scrimped
852. Sculptured
853. Secured
854. Sequenced
855. Selected
856. Sensed
857. Serialized
858. Served
859. Set objectives
860. Set up
861. Sewed
862. Shaped

863. Shared
864. Shredded
865. Showed
866. Signified
867. Simplified
868. Sized
869. Skilled
870. Socialized
871. Sold
872. Solicited
873. Solidified
874. Solved
875. Sorted
876. Sought
877. Spared
878. Sparked
879. Spayed
880. Specified
881. Speculated
882. Spiced
883. Spirited
884. Spoke
885. Sponsored
886. Spread
887. Staffed
888. Stabilized
889. Standardized
890. Starred
891. Stated
892. Stepped
893. Sterilized
894. Stimulated
895. Stored
896. Straightened
897. Streamlined
898. Strengthened
899. Stretched
900. Strolled
901. Strove
902. Structured
903. Styled
904. Subcontracted
905. Submitted
906. Succeeded
907. Summarized
908. Supervised
909. Supplied
910. Supported
911. Surfed
912. Surmised
913. Surveyed
914. Survived
915. Syndicated
916. Synthesized
917. Systematized
918. Tabulated
919. Tamped
920. Taught
921. Taxed
922. Teamed (up)
923. Telecommuted
924. Telemarketed

925. Telephoned
926. Televised
927. Terminated
928. Tested
929. Thwarted
930. Told
931. Tolled
932. Toughened
933. Toured
934. Traced
935. Tracked
936. Traded
937. Trained
938. Transacted
939. Transcribed
940. Transferred
941. Translated
942. Transmitted
943. Transported
944. Traveled
945. Treated
946. Trekked
947. Triumphed
948. Troubleshot
949. Trucked
950. Truncated
951. Trusted
952. Turned
953. Typed
954. Typeset
955. Understood

956. Undertook
957. Unified
958. United
959. Updated
960. Upgraded
961. Uplifted
962. Underscored
963. Used
964. Utilized
965. Validated
966. Valued
967. Varied
968. Vaunted
969. Venerated
970. Ventured
971. Verbalized
972. Verified
973. Videotaped
974. Viewed
975. Vindicated
976. Visualized
977. Vitalized
978. Vocalized
979. Voiced
980. Volunteered
981. Voted
982. Vulcanized
983. Waited
984. Waived
985. Watched
986. Waved

987. Weaned

988. Weighed

989. Weighted

990. Welded

991. Willed

992. Wintered

993. Withdrew

994. Wholesaled

995. Won

996. Word processed

997. Worked

998. Wrote

999. Wrought

1000. Xerographed

1001. X-rayed

1002. Yearned

1003. Yielded

1004. Zeroed (in)

1005. Zoned

*   *   *

Action Verbs Frequently Used on Resumes, Cover Letters, and Business Correspondence

1. Accelerated
2. Accomplished
3. Accepted
4. Accounted
5. Accrued
6. Accumulated
7. Achieved
8. Acquired
9. Acted
10. Activated
11. Actualized
12. Adapted
13. Adhered
14. Administered
15. Advertised
16. Advised
17. Affected
18. Affirmed
19. Afforded
20. Allocated
21. Analyzed
22. Animated
23. Announced
24. Anticipated
25. Antiqued
26. Applied
27. Appraised
28. Approved
29. Arbitrated
30. Arranged
31. Ascertained
32. Assembled
33. Assessed
34. Assigned
35. Assisted
36. Assumed
37. Assured
38. Attained
39. Audited
40. Augmented
41. Authored
42. Authorized
43. Automated
44. Awarded
45. Bought
46. Brought
47. Budgeted
48. Built
49. Calculated
50. Catalogued
51. Chaired
52. Changed
53. Charted
54. Clarified
55. Coached
56. Coded

57. Collaborated
58. Collected
59. Commanded
60. Communicated
61. Compared
62. Competed
63. Compiled
64. Completed
65. Composed
66. Computed
67. Conceived
68. Concentrated
69. Conceptualized
70. Conciliated
71. Conducted
72. Conferenced
73. Configured
74. Considered
75. Constructed
76. Construed
77. Consulted
78. Contracted
79. Contributed
80. Controlled
81. Cooperated
82. Coordinated
83. Copywrote
84. Corrected
85. Correlated
86. Counseled
87. Created

88. Credited
89. Critiqued
90. Cut
91. Dealt
92. Debriefed
93. Debugged
94. Decided
95. Deciphered
96. Decorated
97. Decreased
98. Defined
99. Deflected
100. Deigned
101. Delegated
102. Deleted
103. Delivered
104. Deregulated
105. Demonstrated
106. Derived
107. Described
108. Designed
109. Detailed
110. Determined
111. Developed
112. Devised
113. Devoted
114. Devulged
115. Dialogued
116. Directed
117. Discovered
118. Discussed

119. Dispersed
120. Displayed
121. Distributed
122. Documented
123. Drafted
124. Edited
125. Educated
126. Effected
127. Elaborated
128. Eliminated
129. Emphasized
130. Employed
131. Encouraged
132. Energized
133. Engaged
134. Engineered
135. Enhanced
136. Enlarged
137. Enlisted
138. Ensured
139. Entered
140. Entertained
141. Established
142. Estimated
143. Evaluated
144. Examined
145. Excelled
146. Exchanged
147. Executed
148. Exercised
149. Expanded

150. Expedited
151. Explained
152. Explored
153. Exported
154. Exposed
155. Extended
156. Extrapolated
157. Extraverted
158. Facilitated
159. Faxed
160. Fixed
161. Flowcharted
162. Forecasted
163. Formulated
164. Forwarded
165. Founded
166. Functioned As
167. Furnished
168. Generated
169. Governed
170. Graded
171. Granted
172. Graphed
173. Grew
174. Guaranteed
175. Guided
176. Handled
177. Head
178. Healed
179. Helped
180. Hired

181. Identified
182. Illustrated
183. Imagined
184. Implemented
185. Improved
186. Included
187. Increased
188. Indexed
189. Influenced
190. Informed
191. Initialized
192. Initiated
193. Inspected
194. Inspired
195. Installed
196. Instituted
197. Instructed
198. Insured
199. Integrated
200. Interested
201. Interfaced
202. Internalized
203. Interpreted
204. Interviewed
205. Introduced
206. Intuited
207. Investigated
208. Invented
209. Inventoried
210. Inverted
211. Involved
212. Issued
213. Joined
214. Judged
215. Juried
216. Justified
217. Keyboarded
218. Leased
219. Lectured
220. Lessened
221. Led
222. Linked
223. Loaded
224. Mailed
225. Maintained
226. Managed
227. Manipulated
228. Marketed
229. Mastered
230. Measured
231. Mediated
232. Merchandised
233. Merged
234. Met
235. Microfiched
236. Micrographed
237. Ministered
238. Moderated
239. Modified
240. Molded
241. Monitored
242. Motivated

243. Multiplied
244. Narrated
245. Navigated
246. Negotiated
247. Networked
248. Neutralized
249. Normalized
250. Normed
251. Notified
252. Notaried
253. Obtained
254. Officiated
255. Opened
256. Operated
257. Opined
258. Orchestrated
259. Ordered
260. Organized
261. Participated
262. Perceived
263. Performed
264. Persuaded
265. Photocopied
266. Photographed
267. Piloted
268. Pinpointed
269. Planned
270. Played
271. Posted
272. Practiced
273. Predicted
274. Preempted
275. Prepared
276. Presented
277. Presided
278. Pressed
279. Processed
280. Procured
281. Produced
282. Programmed
283. Projected
284. Promoted
285. Proposed
286. Proofread
287. Protected
288. Proved
289. Provided
290. Publicized
291. Published
292. Purchased
293. Qualified
294. Quantified
295. Quickened
296. Quilted
297. Questioned
298. Raised
299. Reclaimed
300. Recognized
301. Recommended
302. Recreated
303. Reconciled
304. Reconstructed

305. Recorded
306. Recouped
307. Recovered
308. Recreated
309. Recruited
310. Rectified
311. Recycled
312. Re-Designed
313. Redecorated
314. Reduced
315. Re-Entered
316. Registered
317. Regulated
318. Rehired
319. Reimbursed
320. Reinforced
321. Related
322. Released
323. Relocated
324. Renewed
325. Rented
326. Repaired
327. Replaced
328. Replentished
329. Reported
330. Represented
331. Requested
332. Required
333. Requested
334. Requisitioned
335. Researched
336. Resequenced
337. Reshaped
338. Resolved
339. Responded To
340. Responsible
341. (For)
342. Restored
343. Resumed
344. Retained
345. Retired
346. Retooled
347. Retrained
348. Retrieved
349. Returned
350. Revamped
351. Reviewed
352. Revised
353. Rewired
354. Robotized
355. Routed
356. Scanned
357. Scheduled
358. Scored
359. Screened
360. Sculptured
361. Selected
362. Sensed
363. Served
364. Set Objectives Set Up
365. Shaped
366. Simplified

367. Sold

368. Solicited

369. Solved

370. Sorted

371. Specified

372. Spoke

373. Sponsored

374. Staffed

375. Stabilized

376. Standardized

377. Starred

378. Stimulated

379. Streamlined

380. Strengthened

381. Structured

382. Styled

383. Subcontracted

384. Submitted

385. Succeeded

386. Summarized

387. Supervised

388. Supplied

389. Supported

390. Surveyed

391. Syndicated

392. Synthesized

393. Systematized

394. Tabulated

395. Taught

396. Telecommuted

397. Televised

398. Terminated

399. Tested

400. Traced

401. Tracked

402. Trained

403. Transacted

404. Transferred

405. Translated

406. Transmitted

407. Treated

408. Troubleshooted

409. Typed

410. Typeset

411. Updated

412. Upgraded

413. Underscored

414. Used

415. Utilized

416. Validated

417. Verbalized

418. Verified

419. Videographed

420. Videotaped

421. Visualized

422. Vocalized

423. Voiced

424. Waited

425. Waived

426. Wordprocessed

427. Wrote

428. Xerographed

CHAPTER 8

Job, Executive, & Life Coach Practice Simplifying & Critiquing Resumes

To sell or market a person's skills or products, first call in a popular celebrity who practices that same skill set. The celebrity's reputation and familiarity will help to bring in customers to see a design, service, or product *endorsed*, arranged, mentored, or produced by that celebrity. The celebrity's 'simple' presence makes sense and sells more 'product.' In the same fashion, **employers prefer 'simple' resumes that quickly make sense.** Simplicity, branding, and celebrity help to sell almost any service, skill, design, application of an idea, or practical product. Celebrities sell the idea of **commitment** and **value.** It's 100% about connection to clients' values and not about name dropping. A celebrity' presence adds substance and commitment both ways when you market your client's abilities, marketing techniques, or products. Simplify the information in the sample resumes and be able to use a checklist to edit your clients' resumes. As a job coach, writing resumes can be part of your online service business—not only writing resumes (with your clients) but also "righting resumes" as well as evaluating all types of business letters.

You'll learn to see and solve problems in resumes and describe your qualifications using action verbs. You'll soon be able to apply these universal strategies to simplify your own resume. All resumes need visual appeal. As an executive coach, you will have to create a brand for your client to position the individual in first place with prospective employers.

As a life or career coach, presenting your client's competencies will be about creating visual appeal by showing charisma, commitment, and simplicity in your client's honesty and achievements—the way your client gets results and solves problems step-by-step so others can follow the directions and information.

You're repackaging information about your client. The ways you present the information about your clients are based on visual, auditory, and kinesthetic appeal. If you decide to be a spiritual coach, a life coach, or an events planner, the direction won't be that far from running a resume and cover letter/business letter writing service business.

You'll have three goals for yourself as a coach-writer: solving problems, achieving results, and showing those who do business with you how to follow the easy-to-understand information you offer step-by-step.

Your ultimate goal is clarity. To make any information clear about any person or product, you need to create visual appeal. To create visual appeal, get rid of gaps.

The *big picture* is anyone who deals with you wants you to show him or her how to pull together diverse information. That's the secret formula for writing a resume or being a life, career, or executive coach. That's also the secret for being a spiritual coach. To write a resume or cover letter, sales letter or any business correspondence, show others how to pull together diverse information. That's how you reach visual appeal. The *little picture* is about getting rid of gaps—on paper and in life coaching. Life coaching is about commitment and simplicity. Job coaching is about organizing skills and presenting your clients' skills, attitude, and personality as *distinctive.*

Brand Your Clients with Distinction

As a career coach, create branding for your client. To be a brand 'name,' show clearly how your client is distinctive. In your client's resume, what counts most is brevity. Keep the resume to one page.

Your client needs to be portrayed as 'appropriate.' The resume must be a fit with the business and life purpose or goal of your client. Is your client's name easy to remember and pronounce? Work on how to get around this issue, perhaps even putting a nickname that's short and easy to pronounce next to the legal name, when appropriate.

Is your client likable? People hire likable people first. Is there information and eye candy appeal in the resume that can be interpreted visually? Is the resume standing independently? Will the resume land on its legs or end up in the round file? Does it have the opportunity for creative expression or expansion without clutter?

Trademark your client when it is possible to do so. Is your client's resume or achievements suitable for the Web, and will the client want visibility on the Web?

Creating Visual Appeal

Get rid of the time gaps in your clients' resumes. Most resumes are rejected because the employer can't pull together diverse information. Too much information is scattered. There's not enough white space around the printed information.

To make a resume unforgettable, you need to lay out your resume in four bolded, headlined sections divided by surrounding white space. Eliminate holes in time

You can improve your client's resume if you know what to change to get rid of the gaps. When you understand why the visual appeal of the resumes in the examples which follow were changed, you'll be able to apply the strategies and specifics to enhance your own resume.

Resumes suffer from the following problems:

- Impacted design and layout with no visual focus or appeal.
- Scattered information. Employer must become the catalyst.
- Ambiguity—instead of specific information targeted.
- Prominent information featured doesn't relate to the job duties.
- Information featured prominently labels the applicant as too idiosyncratic for the exact job duties required.
- Applicant has "an attitude" of manipulation and control hiding low-self esteem. "I dare you to hire me."
- Too much information is squeezed into a one-page girdle.
- Information isn't arranged logically and sequentially.
- Lack of organization. Employer has to pick and choose without being told what past job duties relate to the new job requirements.
- No variety in the formatting or separation of unrelated sections. The facts blend together into a blur. The employer has to pull together unrelated information visually.

Career or executive coaches who also write and evaluate resumes and business letters are catalysts. They bring together diverse and unrelated facts and make unrelated information appear to flow together. They also bring people together. They smooth out the transitions between unrelated jobs and unexplained holes in each client's work history.

Applicants frequently refuse to apply for jobs if their work histories don't match exact job requirements. Take a chance. Some employers will compromise on qualifications. The strategy lies in making the resume visually appear as if your abilities or basic skills are fully transferable between two unrelated jobs in spite of the lack of prior experience.

Mrs. XYZ's Resume

FIRST DRAFT OF CHRONOLOGICAL RESUME

Overview: "Telecommuting desired" job writing learning materials

Experience:

1963–Present Fulltime freelance writer of home-based business books and newspaper columns on computer businesses.

1990–2005 Adult education instructor/facilitator, Literature and Creative Writing, San Diego Community College District Continuing Adult Education

Taught novel writing to senior citizens at senior centers and in adult education classrooms during summer and fall semester 1990–1991, one day per week, until classes closed after 15 weeks, due to low enrollment.

1980–1981 Typist/Wordprocessor
Various clerical temporary employment agencies. (Type 50 words per minute.)

Typed medical report records for the psychiatry department at UCSD, San Diego in temporary assignments for a variety of temporary agencies for two-week assignments.
Typed medical records and reports for
Sharp Hospital, San Diego.

1976–1979 Substitute English Teacher and aide, San Diego Unified School District, San Diego

Taught English to high-school students, junior high, and elementary school students, kindergarten to 12th grade as a part-time hourly substitute for various one-day assignments until 1978.

Education: Master of Arts in English, SDSU, San Diego
1979. Winner of 1st Sigma Delta Chi Scholarship
Bachelor of Science in English Education,
New York University, 1964.

References: Available on request.

Mrs. XYZ's Resume

SECOND DRAFT OF AN EXTENDED/CREATIVE RESUME

OVERVIEW: Writer of computer career books seeks a position as a courseware designer, instructional technologist, technical writer of software user manuals, training materials designer, or writer and editor of corporate or instructional video scripts.

NON-TEACHING EXPERIENCE:

2005–present
Scriptwriter: Instructional Videos, San Diego County Education Center, also wrote 500-page book business services division at same site.

1987–2004—Independent Screenplay author, Los Angeles, CA.-Screenplays Written for a variety of independent producers: Home Video Feature Film Scripts include: Midnight Shift, Two Astronauts, Metalhead, Kiss Mommy, Playpen Hostages. Animation: The Amazons. Stage Play: A Man's Woman.

1985–1987—Instructional Film and/or Video Scripts: "The Eric Computer System," 1976. "Elderly Abuse," 1987, "Self Esteem," a video script, 1989. "International Child Abductions," 1990. Budget Feature Film and Television Script, "How to produce a great home video," script.
Plus two training film scripts written on distance teaching for independent educational film producers.

1980–1985—Typist/Wordprocessor:
Various clerical temporary employment agencies. (Type 50 words per minute.)

Typed medical report records part-time for the psychiatry department at UCSD, San Diego, in temporary assignments for a variety of temporary services.

Typed medical records and reports for Sharp Hospital, San Diego for short assignments.

1976–1980—Grant Writer: San Diego Unified School District: Wrote Grant Proposal for Miramar Community School.

1975–1976—Chief Technical Writer/Editor, M.A. English/Professional Writing/(Creative Computer Sciences Corp. San Diego (re-wrote Cobol Manuals and scientific/technical reports.)

1973–1975—Speechwriter: Biomedical Media Planning, San Diego, CA. Wrote medical speeches for president of health planning organization contracted for public relations research.

SOFTWARE:
Desktop publishing skills:
Microsoft Word, Corel WordPerfect, and Adobe PhotoShop.

TEACHING EXPERIENCE:

1991–Present—Grossmont College, El Cajon, CA.
Taught Creative Writing 126 two nights per week as part of team teaching for five weeks of one semester with emphasis on scriptwriting and drama.

1990–1991—San Diego Community College District, taught the following Saturday continuing adult education semester-long workshops in creative writing:

San Diego Community College (part time). Creative Writing Workshop for Older Adults: Midway Center: Taught course in composition, playwriting, autobiography writing.
Taught "Homebased Businesses For Freelance Illustrators and writers," screenwriting, writing the novel, writing the and Writers." Freelance business practices for animation script, comedy, writing feature films, writing for desktop video/home video, and corporate scriptwriting for instructional, industrial, 1973–1985—San Diego City College: Taught evening business communications course: Business Communications 119. Additional Fiction workshops include: videobiography, and writing.

1968–1973, Taught Playwriting at North Shores Adult School, San Diego. Taught course titled: Writing The Inner Personal Journal. Taught Personality Type and Writing Style from Both Sides of the Brain. Taught Writing the Historical Action Novel.

1964–1968, Substitute English Teacher, secondary school, and kindergarten teacher's Aide, San Diego Unified School District. Taught hourly and as an Aide, helped teachers with secondary school English on a temporary, hourly basis taking attendance, lecturing, and doing clerical work for teachers as well as tutoring students in creative writing. Helped design learning materials for curriculum for teachers, working with gifted students in creative writing workshops.

EDUCATION

M.A. English, San Diego State University, San Diego, CA, 1979
B.S. English Education/writing and psychology, New York University, NY, 1964.

REFERENCES AND WRITING SAMPLES ON REQUEST

*   *   *

Job/Career Coach Practice

How Job Coaches Evaluate & Critique Resumes

Mrs. XYZ's Resume

Analysis of First and Second Drafts

WHY EMPLOYERS REJECTED THE FOLLOWING RESUMES

Mrs. XYZ's Resumes aren't focused on any specific skill. Visually, it's not making an impact. Abstract ideas instead of concrete/detailed facts are used. The resume takes too much time to read and decipher. The resume is difficult to understand at first reading because of the lack of powerful action verbs and the use of too many unnecessary and redundant, descriptive adjectives.

The information is perceived by interviewers as if the applicant is still in the mind-set of the late 1950s (focusing on decades-old experience as a typist) instead of emphasizing concrete, up-to-date leadership skills in organizational communications management.

Classes closed in adult education courses after 15 weeks due to low enroll-ment did not have to be put on a resume. It's a negative statement that could imply that the low enrollment had been due to the applicant's teaching style or personality rather than to circumstances beyond the instructor's control.

What should appear is only that the applicant taught classes in a particular subject part-time during that year. It's important to keep chronological work histories factual and neutral whenever positive benefits to employers cannot be stated on a one-page resume.

Information is scattered between gaps of time when she was on the mommy-track as a homemaker and part-time worker, 1963–1972. Employers aren't going to take the time to pull together the past 31 years of her life since graduation from college. She has no specific career goal.

It's hard to make sense out of this resume because the emphasis is on her family life instead of her work life. Clarity needs to be improved by stating the subject taught, the dates, and the name of the businesses, schools, or colleges where employed. The format must be reworked with emphasis on the transfer-ability of her creative skills as content. Employers can't follow the logic. To solve these problems in her resume, her work history has to be simplified. This writer/teacher needs a distinctive 'brand' to stand out from the crowd. She needs to be portrayed as likeable and charismatic. What needs to be emphasized is that she's written several scripts and technical manuals, and also is a success-ful creative writing educator and fiction author with specific skills to share.

This information needs to be conveyed in a clear, one-page resume. However, she's applying for a job as a technical writer and is trying to switch from fiction writing of scripts to writing technical manuals. In the final, one-page resume, emphasis will be on her skills as a technical writer. The ability to transfer writing skills will be emphasized.

FINAL DRAFT/Technical Writer

Mrs. XYZ's Resume
Street Address
City, State
Phone, Email address

JOB TITLE: TECHNICAL WRITER/SOFTWARE MANUALS

SOFTWARE EXPERIENCE

*Wrote book on applications software uses for home-based business owners, published by Simon & Schuster, 1985.

*Weekly national newspaper columnist for The Business News (for small business owners). Write business strategies advice columns. Write software reviews. Weekly columnist for national newspaper.

*Wrote video script training teachers in the operation of the Eric computer system for educational research, San Diego County Education Department, Media Center.

TRAINING EXPERIENCE

*Professsional Writing Instructor, San Diego Community College District, 1990–1991. Specialist in fiction. Adult Education.

*English Instructor, San Diego Unified School District San Diego, 1976–1978 (Substitute teacher on assignment.)

RELATED COMPUTER SOFTWARE EXPERIENCE

Writing: Author of 23 published 100-page pamphlets on computer art careers and careers in graphic design.

Wordprocessing and Desktop Publishing: Owner of a private word-processing, desktop publishing, and technical writing homebased business specializing in career information using Microsoft Word, CorelDraw!, and PhotoShop

EDUCATION
* Master of Arts in English (CreativeWriting Emphasis), San Diego State University, December 1979

* Bachelor of Science in English Education, New York University, June 1964.

LIST OF PUBLISHED WORKS ATTACHED. REFERENCES SENT UPON REQUEST.

Mrs. XYZ's Resume

Analysis of Final Draft by Job Coach

Problem Solved

Mrs. XYZ's re-written resume is now focused on the targeted job title, that of a technical writer specializing in writing software user manuals even though her college major had been creative writing and she had taught fiction writing part-time in adult continuing education classes. Although she has no experience in actually writing a software user manual, she has three related skills to emphasize using bold visual appeal:

1) Combined experience writing about software and the operation of home-based computer businesses.

2) Weekly newspaper business strategies column.

3) Prior teaching experience and education. Although these two factors qualify Mrs. XYZ for a job writing software user manuals, this resume writer needs to write a manual to show to employers at interviews.

Related Jobs Using the Same Resume

Mrs. XYZ could also apply for jobs writing, editing, or coordinating the publication of technical or literary training materials, developing curriculum materials, career books, and writing public relations literature for computer publishing companies or software manufacturing and design firms.

In the expanding field of electronic publishing, such knowledge of desktop publishing and word processing software also qualifies a desktop publisher to write sales brochures and press kit materials for desktop publishing software firms. Desktop publishing skills are often used to obtain jobs as proofreaders, technical writers, or technical editors. One growth area is training materials courseware design for teachers of word processing or desktop publishing. Mrs. XYZ wasn't interested in applying for teaching, public speaking, technical training, or sales jobs.

Practical Strategies

1. **JOB OVERVIEW:** The job overview is now focused on the exact job title, "writer of software user manuals" instead of on telecommuting. The overview has been shortened and clarified.

Excess wordiness is out. The employer can read under the experience cluster that Mrs. XYZ's a specialist in writing about home-based businesses and software reviews, fields more closely related to software user manual writing than teaching novel writing to senior citizens.

Emphasis on "telecommuting desired" was removed from the job objective. At the end of the interview, she can ask whether telecommuting is permitted, or whether the hours are flexible. She will get another chance to decide whether to work at home or commute to an outside office, since it's not a strict requirement.

2. **EXPERIENCE:** Experience in the final draft is now focused and organized into three clusters that make smooth transitions from one to the next without holes in time or other visual gaps in employment.

Clusters of similar kinds of work are grouped together—writing with writing, teaching with teaching, and word processing with desktop publishing (listed under Related Software Experience). Her office skills are used on a professional level to operate her own desktop publishing/word processing/writing business rather than given visual appeal as clerical skills by listing typing speed.

The chronological work history dates were subdued. She left off her resume the "missing time gap" when she was on the full-time "mommy track" from 1965 to 1973 and from 1981 to 1991. Experience needed to be strengthened. So she organized her experience in segments that have a direct relation to the exact job title of "software user manual writer."

She didn't list her occasional temporary typing jobs, which spanned the years from 1959 to 1981. Her temporary assignments all lasted from a week to seven months on each job and were for many different firms: from hospitals to law offices, to construction, to typing badges at convention registrations, to selling classified real estate ads on the phone for a weekly newspaper.

3. **RELATED SOFTWARE EXPERIENCE:** Mrs. XYZ wanted to play up the importance of her familiarity with computers and software, even though she had never taken a computer or software course. She's entirely self-trained in several kinds of desktop publishing software and owns her own computer.

To deemphasize the lack of formal training, she emphasized running her own home based desktop publishing and word processing business. She lists the software as well as the specialty. The focus emphasized her experience or interest in writing materials about computer careers, specifically computer art (graphics, animation, and illustration).

With each "Related Software Experience" specialty listed in a cluster, the job interest becomes more focused. To create visual appeal she bolded the headlines of her specialty.

Employers can refer back to general experience to see that she reviews software in her weekly column for a national business newspaper. These facts in sequential order build up her credibility and qualifications for the job objective or title.

Instead of emphasizing that she 'keyboards' using word processing—which would lead an employer to place her in the typing pool, she focuses on the fact that she owns her own home-based business, directing and overseeing word processing and desktop publishing design.

She's removed her typing speed, which is a dead giveaway to employers that she'll accept a lower-paid clerical job instead of a professional job as a higher-paid technical writer or editor. Typing speed spent typing on an old IBM in use during the 1950s through 1980s reflects skills that need to be updated with computer keyboarding skills and knowledge of Excel, Access, and Microsoft Word or Corel World Perfect software if applying for a general office clerical or administrative assistant job as what used to be known two decades ago as an executive secretary.

When applying for a professional job, omit your typing speed. It's usually women who list it. Typing speed is a throwback to the fifties, white-gloves mentality when most degreed women were shoveled into typing pools for decades. Use it only if you're applying for a word-processing, medical transcription, secretarial, court reporting, or data-entry job where you're hired mainly for your 'keyboarding' speed.

4. **EDUCATION:** Mrs. XYZ's fine educational attainment of a master's degree in English/creative writing remains listed. Since she's not looking for a teaching job, professional writing is emphasized, especially the writing of non-fiction computer-oriented-educational and training materials. Her main problem is making the switch from majoring in a specialty of fiction writing, to finding more plentiful jobs available writing non-fiction in either medical journalism technical writing, or writing multi-authored (or single-authored) computer books and software manuals. She understands that computer books become out of print and obsolete quickly.

Her degrees in English automatically qualify her for a job as a writer or editor as well as proofreader and indexer (with instruction in how to index books) whether in the software field, instructional design, or in education.

It's easier to train a writer in programming than it is to train a programmer to be a writer specializing in making complex terms simpler and clearer to non-technical readers. Technical writers also are needed to write easy-to-follow instructional flyers and booklets on how to assemble toys and furniture, or how to set up gadgets. Every type of device or software comes with a user manual, booklet, or brochure.

5. **LIST OF PUBLICATIONS ATTACHED:** Instead of the usual "references on request," it's better (for credibility) for a creative person to attach a

one-page list of books, pamphlets, articles, art, videos, or interactive fiction—with dates of publication/production.

In final analysis, Mrs. XYZ's revised resume is unforgettable, impressive, powerful, and competitive with the hundreds of resumes that her targeted company will receive. The cleaned-up revision has a better chance of being taken seriously than the original resume she used for two years without one resulting live interview.

         *   *   *

Job Coach Practice: Analyzing Mr. XYZ's resume

Mr. XYZ

FIRST DRAFT OF AN ABILITIES RESUME

OVERVIEW: Applications Programmer, any field except finance.

EDUCATION:

1985   A.S. Computer Science & Information Systems
San Diego City College, San Diego, 3.45 grade point average

1977   Attended AT&T 4ESS Switching Machine School to learn how to repair 4ESS Switching Machine.

1962   B.A. Anthroplogy, American University, Washington, D.C. 3.0 grade point average

1963   18 graduate credits in Middle East Area Studies, American University, Washington, D.C.

HARDWARE: 4ESS, IBM 486, MAC, AMIGA, Video Toaster
SOFTWARE: Microsoft Word, Word Perfect, DeLuxe Paint
DBase IV+, Paradox, Lotus 123.
Local Area Networks with Novell

COMPUTER LANGUAGES: Assembly, Pascal, C, C++, Basic

EXPERIENCE: AT & T Corp, San Diego, CA 92103
June 1977
to Aug.1993   **COMMUNICATIONS TECHNICIAN & SWITCHMAN**

Personally responsible for maintenance
and repair of a 4ESS switching machine.

Worked on machine translations and
also fixed carrier systems that
go to different cities.

Analyzed schematic diagrams and
analyzed Assembly language of
maintenance programs.

1963–
1977

AT&T Corp., Los Angeles, CA 90028

COMMUNICATIONS TECHNICIAN AND SWITCHMAN

Repaired microwave and carrier systems including private line circuits.

References on request.

Mr. XYZ's Resume

ANALYSIS OF FIRST DRAFT BY JOB COACH

WHY EMPLOYERS REJECTED THE RESUME:

Experience is subdued in the bottom third of the resume and listed too broadly without itemizing what he actually did for the past thirty years on a daily basis that is fully transferable to a programmer's job. He doesn't link his thirty years as a telephone company switchman to new areas of telecommunications.

Mr. XYZ briefly lists three tasks he repeated daily for three decades at the telephone company, but the details do little to convince an employer that he is a competitive programmer. Also, he asks to work in "any field except finance." He needs to focus on specific fields that welcome his skills.

PRACTICAL EVALUATION:

Job Overview:

1) Mr. XYZ wants to find an applications programmer's job in "any field" except finance. Employers are looking for focus when they begin to scan the resume.

2) Focus is lacking in the upper half of the resume, especially in the job overview statement.

3) There's no play up of his 30-year outstanding performance as a telephone company communications technician/switchman. He needs to replace his job objective with more realistic job titles that answer the question, "in what field?" Several possibilities include the following:

- Applications programmer in telecommunications.
- Sales of applications software to telephone company spin-offs.
- Database management for telephone or telecommunications firms selling to corporations.
- Specialty items technology such as repair and installation of distance teaching telecommunications linkage equipment and related programming.

- Information systems technology or management.
- Local Area Networks technology.
- Corporate telecommunications technology/repair, programming, or installation.

4) His resume is unfocused as far as the exact nature of his job objective. All we know is that he doesn't enjoy working in a finance-oriented environment.

Education:

5) He has attended annual training at AT&T school to learn repair of the various telephone company machines, but has left this off of his resume, assuming that none of the skills are transferable to work outside the telephone company. Mr. XYZ has had over 20 annual training sessions lasting from two weeks up to five months per year at locations all over the nation.

6) His itemized liberal arts education in anthropology and Middle East area studies is irrelevant to his job goal as a programmer. It shouldn't take up half the page.

7) He has overpowered his communications technician qualifications by emphasizing his early general education at the top of the resume.

Experience:

8) Mr. XYZ needs to show how his perceived 'narrow' daily job experience reading computer program errors in Assembler language code transfers to 'wider' fields outside the phone company. Emphasis on correcting errors in computer code serves as a bridge between the old communications technician job and a new job goal in applications programming. He's switching from repair and maintenance to programming.

9) Mr. XYZ needs to detail his knowledge of programming in C Language, Pascal, Basic, and Local Area Networks using Novell, learned in his community college courses paid for by his employer. These are professional quality skills that can be transferred to the new goal as a programmer.

10) The revised abilities/competencies resume can show how skills learned from his evening computer courses at community college and daytime job can

be transferred to related fields. His whole career is not bound to phone-company switching machine maintenance and circuit repair.

11) Mr. XYZ needs to position the most programming-relevant skills at the top of his resume and bold the most important competency titles. Only practical skills and experience which can be easily transferred to other companies need to be emphasized.

12) In the cover letter, Mr. XYZ can refer to his excellent work evaluations and attendance award and use them later as references.

References:

13) There's no need to take up a line on the resume stating, "references on request," for a person who has only worked at one company for many years. The employer already knows how to call the phone company to verify the employment or ask for the name of Mr. XYZ's immediate supervisor. Note all the powerful nouns or action verbs are highlighted. Nouns are placed in the left hand column. Use one action verb or one noun in the left hand column to describe education, skills, or experience.

Mr. XYZ

Final Draft

APPLICATIONS PROGRAMMER: TELECOMMUNICATIONS

OVERVIEW:

- Communications technician
- Software troubleshooter for 30 years
- Maintenance and repair service
- Programming position wanted
- Machine translations, analysis specialty
- Assembly language maintenance programs
- Analysis of schematic diagrams

PROFESSIONAL SKILLS

COMPUTER LANGUAGE ANALYSIS:	Assembly language (4ESS) Machine language translations
PROGRAMMING LANGUAGES:	Assembly, Pascal, C, C++, Basic, Cobol, Local Area Networks with Novell.
DOCUMENT PREPARATION:	Prepare reports and schematic diagrams. Use of word processing software, advanced use of database packages and spreadsheets.
EQUIPMENT REPAIR AND MAINTENANCE:	**4ESS Switching Machines:** Troubleshooting, maintenance, and repair of private line systems, microwave, fixed carrier systems, and telecommunications equipment which route to different cities.
EXPERIENCE:	
<u>June 1963–Present</u>	Communications Technician and Switchman, **AT&T Corporation**, San Diego, CA & Los Angeles, CA

EDUCATION:	Associate in Science (AS) Computer Sciences and Information Systems San Diego City College, San Diego, CA, 1985
	Bachelor of Arts (BA) Anthropology American Univ. Washington, DC,1962
REFERENCES ON REQUEST	

Mr. XYZ's Resume

JOB COACH'S ANALYSIS OF FINAL DRAFT

Problem Solved

Mr. XYZ's resume is now focused on his competencies in the specific area of telecommunications. This industry reflects the marriage of computers to a vast network of corporate telephone systems. He's now prepared to apply to the burgeoning field of wireless telecommunications for job descriptions so new that no one has yet had time to get experience in them.

The revised resume applies his thirty years of 'craft' level experience working for one telephone company to new technology opportunities with a wide variety of telecommunications firms that link telephone systems with computer equipment and peripherals. His unique combination of experience, company school training, and employer-paid computer training in outside college courses enables him to use his programming skills and technician experience.

The new resume has helped Mr. XYZ transfer his competencies to a wider variety of businesses within the familiar—and technologically expanding 'new' telecommunications industry. His main problem was to find out how his former job competencies and continuous retraining in new programming languages could be used outside of the deregulated phone company.

Related Jobs Using a Similar Resume

He can choose from telecommunication companies involved with the maintenance and repair or distribution of satellite, fax, and modem equipment used for global teleconferencing. He can apply for programming and technician positions with local area networks.

Mr. XYZ can apply for positions as a programmer or technician or use a combination of both competencies. Corporations receptive to an applicant with such skills include the new field of wireless telecommunications, manufacturers of equipment used for distance teaching, global videoconferencing, electronic mail, and telecommunications firms involved in information retrieval from databases.

Practical Strategies

Job Overview

1) Mr. XYZ has targeted the telecommunications industry. The revised resume now applies the specific job title as applications programmer to a field

that can use all of his competencies rather than only his mid-career training in programming.

2) He clarifies his telephone company technician skills which ads to his ability to link computer equipment with telephone and wireless systems. His job objective prepares the interviewer for the wide variety of competencies that are itemized in the order of their importance to a wide variety of businesses.

3) Focus is now on a specific specialty. Mr. XYZ tersely explains that after thirty years in maintenance and repair with the phone company, he is transferring thirty years of continuous annual retraining and (outside of employment) learning of computer programming to a new company in the expanding telecommunications industry.

Professional Skills

4) Since Mr. XYZ desires an applications programmer's position, he emphasizes his competencies in computer language analysis, programming languages, and document preparation using advanced database packages, spreadsheets, and word processing software packages. Only last on the list does he enter his equipment repair and maintenance skills, inspite of the fact that he's done this routine daily for three decades. It's obvious he wants a break in the routine and prefers to program.

5) His repair work consisted mainly of weeding out and repairing mistakes in the Assembler computer language code on the 4ESS machine. This task focused on reading computer code from printout sheets many hours during the day and night shifts.

6) The order in which the professional skills are listed show how important they are in seeking a new position as a programmer.

Experience

7) He's worked only at one company since his graduation. There's no need to list companies in the order of importance or break experience into subdivisions, as would be done if he had worked at numerous firms.

Education

8) Mr. XYZ's training was listed at the end of the resume. His 30-year career with the telephone company presupposes that the corporation sent him to

company school to learn how to maintain and repair the 4ESS switching machine he worked on full-time.

9) His computer-related education leading to the Associate in Science degree in Computer Sciences and Information Systems was listed first. It shows he spent two years in evening community college learning six new computer languages and specific technical competencies.

10) His general education is singled out and not mixed with job training. The general education B.A. degree he received in anthropology was listed last to show he completed a well-rounded education in the study of humankind before starting his technical career.

Resume Summary Checklist

Many job coaches, employers, or human resource managers have individual pointers about what's organizationally correct on a resume. Visual appeal is subjective. Resume readers and writers prefer uncluttered resumes that draw attention to job-related successes. Brevity and simplicity are important.

The following checklist is a summary of 50 commonly accepted do's and don'ts of resume writing. Use these tips as you edit your clients' resumes.

Give this check-list to your clients before they begin to compile information that will eventually be sorted and analyzed. The goal is whether selected information will be placed into a resume or included on brief, powerful, and concrete cover letters.

Organizationally Correct

1. Clarify only those competencies valued by the employer in the job objective and overview section of your resume.

2. Plan your resume as if it were a personal display ad designed to sell the benefits and advantages of hiring you.

3. All facts on your resume are true. They can be checked and verified at any time.

4. At the top of your resume are bold headings or important titles which state your competencies and responsibilities.

5. Use large amounts of white space to create visual impact.

6. Keep the resume simple.

7. List only your most important degree first.

8. Leave salaries out.

9. Use active verbs to describe your competencies.

10. Persuade and market.

11. Leave out employers' names.

12. Resumes do not need to contain personal information such as your age, height, weight, or marital status.

13. Be specific and practical.

14. Show how your preparation for the job fits the company's requirements.

15. Use bullets, to draw attention to the statement "why you're best qualified for this job."

16. Only put required items on your resume.

17. Summarize your qualifications in an overview at the top of your resume.

18. Use three-word phrases to highlight your specifics and link competencies to job.

19. Explain why you left your last job as it relates to the new job duties.

20. Be clear about your most important qualifications.

21. Don't flout tradition.

22. The word 'Resume' never appears on your actual resume.

23. Mention how much you increased your company's profit or how much money or business you brought in, such as your high sales record, to improve

your visibility and credibility. Mention percentages, increases, or dollar amounts per year.

24. Write your resume as if it were a press kit going to the media.

25. Include patterns and similarities between your competencies and the company's patterns and trends.

26. Give concrete evidence of good work evaluations.

27. Itemize how much profit you made for the company recently in dollars and cents.

28. List your accomplishments in terms of the company's profit, not personal profit.

29. Keep the tone or mood of the resume objective, neutral, and professional.

30. Show patience and dedication to climb the ladder.

31. Include dates on all types of resumes as a reference point.

32. Itemize the profit, the competencies, benefits, advantages, and skills that make future employers want to label you as a hard worker. Show how you reduced costs for your former employer.

33. Desktop published resumes are preferred. Use a word processor or desktop publishing software to typeset your resume so that it looks professionally printed or clearly typed with bold contrasts for the headings and titles. Use bullets to attract attention to facts.

34. Shorten run-on job responsibility paragraphs to three 10-15 word sentences or two tight paragraphs per job.

35. Sell only what you realistically can offer.

36. After using a computer's spelling and grammar checker, proofread your resume again for computer errors—three times—on different days, before having it duplicated for mailing.

37. Use 20 pound bond laser printer and duplicating paper, 100% cotton paper, or linen 'laid' resume paper to prevent smudging and tearing. The envelope, cover letter, and letterhead should be of the same color and weight.

38. Address your resume to the person with the authority to hire you in the department for which you want to work. Name the person specifically.

39. List business phone numbers, not people's home phone numbers.

40. List your most recent job, business or accomplishment first.

41. Relate your military service to specific civilian job objectives. If you're retiring from the military, include what you did in the service as a bridge toward a specific career.

42. List only memberships in professional associations, and trade or business organizations that relate to the occupation.

43. List all volunteer work for professional associations that relate to the type of job you want if you have not worked for pay outside the home for a long time or are a student, a retiree, or serving an internship to obtain work experience.

44. Use volunteer work with business organizations to show job progression, networking with colleagues, activity, enthusiasm, or to showcase employers.

45. Interview employers or professional association members and officers for resume research. (Offer to give them a benefit by publicizing or creating visibility for them for free.)

46. Summarize a job-related premise about yourself in one line on the resume overview.

47. All action verbs used in your resume illustrate an image of what you're all about at work in positive, concrete business, not boastful terms.

48. No information appears on your resume regarding your driver's license unless you're applying for a job where driving is a requirement.

49. Your resume reflects how you work under pressure in high-stress jobs.

50. Your age is not on your resume. Any physical challenges are not listed on your resume. Employers are looking for work-related challenges you overcame to be highly productive and profitable.

*   *   *

Additional Resume and Cover Letter Pointers for Job Coaches to Discuss with Clients

Don't be redundant or a space-waster on your resume, and don't repeat yourself at the interview. Some employers prefer that you keep the names and addresses of all your references to yourself until asked to supply them upon hiring or at the final interview. Others insist that you state on your resume that references are available. Use your common sense.

Tell the interviewer on the phone that all references are available on request, or mention it in your cover letter. The employers who complain state that it's redundant for an employer to have to read at the bottom of every single resume that comes in the same line "references on request." It irritates some employers.

Use your discretion and individual preference to decide whether or not to include the phrase on your resume. Personally, I'd leave it out of the resume, but make it known immediately that it's available. I'd also leave out the word "resume" at the top of a resume. That's also redundant and a space waster.

The reader knows what you're sending from the format and overview. You will have to supply references and sometimes work samples, writing samples, software designs, videos, or art and slides in a portfolio when asked, if you're going for one of those creative expression jobs in the computer industry. Creative doesn't mean "far out." It means profitable by filling voids or gaps in the community. The computer world always needs better and more profitable tools.

*   *   *

Organizationally Incorrect

1. Use the reader's time to pull together many unrelated facts and experience.

2. Give no practical reasons why they should hire you.

3. Exaggerate your achievements, awards, and educational background.

4. Use long, confusing sentences and run-on paragraphs up front.

5. Crowd too much typing into a one-page corset or use so much white space that you make your resume too long.

6. Expect the reader to pick and choose from scattered facts to fill "any job" in the computer industry.

7. Include all degrees and diplomas not relevant to job.

8. Include your minimum acceptable salary required.

9. Boast with many passive adjectives.

10. Plead for the job.

11. Complain about former employers.

12. Refer to ageism. List any health problems.

13. Force the employer to read between the lines by using abstract descriptions.

14. Learn nothing about the job and the company.

15. Distract the reader with italic script or fancy fonts.

16. Send unnecessary photographs, portfolios, tapes, videos, and list hobby preferences.

17. Run your summary two paragraphs so it overpowers your resume or makes it redundant.

18. Let the reader try to make sense of how your education fits the job requirements.

19. Reveal negative emotions or judgments about why you left your previous employment.

20. List all your skills. State you'll work at any job open in the firm.

21. Disregard a particular corporation's tradition, modeling, or orientation toward change.

22. Take up space on your resume by writing what the employer already knows.

23. Leave it to the reader to know what's important and what's not.

24. Encourage the invisibility of your resume by blurring your achievements and skills.

25. Elaborate how autonomous and different you are in operating your own business.

26. Boast how important and competitive you are, how creatively original as an entrepreneur

27. Emphasize how much more important your ideas are than production or profit.

28. Tell how hard you worked or how loyal you were when the company betrayed you by making you a temporary employee to save money.

29. Reveal an undertone of hostility, resentment, and anger.

30. Demand a top-level position only because you have a recent degree from a prestigious school.

31. Focus your resume on the importance of the dates and bold or underline the years you worked.

32. Keep repeating throughout the resume how hard-working you are and how devoted, determined, or dedicated you are to jobs you no longer have. Tell how aggressive you are and how you can beat out the competition.

33. Type your resume with a faded ribbon and photocopy it on cheap paper marred with grey photocopy machine marks. Submit a colored-paper resume with blurred lettering of low contrast.

34. Use a few long paragraphs to tell everything about your work history.

35. Promise what you wish you could be.

36. Send your resume off the first day you write it without letting it "cool off" a few days. Typos are sure to appear.

37. Use black paper with white lettering because you think it will imprint the reader's brain as a reverse display print ad.

38. Send your resume to the human resources manager whose job it is to screen out the wrong applicants the majority of the time.

39. Give out phone numbers of personnel department people who don't know you well, aren't familiar with your business skills, and who will respond negatively to questions about your competencies or work history.

40. Emphasize equally all your jobs, even those unrelated jobs from many years ago. List all your clerical jobs, and then ask for a job in a non-clerical capacity without bridging the gap from one type of work to the other.

41. Ramble on about all your military honors, travels, or experience which never relate to the job competencies requested.

42. List only membership in social and high IQ groups, civic and community or religious and ethnic groups.
Summarize all the work you did for community service clubs.

43. Advertise yourself as a down-heeled, bored to tears housewife or househusband with no previous bad job experience to unlearn.

44. List on your resume all the colleagues with whom you recently exchanged cards and expect them to give you good job references and referrals.

45. Use your cover letter to beg employers to create non-existent jobs especially to fit your talents—after you volunteer to be a public speaker on a panel.

46. Every item in your resume points to the conclusion that life at work is bearable only if lived elsewhere in the imagination.

47. You include your I.Q. on your resume, grade point averages below 3.5, and the results of psychological questionnaires. List your illnesses.

48. You state at the top of your resume that you're a non-driver who will work only near a bus line. Then you explain why you don't drive in negative terms such as "I'm too nervous to drive and failed the driving test numerous times before I abandoned all hope."

49. You dare the employer to hire you because you're a victim and need rescuing.

50. Your resume states that you're a senior citizen, retiree, displaced home-maker, battered spouse, or uses the word 'elderly' instead of 'mature.' You note that you were fired due to covert ageism. Or you state that you're handicapped, disabled or 'handi-capable.'

More Tips from a Job Coach on What Not to Put on Resumes

Don't explain, for example, that the reason you didn't work for the past number of years was that you were housebound with agoraphobia and panic disorder and had to work online at home because of being unable to leave your home. Medical situations should not be on a resume. Your medical records are confidential.

Employers only want to know whether you can perform the job. Instead of listing what you can't do, emphasize what you can do and what hours you want to work or whether you will only work online at home.

You don't have to give a reason for wanting to work online at home during certain hours you specify other than you prefer flexible hours for personal reasons. State the hours you will work and whether you want to work only at home online. Don't put on your resume that you don't drive unless the job requires driving to reach the office or do errands.

*   *   *

PRACTICAL JOB COACHING THROUGH EVALUATION

1. **Job Overwiew:** The job overview isn't specific enough for the majority of time-pressured employers to understand. They'd have to read between the lines. Employers scan resumes for sequential facts and easy-to-follow logic. There's no way to tell how long applicant worked.

2. **Experience:** The chronological work history is unclear and not chrono-logical.

Too much emphasis is on issues not related to the job in question.

3. The sections aren't separated. Long gaps of unemployment exist.

4. Experience isn't sorted or organized into related segments that show how skills are transferred. Resumes need smooth transitions.

5. Superfluous experience is merged with important skills.

6. **Education:** The degrees are relevant to the job objective. There's no problem with the visual placement of the general education and degrees.

Improvement could be made by detailing the professional writing emphasis of the two degrees, rather than only listing the major, 'English' and "English Education." Mrs. XYZ needs to specify the emphasis within the major: literature, linguistics, teaching, professional writing (nonfiction), or creative writing (fiction). An area of focus helps to fit the exact job title to the person's specialization within college majors or job responsibilities.

Considering two applicants who majored in English, the 'ideal' person most likely to be hired as an interactive fiction writer for a computer software game company manufacturing entertainment on DVD, CD-Interactive or CD MP3 audio, would be someone who majored in creative writing (fiction) or earned a Master of Fine Arts in creative writing, script writing, or combinations of digital animation design, film/video, digital media, and writing.

CHAPTER 9

A Job Coach's Guide to Writing Non-Traditional Resumes

Back up your client's strengths with concrete evidence that your client really *connects* with both the company leadership and its bread-and-butter customers. Write a non-traditional resume so clearly, that your client's skills can't be misunderstood. What your client's resume needs is market appeal which is called buzz appeal in the media—good public relations visibility. You create visibility by supporting the statements made in your resume. Even resumes can have their own spin doctors. You certainly are putting a spin on resumes. Do resumes need a spin? Actually, resumes only need promotion through factual information briefly stated and written for clarity.

When Your Client Needs a Nontraditional Resume

Your clients need nontraditional resumes after the following experiences:

- Taking a long time out for study (more than a year).
- Running a business.
- Rearing children, or caring full-time for aged or disabled relatives in the home for more than one year.
- Retirement from many years of military service.
- Unemployment of over one year's duration.
- Switching careers after retirement.
- Working flexible hours.
- Immigrating from another culture.
- Applying for an internship or a cooperative work-study arrangement.
- Seeking a work-travel assignment.

- Working part-time for more than a year or switching from full-ime work to part-time work.
- Job sharing for more than a year.
- Public speaking full-time.
- Many years work as a freelancer, consultant, independent contractor, entrepreneur, or 'intrapreneur.'
- Assignments for a temporary employment agency.
- Many years spent unemployed because of illness, disability, or confinement.
- Work outside the country for more than a year.
- Creative artists, computer midi synthesizer musicians-composers, and staff writers entering the fields of software design, interactive education/entertainment, or instructional technology for the first time.
- Anyone switching from one career to an entirely new industry.

Why Clients Need Nontraditional Resumes

Nontraditional resumes break patterns. You're drafting a nontraditional resume because you're a person who diverges from corporate personnel habits. You're different. Therefore, you need to be convincing.

Your resume can be made so persuasive, that the employer will find your competencies profitable. Here's how nontraditional resumes also break patterns.

Collect Work Style and Job Preference Data About Your Clients

Nontraditional resumes support statements with collected job-related data about all the benefits they offer a company. Collect data about yourself on index cards. Mark the significant facts that specifically offer the company benefits and advantages.

Ask yourself, which of your ideas do you find interesting and exciting? Now get specific. Back up a selected few ideas with facts and details that clearly show benefits to the company. You need to retrieve the facts that gave you ideas in the first place.

Fitting Into the Group

Strengths need to be emphasized in such a way that the nontraditional job applicant (who doesn't fit into the group) appears attractive and competent. Nontraditional resumes need special drafting to earn respect by their presentation.

Ask your client how all the facts revealed about that person are connected. What generalizations can be made that would fulfill the job-related needs of the employer? All day long employers listen to facts and give back facts.

How can you tie together all the relevant facts about yourself and connect it to a specific part of the computer industry? How can you give meaning to all those facts about yourself on your resume?

If your clients don't fit into the selected group, your clients can fit into a company niche or fulfill a specific need. Your client can target specific needs by researching hidden markets or industrial and educational niches.

Your client's resume isn't only composed of facts. There's an important theme to each resume and cover or follow-up letter. Even direct mail sales letters and other business correspondence have their own symbolic themes. This theme is the big picture. Themes recur, like needs and niches in any company. Tie together the facts by stating the exact need you'll fill in the company, or the niche you'll develop. How will you carry out the job requirements?

By tying together your facts and connecting it to a specific need in the company, you're wrapping up the theme of your resume.

Talk about making connections with the employers. Your resume is there to make connections. How are your skills connected to the computer industry? Use your resume to network, make connections, and specify benefits. That's how you leap the hurdle of not fitting into the group.

Likes Hire Likes

People hire people most like themselves in age and education, and bosses hire people smarter than themselves to innovate new and productive products. Employers in the computer industry prefer job applicants who are already working full time in a job similar to the new position. Outsourcing is taking over most of the technology and computer animation fields. For example, an advertisement for a manager of information systems (MIS) usually draws groups of applicants from across the country or overseas that are already employed as managers in similar settings.

As many corporations downsize or hire temporary employees and independent contractors as computer consultants, many middle managers aren't currently employed. These managers are competing with a large group of computer professionals who have not yet worked as managers, but who are applying in hopes of being hired.

Job applicants applying for the MIS position include military retirees reentering the civilian workplace after 20-30 years of logistics administrative work in the services. Other job applicants may be displaced homemakers carving out their own niches after recent re-training. Some job applicants are recent "MIS graduate degree" recipients looking for "management trainee" positions.

Applicants include former entrepreneurs seeking to be 'intrapreneurs.' Some are computer consultants who want to work for one company on staff. There are many systems analysts, software engineers, local area networks specialists, and programmers who intend to move into management.

The days when one ad for a manager of information systems brought in only groups of employed managers who wanted to move laterally are gone. Today, many individuals are trying to get into a door at the top to avoid the crowd at the bottom.

To open that door for you—at any level—you need to approach employers with persuasive advantages and benefits. Let's discuss each type of nontraditional resume and the best strategies for marketing yourself to the computer industry.

The No-Job-Continuity Resume

Use these resume strategies if your client has one of the following situations:

- First job after graduation.
- A displaced homemaker.
- A mommy-tracker or house-husband returning to the workplace after a long absence to take care of children.
- A long period of self-employment.
- Part-time employment.
- Merger mania—a loss of employment due to a merger.
- Time out for education in order to change careers or job level.
- Temporary work or freelancing.
- Consulting full time.
- Retiree returning to workplace in an entirely different career.
- Military or government service retiree (or detachment)—entering the civilian or non-civil service workplace in a new career unrelated to your former job.
- Entering the job force after a long absence due to mental or physical disability or illness.
- Returning to the U.S. after a long absence overseas and changing careers in midlife to a completely new field.

- Tired of telecommuting in a home-based business or assignment.

NO-JOB-CONTINUITY STRATEGIES

- Collect Transferable (Lateral) Competencies

Your first task is to explain the breaks in your employment or the reason for your career switch to a new field. Instead of climbing the ranks from clerk to president in one firm, you're moving laterally through many careers, collecting transferable experience and competencies that can be used equally well in many careers.

Job continuity is no longer promised. Technology changes job descriptions. You move forward only by training continuously how to use the newer products.

- Show Transferable Objectivity

If you can show that what you can do is neutral, that is, useful to many types of firms, you can transfer skills from one career to the next. What you're selling to the employer now is transferable objectivity. You're trying to convince the new company that your competencies are neutral and useful.

- List Marketable Strengths

What strengths can you sell? What strengths can you use to persuade, motivate, and inspire an employer to hire you? You bring your marketable strengths to the attention of an employer by showing exactly and concretely how your strengths are going to be used by the company. Then you create visibility.

If you're a displaced homemaker with no outside paid experience, you sell your ability to inspire, motivate, and promote other people or products in the computer industry. You promote your ability to make things grow—by creating visibility for the product as you're doing for yourself. You're selling your ability to oversee and parent a product from its inception through all stages of its growth. Your client is transferring parenting skills from person to product.

Market the usefulness of your client's competencies to an employer. Whether your client obtains the job or not depends on the ability to create enough visibility in a resume and cover letter.

- Market and Promote Your Client as a Consumer Offering Feedback

Feedback from consumers of computer products is coveted. Market your clients as consumers of products offering specific skills that solve problems and achieve results. To show how active your clients are as consumer with attitudes, have the clients write product reviews and send them to throwaway newspapers, magazines, and special interest group newsletters.

Your clients' common sense as consumers of products can carry heavy weight by convincing others in power to listen, improve products, and hire spokespersons or representatives. Your client's and your own consumer experience are valuable sales tools.

The business, medical, and academic world listens to consumers. So does the government. That's why many corporations use volunteer beta testers on new software, book reviewers, and product opinions gathered by marketing firms on consumer opinion.

- **Beat Ageism**

The computer industry is marketing to mature people, including senior citizens computer clubs that network nationally. If you're a retiree returning to the workplace, show how you can offer computer information or products to the rising tide of "over 48" baby boomers—75 million aging computer users. Computer interest among people over 50 is rapidly increasing. Who's going to serve this market's needs in marketing computer products from investment software to creative innovations?

On the other hand, if you're very young and inexperienced, use the same strategy to appeal to the youth market. Children begin using computers in preschool and will use software until they graduate from college. The computer industry is intergenerational.

- **Use A Nontraditional Abilities Or Creative Resume**

Show how useful, profitable, and productive your skills, talents, and abilities are. Don't use the chronological work history resume if there are large gaps, "holes in time," or breaks in the continuity of your work between graduation and the present. Instead, emphasize all your transferable competencies.

- **Enroll Clients in Current Skill-Building Courses**

Nobody networks better than working adult weekend/evening computer students with a course in common. Learn the latest technologies and software. Exchange business cards.

Find out what applied artificial intelligence is all about when used to forecast stock market trends. Learn the meaning of neural networks and fuzzy logic in the biotechnical or genomics industries.

Encourage your clients to enroll in courses to update skills and to join professional or trade associations. Network, and really work a room as an extrovert for a day.

- **Show What Your Clients Can Do**

Use your client's personality preferences to find out what feels healthy and comfortable in the world of work, what's easiest to do, and what competencies come naturally. Have your clients take one of the personality classifier questionnaires such as the Myers-Briggs Type Indicator (MBTI)™, The Keirsey Temperament Sorter II, or other vocational and personality quiz questionnaires. Most people will prefer to do certain tasks at work. People choose to work alone with the office door shut, to work with a team of a few familiar coworkers, or with open office doors and constant interaction with new people each day. Others want to work outdoors most of the time. People choose work tasks and styles according to what their personalities reveal, if given the choice of specific tasks and environments at work.

Emphasize your client's best skills to create a niche. The idea is to find your client's abilities and preferences for what feels healthy. Then, as a job coach, help your client choose which careers make the more comfortable fit for those preferences. When you know what type of person your client is on the most basic level of activity, it's easier for your clients to do what they are on a variety of levels. When practicing a skill motivates your client, help your client look for a role to fill which uses that skill. Motivation urges anyone to become more qualified.

- **Why Should The Outside World Hire Your Client?**

Help your client to develop a list of all the pros and cons regarding why an employer should hire your client—from the employer's point of view. When your client can get the pros to outweigh the cons, list the pros on your client's abilities and resume plan for the first draft of that resume. Then select a chosen few pros to include on your client's polished final draft of a resume. After the final draft of each resume is finished, work on the cover letter. After the interview, write the follow-up letter with your job coaching client.

Realize that most people won't spend much time on a half-page follow-up letter. Keep follow-up letters brief. Research the company you want to hire your client. Then research the job there. If your client has no experience, use practical examples of how your client uses specific abilities, skills, talents, or competencies. If you think your client has few skills to offer, or no experience that's transferable in a traditionally practical way, then emphasize how your client motivates and inspires people to take action about something. Being a motivational speaker, writer, or researcher is a practical and up-to-date job skill.

Your summary or overview placed after the job objective and before you list your client's competencies contains the action you take. For example, if your client is a volunteer fund raiser for a local charity, use one action verb to describe the skill—"fundraiser." The one action verb acts as a hammer to describe what your client actually did. Emphasize the "fundraiser" not the "volunteer."

- **Show How Your Clients Are Motivated By The Realities Of The Employer's Needs**

Find many links between your clients and the employers—working on professional association panels or committees together, doing volunteer work, or taking the same hobbies or courses. Being qualified really means being motivated by reality.

Being motivated by reality is about knowing the realities of each company's special needs. "How can I serve you?" becomes, "This is how I can solve your company problems regarding the niche you value most. Here are the results achieved. You can follow the solutions and results step-by-step as I outline them in clear, easy-to-understand language."

To give your clients credibility, translate accomplishments into skills highly valued by the companies selected. Your clients' past achievements must be relevant to both present and future company plans.

Hand the employer a resume itemizing the ways you intend to meet the company's most important needs. To be hired, your resume must become a list matching a company's needs to your skills. In the computer industry, such a resume is called "the cache."

Use these techniques for bringing your ideas into reality. Writing a resume is a hands-on exercise. All an employer wants is for you to be clear and detailed and to generalize from the data.

Place a classified ad under the heading "employment wanted" in a trade journal (industry-related publication). When you advertise the best you can offer an employer, chances are you'll get more responses by employers calling you in for an interview than if you send your resume in response to a "help wanted" classified ad appearing in a general daily newspaper.

- **Student Strategies**

As a job coach, you find that your first client is a full-time student with no paid job experience. And you wonder how you can find a job when all the jobs require experience. To find a job when your clients have no experience, show employers how much your clients are interested in a specific type of job.

If every job offering your client looks at requests experience, should your clients only look for help wanted ads that begin with the words "management trainee" or simply 'trainee?' No. There's a whole wealth of ways to connect with companies for years before you graduate.

Use the following student strategies as *bridges*. Select what's most comfortable for your clients to do, and then list the involvement on your resume. These strategies will connect your school experience to the workforce.

- **Use Professional Associations As A Bridge To Employment**

Your first step is to connect with companies and begin relationships in capacities other than traditional employment. Look at trade journals, the newsletters of professional associations, and the *Encyclopedia of Associations*. This reference book is in most public or university libraries. Have your student client choose several national and local business, educational, or professional associations to join at reduced student membership which are related to your client's field of interest. A student can volunteer to serve on a special interest group or panel, help to write the national association newsletter, or start a local chapter of a national organization.

Pick those associations which relate to your client's deepest interests. For example, if your client is a student or recent graduate with no prior paid work experience interested in computer graphics, there are many different organizations dedicated to the use of computers for creating designs. Look for internships/externships, and volunteer work on publications or panels that choose speakers at conventions for various national professional or trade associations.

One example is SIGGRAPH (Computer Graphics) special interest group of the Association for Computing Machinery, or AIGA (American Institute of Graphic Art) for commercial artists using computer illustration. If you're interested in technical writing, there's the Society for Technical Communication and the Association of Professional Writing Consultants.

There's probably a national association to benefit almost any area of most industries. Most of these national associations publish newsletters or bulletins that take volunteers to work on at home online. Some offer internships. National organizations may also have job referral services.

If there's no chapter in your client's city, your client can start one. Have your client ask selected or favorite employers to assist your client in starting up a local chapter or to provide a meeting room at their company for after-hours seminars. This gives your client a foot in the door through making friends and business contacts. It's part of networking. People are hired mainly by other people who know them.

- **Have Your Student Clients with No Prior Paid Work Experience Start the Following Networking Activities**

Ask several employers to volunteer as speakers for the local chapter meetings. Or plan an annual conference and invite those people you'd love to work for in the future.

At the very least, join one of those professional or trade associations related to your goal somewhere in the computer industry, or in industries using computers as tools.

Work on task forces, committees, and planning teams inside the special interest groups of national associations with a variety of computer-related interests. If there's an annual convention, ask to help on the planning team. Offer to speak on a panel or to find experts to speak at conferences or meetings.

Publicize the professional association. Edit the newsletter for a year. Volunteer to do "take charge" activities that create visibility for you in the club. Leave the envelope stuffing and mailing chores to members not looking for a job in a hurry.

Involve yourself in fundraising or event planning. Or start local chapters. Find corporations willing to let their conference rooms be used for evening or weekend meetings. Join Toastmasters and other public speaking groups which cater to a similar crowd of office workers, professionals, sales persons, business owners, etc, or start your own chapter of Toastmasters or related public speaking groups for computer personnel in a variety of firms. If speaking on panels or public speaking in general isn't your way of creating visibility, try the written word. Become a reporter or editor for the special interest group's newsletter and use that as a bridge to writing company newsletters.

Having never worked before is no excuse not to join a team at a professional association. Look for as many resources as you can find related to clubs composed of people who work in similar industries. Use computer magazines, newspapers, and national periodicals to report on your client's organizational research.

Start projects on your own, relating them to committees and task forces within a national association. The affiliation with a national association gives you credibility and backs you up when you present your experience to employers.

Summer and part-time jobs come out of working on task forces and committees of professional associations. That's how you make business connections to use as a bridge between school and employment outside of your university department office.

If you're looking forward to a career as a technical trainer or teacher of computer-related subjects, join national computer trainer's associations, such as the Trainers Association of Southern California, or similar associations in your own state. Consult the *Encyclopedia of Associations*.

- **Tutor Using Skills**

If your clients with no prior work experience have skills learned in college or other technical or health care training and are interested in education or corporate technical training, have your clients offer to tutor others in adult education, at libraries, in literacy, and in various schools and community colleges as teaching assistants or tutors. Have your clients choose a specialty or subject they know well such as a college major.

Encourage clients to volunteer or apply for a job as an instructional aide in a school that uses many computers. Or have them volunteer to train the staff at corporations in new software and hardware equipment use within your specialty.

Use what you learned in computer school to instruct workers who are being trained on-the-job. If your background is in the humanities, train workers with basic literacy problems in written communications.

Computer training programs sponsored by the government and private industry councils are offered to low-income students. These programs are offered to people over 55, displaced homemakers, the homeless, and persons in recovery or recently released from prison.

Opportunities exist to become involved as trainers, aides, tutors, fundraisers, grant proposal writers, or volunteers to share your computer skills with others. The people you meet in the training business can form solid business relationships when you graduate—especially if your clients want to become corporate trainers.

- **Students Can Tutor Workers with Disabilities**

Many community colleges have special programs in computer instruction for the physically challenged. Volunteer to help these students learn computer skills. Work with computer students with disabilities. Volunteer as a student aide or tutor, or work on a team that trains them in their homes or in adapted classrooms.

Computer programs for students with disabilities emphasize such fields as computer aided drafting and design, word processing, programming, desktop publishing, circuit design, robotics, and software specialist training. You can become involved with teaching computer skills to the disabled while you're still a full-time student.

- **Show How Much Your Clients are Interested in a Specific Job**

Encourage your clients with no prior paid work experience to apply for summer or part-time work which leads directly into your preferred career track. Ask for an internship. Express more interest in the company than in the position, without putting the position down. Don't mention advancement yet. Instead, emphasize how much you're interested in the job in your cover letter—and—how much you're interested in where the company's heading.

To find out the firm's direction and position, in comparison to its competition, research the company in the library or call the firm's public relations director and ask for a press kit with annual report. Find out the same information for several companies you wish to target and compare them in relation to growth as well as your goals.

- **List Positives about a Company**

In your client's cover letter, include positive statements about the firm. Emphasize how much you welcome hands-on experience in contrast to the theory you learned all through college. Point out how many good facts you've heard about the company at college

Giving a few examples, state how wonderful the company's reputation is in the computer industry, how durable or beneficial the products are, and how much they fill a deep need in the computer community.

Sum up with how much your client will learn from the company if your client is hired—even if it's only for temporary work. In your client's job objective and overview at the top of your resume, list the exact job title of the summer or part-time job you want. Be sure the letter sounds as if the client wrote the letter. A business letter writer is a ghostwriter.

- **How are Your Clients Qualified To Perform Specific Job Duties?**

Resumes can't always reveal work history. Therefore, let that type of resume qualify your clients by concrete evidence of their competencies. Briefly point out how their competencies and skills qualify the clients for each of the duties required in a job description.

Emphasize your clients' motivations for each job. If a specific job actually leads to a career goal or is on your clients' career tracks, mention that. Be honest and direct. All you're stating is what the job duties are, why your clients are qualified to perform those duties, and what motivates each client to work for a selected company.

Indicate on a resume or cover letter that when your client will graduate, that individual will still be working for the company if the job isn't seasonal or temporary. If the job ends in a few months or is strictly part-time, note that your client is willing to stay on if any full-time employment opens with the same firm within a reasonable time. Make sure you write as if the client did the writing.

No employer wants to hire anyone using a ghost writer on a resume. Yet the idea of hiring job coaches and executive coaches is approved and used by many corporations.

Encourage your clients to train in writing skills to be able to write their own resumes, cover, and follow-up letters by evaluating what they write. Show clients how to improve writing skills specifically related to writing resumes with cover and follow-up letters. Emphasize powerful nouns, action verbs that make a positive impact, time spent on reading resumes, being brief, and clear.

- **Evaluate The Job Experience as it Relates to Your Client's Career Goal**

Ask your clients what value they will get out of working for a specific corporation. Will it pay off their student loans? Will they learn more about their chosen field? Is there any on-the-job training your client can't find at college? Or will your client leave with experience in a field totally unrelated to a specific career goal?

- **Summarize Intentions in an Overview**

Each resume packages your client's strengths in relation to one job. In your client's one-paragraph *Overview*, listed right under the *Job Objective*, summarize your client's specific intentions. For clients with no prior paid work experience, the intentions are the most important visible concrete evidence of skills in a resume. The *job overview* was 'made' for students and re-entry individuals without prior paid job experience.

Three sentences should accomplish the summary which will market your client's abilities. For example, an overview might look like the following paragraph:

Overview:

- Second year Computer Information Systems student completing the B.S. degree in Information Systems, School of Business Administration, New York University, applying for the summer position as Software Engineer. Exceptional skills with Windows, Macintosh, OS/2, Unix, and DOS working in C++, C, Assembler, Basic, Cobol, and Novell Netware.

- Commercial PC software development, file systems, compression, networking and localization courses qualify me for the software engineering position as well as the goal of exploring future permanent work with C. C. Corp.

*   *   *

- **Use Online, Home-based Facilitating and Telecommuting Opportunities**

Full-time students online seeking flexible work hours may also work at home using their computers and Internet connections as facilitators, tutors, independent contractors, sales representatives, help desk assistants, appointment setters, digital artists, videographers, or freelancers in research, editing, writing, indexing, mailing, or proof reading.

Students and independent contractors can contribute articles, cartoons, or illustrations to computer publications. People can work at home indexing medical or computer books, preparing databases, or performing record keeping online. Works can be connected by servers to office headquarters from home or while traveling by mobile van. It's called extreme telecommuting when you work by wireless Internet while traveling around the world.

This work-at-home employment is called telecommuting. It's different from work your client does at home in as an independent contractor because the individual would be on a company's staff yet working at home. Some marketing firms pay for opinions. Others pay for reviews of products. Almost anyone can sell or advertise online from Web sites. For example, a student can sell used textbooks on eBay. This represents sales experience online if put on a resume.

Ask whether your client can connect a home computer by modem to a school or company to help process information or research databases. Doctors and lawyers sometimes hire information brokers to search professional library databases by computer. These can be either freelance or staff employees.

The 'online' field of information retrieval is called "the competitive intelligence industry." National clearinghouses of information and specialized as well as public libraries are linked to researchers through many private and government databases. Your clients can use home-based computers to assist a firm with data analysis, informatics, or other research in many fields of interest.

- **Use Work-Study Plans Or Cooperative Education**

As a job coach, encourage student clients to create their own cooperative work-study plan focusing on companies most likely to hire them after graduation. Many colleges arrange paid internships or part-time work and study arrangements in the computer industry. Use these opportunities to create a link between schools and the 'real' world of work.

Use a work-study situation to obtain increased perspective on the computer industry, the company, or your special focus. In your cover letter, explain how your client will adapt skills to the work-study environment. Let the employer know how your client manages time. Summarize how your client will juggle school requirements and work responsibilities in the cover letter.

Don't send your client's cover letter randomly to companies in a chosen area. Look for the newest innovation on the cutting edge the industry of choice to follow. One example is DNA-driven genealogy. Another is nutritional genomics, or in the artist's world of digital imaging, new color separation software.

Show interest in the newest technology of your client's field. Encourage your client to attend trade shows and exhibits and offer resumes to vendors and speakers. This arena is excellent for job coaches who set up booths at trade shows and conventions.

For the student with no prior paid work experience, it's better to obtain a work-study position or internship in a growth area so new that few in that field has had time to build up experience. Students without any experience have a lot in common with retirees re-entering a totally new career. In the following chapter you'll learn resume tips for helping mature clients switch careers or find part-time work with flexible hours and less stress commuting.

For communications majors who want to work as technical editors and writers or documentation analysts, the technical writer most likely to be hired as a software user manual writer or editor would be a "professional writing" major (nonfiction), a "digital media journalism" graduate student, or a person studying for a degree or certificate in technical writing or medical writing.

Also hired for technical editing work would likely be a person who majored in English with a specialization in technical or science writing or in technical journalism. Pharmaceutical firms prefer life science majors with minors in journalism or science writing, or a person with a degree in one of the life sciences attending graduate school for a Masters degree in journalism or medical writing.

In reality, persons who majored in almost anything from computer science to history actually are hired for writing jobs with software companies—as long as they know how to simplify computer software instructions.

Employers won't sort your clients' experiences and separate the sections into superfluous and important information. Therefore, only feature prominently the information that labels each client qualified for the job in question. It's time to focus. So let's analyze, evaluate, and do some problem-solving.

Working with older, re-entry job applicants is a special niche area for the career coach. As people return to the workforce after retirement, emphasis may be on finding part-time work with flexible hours, working online at home or extreme telecommuting (traveling around the world while working online from mobile vans, planes, trains, and campsites). Others way wish more creative work or helping people enjoy leisure connections.

The life coach, who also is a career/job coach and an executive coach, wears many hats. Add the role of spiritual coach, and you find a special niche planning for retirement, leisure, and more rewarding work experiences as well as relocation and combination living, travel, and working environments. Let's explore how to work with re-entry job applicants and retirees seeking income.

CHAPTER 10

Re-Entry

The Military Retiree Resume

In this decade, as many of the Baby Boom generation pass the age of 60, more job seekers are waiting longer to find employment compared to older job seekers in the 1990s. According to an employment analyst at the Conference Board, a New York-based business research group, in 1992, unemployed workers in the United States over the age of 44 (with many years of experience and high seniority) waited more than 27 weeks to find a new job. In comparison, workers age 35-44 were unemployed only 21 weeks in 1992—compared to 1991 when they spent only 16 weeks out of work.

Labor trend forecasters report that there's no shortage of jobs for college educated persons, only a shortage of 'good' jobs—that is, permanent staff jobs with incomes $30,000 a year and above offering the kind of lifetime job security you used to have in the 1950s if you worked for the telephone company, government, or the Gas and Electric company. Those days are gone. The weekly national news magazines forecast that the jobs requiring a college degree are increasingly becoming a series of temporary assignments for contingency professionals. In addition, there are always many more college graduates available than jobs offered requiring a college degree.

With recent college graduates facing tough competition, the older worker often falls victim to covert ageism in the workforce. If you're an older worker or military retiree, you need to have a selling point in your resume and pitch a good closer at your oral interview that markets your experience, visibility, and stability. You need an edge.

Therefore, to give yourself an edge, and cut the time you may have to wait before finding your next job, begin your cover letter by showing your future employer how to reduce costs by hiring you. In your resume job overview paragraph, state that you're not retired; you're in transition.

You're moving between levels of responsibility. Emphasize commitment and enthusiasm on your resume. You'll always use a combination of practical skills, people management competencies, and task-oriented qualifications at each level of your career, regardless of the type of company.

Many military retirees apply for civil service jobs where they can earn veteran's preference points on civil service exams. Government applications require special resumes for government or civil service work—called Form 171s. You answer the questions directly on the form instead of sending a resume. Request a Form 171 from your local State Employment Office.

The United States Office of Personnel Management, Los Angeles Service Center has specific instructions on how complete an SF-171 Application for Federal Employment on its form FL-1216 (8/92), entitled "How To Complete An SF-171 Application for Federal Employment." You can obtain instructions on how to fill out the SF-171 form from the United States Office of Personnel Management or from most community college student job placement offices.

* * *

Job Coaches Working with Standard Government Job Applications

Here's what the United States Office of Personnel Management's flyer entitled "How To Complete An SF-171" states:

The SF-171 is the standard application form used by most Federal agencies. It is also a Federal employer's first impression of your client. As with any other application, a completed SF-171 is not only a reflection of the experience and knowledge your client possess. It is also an indicator of the kind of employee your client would be.

When reviewers evaluate your client's SF-171, they assess the extent to which your client's experience and education will allow your client to successfully perform the duties of the position for which that person is applying.

Although you may have described your client's educational background and work experience clearly, spelling errors grammatical errors, and/or a sloppy appearance could give an employer a negative impression of your abilities as an employee.

An SF-171 which is neat, clear, and error free is to your benefit. It is extremely important that all the information you provide is factual. The SF-171 is a legal document: falsifying any portion could prevent your client from being hired, lead to your dismissal, or be grounds for criminal prosecution.

How to Complete the Form:

First, read the front page of the SF-171 carefully. It explains how to describe your experience, how to claim veteran preference, and how to reproduce the form for your future use. The SF-171 may be photocopied. In addition, you may describe your experience on separate sheets of paper. Be sure to include your name, social security number, and all other information requested at the top of the experience blocks. Every SF-171, or photocopy, must have an original signature and date in order to be accepted. Guidance on how to complete the SF-171 follows:

Availability:

You will only be considered for positions for which you have indicated willingness to accept the pay rate, working hours, and the location. In most cases, the pay and job site are not negotiable. Please do not indicate that you are willing to work "anywhere." Indicate only those geographic locations where you are willing to work or are willing to relocate.

Military Service and Veteran Preference:

If you have never served in the U.S. military, answer "no" to question 17, and mark the "no preference" box in question 22. If you have served, be sure to read the "Veteran Preference in Hiring" section on the front of the SF-171 carefully." Item 21 is especially important to complete if you served in Operation Desert Storm and have earned a campaign badge or expeditionary medal.

Work Experience Blocks:

It is to your client's benefit to describe work experience as clearly, concisely, and truthfully as possible. You will want to describe your experience in familiar, non-technical language. The initial reviewer of your application may not have direct knowledge of the positions your client has held.

Be sure not to use excessive abbreviations or technical references that only apply to specific projects. You will want to describe the actual duties that you have performed and indicate the percent of time you spent performing each duty.

Provide the actual month, day, and year you started and left each position, and the number of hours per week you worked in the position. Do not include excerpts from formal descriptions of your duties. Instead, describe the actual activities you performed and your professional accomplishments. If possible, briefly describe how your level of responsibility for accomplishing specific tasks increased with the time you spent in each position.

All this information is used by reviewers to quantify the extent of your experience and to determine its relatedness to the position for which you are applying. Please claim any experience you have gained through volunteer work, or hobbies, if this information is applicable to the position for which you are applying.

Education:

Indicate your client's baccalaureate and/or associate degree major on the first line of item number 29, and your graduate major on the first line of item 30. The "Number of Credit Hours Completed" is the number of total units you have completed. Only <u>Completed</u> courses will be credited. Also, remember to enclose a photocopy of your transcript (or 0PM Form 1170/17, List of College Courses and Certificate of Scholastic Achievement) for verification.

Special Skills, Accomplishments and Awards:

This section gives you the opportunity to claim credit for special skills your client has acquired, achievements made or honors earned that are not appropriate to mention in the course of describing your client's experience. This is the place to mention computer skills, public speaking skills, even personal developments that are pertinent to the position for which you are applying.

As with the experience blocks, attach additional sheets of paper if you need more space to describe the individual's accomplishments. Items 33 through 35 ask your client to claim typing skills, licenses or certificates, and language proficiency.

References:

The references you list will be contacted. Include the full names, addresses and phone numbers of individuals who can accurately attest to your character.

Background Information:

Answer questions 37 through 47 carefully and honestly. Be sure to review your responses in this section, and in all of the others. Re-read your SF-171 while imagining that you are the reviewer. **Each application must have an original signature and date.**

How Does Your Client Transfer Skills From One Job To The Next?

Many career switchers, Military retirees, re-entry persons, and newcomers to the United States are seeking different careers unrelated to their past experiences, learning, or skills. Best selling points are the practical skills which can be transferred from one career to the next, because the different, unrelated career really is a higher octave of your past job. You only have one career, but different jobs. Look at each of your past jobs as platforms, levels or foundations within one career.

Your Client's Past Jobs Are Platforms

Every job's a platform, and all the workers, climbers. Military retirees who spent 20 or 30 years in the service have a lifetime of 'increments' or 'stages' to transfer to new jobs. Use the military service as a projection of your client's qualifications to the new job.

Strategies:

- **Military Retiree Resume Strategies**

The use of action verbs gives your resume the feeling that you're blazing with energy. Show how efficient you are by listing measurable achievements on your resume.

The long service record sells your client's commitment to service and loyalty to duty. What's left to market is your client's enthusiasm and practical skills with data, objects, or people.

As a job coach, you'll realize that your client has never felt more alone than when retiring from one career and trying to convince someone to hire you in another. List ten transferable values next to ten skills you're going to offer an employer.

- **Administrative Work Is Easiest To Find**

The majority of retiring officers prefer to transfer to administrative work. One example would be working as a law office administrator. Your main responsibility would be to free time so the lawyers could handle their cases while you take care of the office and staff administrative tasks.

Law office administrative work is similar to what many officers did during their career with the military service. However, you'd be competing with experienced legal secretaries who want to rise to a career in law office administration.

- **Chronological Work History Resumes**

Your military career fits easily into a chronological work history resume. Neither the expanded nor creative resume usually fit twenty or thirty odd years in military service. An abilities resume wouldn't show the length of your service. Since your selling dependability and reliability in terms of concrete skills; loyalty, and military honor, the chronological resume becomes an extension of service.

- ## Use the Abilities Resume with Re-Entry Former Retirees

Retirees could successfully use the abilities resume rather than the work history resume. Mature people switching careers may use the abilities resume to reflect a transition of competencies rather pack a long-winded, long-time service resume running several pages to express work done with one or several employers. An exception would be noting on a resume the winning of major prizes such as noteworthy medical discoveries, a Pulitzer or Nobel Prize, or special government appointments.

For the military or civil service retiree, the chronological work history resume or the abilities resume works well, in opposite circumstances. The abilities resume places your client's diversified experience in increments. A work history resume highlights your client's long track record with the military or government as a single employer.

- ## Short-Length Military Service

The job coach needs to find out the length of a client's military service. If your client's military service was relatively short, simply state your branch and dates of service, and provide the date that you were honorably discharged. Stating your military service avoids time gaps or unaccounted for holes in your employment record.

List any specific, job-related training each client received in the military service. Give the highest rank achieved, and include any training which could be transferred to a new job in a similar or unrelated industry. For example, a military support clerk retiring from the service might work well as a law office administrator.

- ## Tie Together Qualifications

If you're retiring from military service after a long career, it's necessary to include in your resume a continuity section for tying together your qualifications. This could be a brief paragraph at the end of your resume.

- ## Expanded Two-Page Resumes Emphasize Responsibilities

You may wish to use a two-page expanded resume to explain your client's responsibilities. Don't elaborate on your rank or dwell on how much control or power you wielded in the service. Responsibility should never be confused with rigid control. Responsibility means flexibility and adaptation to change.

All the techniques for military retiree resumes can be applied successfully to the resumes of persons retiring from any type of work or for those switching later in life to new careers. The computer industry contains niches new enough to absorb those with little or no experience as long as training is current.

- **To Create Visibility Update Skills**

Keep your client's competencies fresh. If your client is a re-entry former retiree trained long ago, it's time to take update skills, attend conventions, and organize workshops and seminars. Clients need to attend meetings where volunteer guest speakers who sell products to a captured audience can give tips to your client on updating skills.

As a job coach, encourage your client to act as a liaison between associations, schools, and corporations. It will keep your clients actively seeking contacts. Individuals out of the workplace or retired for a number of years also need to learn how to use the most recent equipment and the latest software. Older adults who join computer user groups and professional associations are able to keep in contact with people with the authority to refer them to others in the workplace with the power to perhaps hire them.

Clients can remain encouraged by volunteering in those associations that allow members to call upon companies. The same advice on creating visibility works equally well with retirees, students, and among those with no previous paid experience. Create visual and visceral positive responses in the person who first reads the resume. The idea is for the client to become as memorable as the outstanding resume.

- **Creating an Extra Edge by Evaluating Skills**

What qualifications give your clients an extra edge over the rest of workers in a selected job? Evaluate skills. Keep a list of those unusual skills. Keep dates off resumes if your client is concerned about covert age discrimination.

It's unlawful under the federal Age Discrimination in Employment Act to be turned down for a job because of age. The law applies to anyone over 40. However, the law is hard to prove if employers give competency, experience, or personality-related reasons for not choosing your client.

Employers are looking for seasoned job applicants—*if they can wear more than one hat.*

This is borne out by research done by the American Association of Retired Persons (AARP) Work Force Programs Department. The AARP studied how human resource managers viewed older workers. Does your older client wear more than one hat?

Employers would prefer to save recruiter's fees and hire older workers who come to them first, but many are frightened of high medical insurance costs of older workers. More experienced works also are paid more. Employers hire those who are the least expensive to maintain. Low-maintenance is preferred over high-maintenance workers and executives.

Some employers don't have the budget for paying agencies to recruit new graduates, or younger professionals. So they turn to the older worker more willing to share a job, work part time, be outsourced, offered temporary work, or paid less as an independent contractor.

Employers in some industries, including online university course facilitating, may figure that the retiree returning already has medical insurance and a pension from a previous job, is possibly taking social security, and can work part time for less as an independent contractor where no insurance costs are paid by the employer. This is true with many adjunct positions such as part time 'facilitator' teaching university courses part time online.

- **Do Older Workers Undervalue Themselves?**

Reveal exactly how you see a task through to completion. Emphasize commitment. Estimate the value of your work ethic. Older workers undervalue themselves. They downplay the value of maturity and business experience.

Don't chronicle past job titles. Instead, emphasize how your clients helped to solve problems for past employers and brought profit to the company. Show with action verbs how they increased production. What can your clients look forward to if those individuals are military or civilian retirees or older workers trying to find less stressful, paying jobs?

- **Evaluating Older Workers' Resumes**

Some personnel managers who look at resumes all day long reject older workers on the false stereotype that they are inflexible and cost more in terms of health care insurance and salaries. Other personnel managers hire older workers specifically because of low absenteeism and high work ethics. They emphasize the older worker's dependability and respect for authority (especially true of retiring military senior enlisted personnel).

Your client's resume could land on the desk of either of those types of managers. The more managers you interview, the better your chances are of finding a job in due time. Two interviews a day is what most job-hunters prefer.

- **Jobs are Filled by Word-of-Mouth and Professional Association Members Referring Friends**

Older workers are most frequently hired by word of mouth, friends who are members of the same professional or trade associations, and not through newspaper ads. That's also how the best jobs are filled.

As a job coach, use your client's and your own circle of business contacts, professional association members, neighbors, and friends to recommend your client to a specific job or industry. Advertisements placed by recruiting agencies force your older client to compete against thousands of younger applicants. Ninety percent of openings are filled through unadvertised jobs.

Whether clients are hired depends upon how you as a job coach can package your clients and how you market each person's qualifications. Some older workers find employment by building friendships at working vacations which draw older volunteers. Hospitals are notorious for not hiring volunteers in paid positions unless they first apply for the paid job.

All resumes are advertisements, but employers don't read them to be entertained. Keep resumes serious. For anyone, and especially for older, artistic or creative-type clients, also use a work *portfolio*. According to C. Handy, it's "a way of describing how the different bits of work" done during your lifetime "fit together to form a balanced whole."

- **Shamrock Employment for Temps**

The term "Shamrock Employment" was coined by Charles Handy in his book <u>The Age of Unreason</u>. He describes a three-tiered workforce or 'Shamrock,' and one level is known as the temporary worker.

It's not necessarily a different category of employee than the usual temporary employee. A temporary worker may be a "Contingency Professional," a temporary technical worker, day laborer, or temporary clerical employee.

When referring to temporary work, the term 'agency' is never used in conjunction with temporary employment. It's called "temporary service." Agency refers to an employment agency which places job seekers in permanent positions for a fee. Not all temporary services have employment agency divisions.

Some temporary services charge the employer one fee per hour for a temporary clerical worker; for example, $15 per hour, for a 1990's-style word processor who knows how to keyboard Microsoft Word, and use spreadsheet software such as Excel and Access.

The word processor has been largely replaced by the administrative assistant and computer operator. Technical writers in some cities that are outsourced as temps may command more than $30 an hour. A temp agency would get a certain fee for the temp worker, but pay the worker less. Independent contractors could command more pay for temp work, but might not know how to find the jobs unless they first worked in a temp personnel agency that drummed up job orders for technical writers.

The temporary service may pay the actual worker another fee, such as $10 per hour as the current rate for word processing specialists and $15 to $20 an hour or more for the technical writer working on contingency. The employee is never charged a placement fee for referral to a temporary job, regardless of the length of the assignment.

Computer personnel are often contingency professionals working on temporary jobs for long or short-term assignments, such as technical writers, desktop publishers, database managers, programmers, or computer operators and paraprofessionals. Contingency professional employment often entails hiring persons on a continuing, but temporary basis.

It costs the employer less than hiring full-time permanent employees. Insurance costs for the temporary employee, such as health benefits or pension plans often are paid for by the temporary service. In contrast, independent contractors working solely on their own as freelancers have to pay their own health insurance and retirement plans.

Sometimes retirees return to contingency work within a year after retirement, frequently asking for flexible or part-time hours or work online at home. Some temp workers may choose to work two or three full days per week. Others might want work during a season in different parts of the country, or as a traveling temporary worker.

Retired teachers with at least a Master's degree may be able to find part time work as a facilitator, 'teaching' part-time courses online for a university as independent contractors or pat-time employees. Sometimes older adults are hired to live in a rural park area where campers go in the summer to management the camping area. Some older people work on cruise lines offering lectures on archaeology, play behavior, or other subjects in demand.

- Temporary Service Employment

Temporary employees may work for many temporary employment services or only one. The temporary worker is sent to one or many businesses for each assignment of varying length from one day to several months.

A larger number of temporary workers are office staff replacements doing word processing, desktop publishing, retail store demonstrating, convention registering, or related clerical work. A smaller, but rising number are technical professionals, computer programmers, software manual writers, or day laborers. College students often apply for temporary work during the summers to gain more experience.

- Temporary Work Increase

Temporary clerical employees and certain paraprofessionals don't have the continuity of working for one service which leases out the worker to a company for many years, like the contingency professionals do. Temporary clerical workers and some technical paraprofessionals, such as desktop publishers and word processing specialists have the 'feel' of doing temporary work with an emphasis on short assignments to fill in for staff employees who are on vacation or sick leave.

- **Strategies for Temps And Independent Contractors**

Temporary Employees

If your client seeks temporary employment, use a chronological work history resume. Skills are most important. List the competencies, practical skills, and speeds of data entry, such as: "Word processing on an IBM Pentium 4 and beyond with Microsoft Word at 80 words per minute, and spreadsheet experience with Excel and Access." List past employers and exact job duties as applies to the skill you're selling.

The skill could be word processing, programming, accounting, desktop publishing, or software manual writing. List the computer languages you work with or your experience as a computer operator detailing the machine and the software.

The temporary employment service receives a fee from the employer and divides that fee with the temporary employee. It's safer than being an independent contractor or freelancer where you pay your own your health insurance fees and save your own income for your pension.

- **Contingency Professionals, "Shamrock Workers" Or Three-Tiered Workforce Temporary Workers (Long-Temps)**

Use an abilities resume, an expanded resume, a creative resume, or a chronological work history resume to focus on your client's individualized abilities, competencies, and responsibilities. Special work history resumes are needed for approaching Contingency Professional employment-type services.

Highlight different areas of unique skills and training background. Flexibility is emphasized. Many contingency professionals prefer flexible hours. Your client usually is judged by perceptiveness.

Customize each client's work history to fit many individual employers. Independent contractors may enjoy contingency employment. As an independent contractor on long-term assignments, three-tiered employment keeps clients perpetually at arms-length from employers looking for permanent employers part time or other.

Re-entry, formerly retired professionals may accept two or three-year leases to work for one employer. "Shamrock employment" at least gives an employee health benefits and possibly other perks. Many times temporary work does not offer as many benefits to the shorter-term workers. Some temporary employ-ment services offer pension plans. The perks differ with each agency.

- **Group Competencies Together on the Resumes and Cover Letters of Older Adults**

Group competencies together, and put them on each one-page resume and cover letter. Can you name each job-related task your client can perform? Every part-time or shared job consists of a series of competencies and practical skills used on an as-needed basis. If flexible hours are your client's goal, sell qualifica-tions as process-oriented behavior tied together to fit a specific business.

- **Senior Citizens Sharing Jobs**

When you open a job-coaching business online at home, you're also creat-ing and customizing a job according to your client's individual preferences. Use an abilities/competencies or creative resume when working with people who want flexible work hours and with older adults. Itemize each client's prac-tical skills, and sell your client's technical, mechanical, data, or people-oriented competencies when working with older adults or re-entry former retirees and students with no prior paid work experience.

Ask your client to pick someone in the same boat as himself or herself, maybe a person close to retirement or a younger person with a double income-with-small-children family with a full-time job. Job sharers, like flexible time seekers (flexitimers), are looking for a chance to work flexible hours or to come into work on preferred days.

Advertise in a business magazine and professional association newsletter for someone with whom your client may share a job. Clients may be looking for new friends with full-time jobs who wish to cut back to two or three days a week or half-days for several years. Women taking time off to stay at home with children also may wish to share a job half time or quarter time with an older adult seeing part-time work.

Look for people who might offer to work half the week so that employee can take time off for family responsibilities, training, or creative interests. Or advertise for people offering to work mornings so the other person can come in only afternoons.

Maybe your client is on the mommy track after a long career or recent grad-uation, (or daddy at home while mommy goes to school). Or your client sim-ply prefers to work at home. Certain types of part-time work can be appealing. Older adults seeking useful, paid work may want to come back into the work-force a few days a week where they have contact with people and activities.

Your client may wish to share a job with someone having similar skills and interests, each working the hours of individual choice, perhaps in academia, museums, or art galleries and live theaters. Perhaps your client is going to school. Or temporary work is desired for a few years, not a few days. Whatever the reason for working tailored hours, you'll need to write a nontraditional resume for those who come to you.

- **Independent Contractors**

Use a creative resume as a brochure or flyer to offer your clients a healthy bottom line. Independent contractors prefer the creative or abilities resume made to look like a business brochure to secure clients or customers. Attached to the resumes are client reference lists.

In back of the resume, attach a one-page listing of clients, companies, and services provided. If you're an artist or writer, include a mini-portfolio attached to the back of your resume or a list of publications.

A resume-with-business-card introducing you as an independent contractor can get your foot in the door of a company on a temporary or part-time basis at first. Include brochures or flyers about your services.

Independent contractors often use Shamrock employment to gain entrance to a large corporation as an in-house intrapreneur (instead of an entrepreneur seeking clients). An intrapreneur works as an independent contractor within a corporation.

The entrepreneur owns a small business. The independent contractor is a freelancer continually seeking new customers or clients. Many independent contractors work at home, at least until they can afford a business listing or office space.

In the computer industry, the use of independent contractors, intrapreneurs, and consultants is increasing as fast as Shamrock employees and temporary workers. The trend is heading towards leasing personnel on long-term contracts which last as many years as needed.

- **Clients of Independent Contractors**

As a job coach, you are an independent contractor until you're put on the payroll of a corporation as an employee. When you offer a resume-writing service, you're also an independent contractor who must pay for your own insurance and create your own savings. You don't get perks or pension from your client corporations or individual.

You're like a private eye in the sense that you're observing as a freelance writer and information packager what management wants from labor.

The independent contractor can be anyone who sells a service or product on an as-needed basis by contract with a client. The independent contractor may work alone as a freelancer or work with assistants or partners.

The client or customer can be an individual or a company. Independent contractors also may work as 'intrapreneurs,' entrepreneurs, contingency professionals, temporary or part-time workers, faciliatators, online adjunct educators, and as permanent staff employees (moonlighting after work) at various times.

Examples of some *independent contractors* include the following occupational titles:

- Adjunct Educators
- Animators
- Architects
- Beta testers
- Biotechnology Paraprofessionals (DNA-testing technicians)
- Cable television/producers
- Care Givers
- Caretakers/Campgrounds
- Coaches/Job/Executive/Life
- Computer graphics presentation specialists
- Computer presentations graphics designers
- Computer press: journalists
- Computer technicians
- Computer trade show planners
- Computer-aided designers
- Designers
- Desktop publishers
- Desktop video producers
- Desktop videographers
- DNA-Driven Genealogists
- Documentation analysts
- Dog Trainers
- Drafters
- Editors
- Engineering graphics specialists
- Facilitators
- Genomics Technologists
- Graphic designers
- Human resource recruiters
- Indexers
- Informatics Database Managers
- Local Area Network specialists
- Managers of information systems
- Manufacturing technicians
- Multimedia specialists
- Nurse Practitioners
- Nutritionists
- Online Retailers & Wholesalers
- Podcasters
- Programmers
- Retailers
- RSS Content Syndicators
- Robotics and numerical control technicians

- Sales and Marketing Representatives
- Software Engineers/Designers
- Software reviewers
- Software talent agents.
- Special effects specialists
- Systems analysts
- Technical and software user manual writers
- Technical illustrators
- Technical trainers
- Tutors
- Video game artists/designers
- Visual Anthropologists
- Web Designers
- Wireless Communications Technicians
- Wholesalers
- Word processing specialists
- Writers

- **Advantages to Corporations for Hiring Independent Contractors**

An employer doesn't have to pay any health insurance or benefits to an independent contractor. Independents can't get worker's compensation from an employer. The independent contractor is a freelancer and a consultant, working alone.

Financial responsibility rests with the independent contractor, not with the client or company hiring you. However, you take orders from the company contracts with your client to perform a service or supply a product.

Clients won't contract with you based solely on resume or cover letter you write for other people. As a job coach, you'll be hired by corporations to train employers and human resource management workers. In addition to a creative or abilities resume, you'll need a brochure or flyer and business cards. Include a list of clients as references.

Written communication will bring you into corporate or institutional offices for interviews. There, you'll bid for your service or product against competing businesses offering similar ware. Evaluate honestly what you will offer.

Bidding independent contractors may deal with competition from foreign businesses which import and export computer peripherals, software, and services. There's a burgeoning foreign market for computer industry independent contractors and consultants, for example, foreign computer animators.

There are a tremendous number of immigrants coming from all parts of the world seeking jobs, clients, or customers in the world of computer technology. What does a recent newcomer to the United States or Canada seeking work put on a resume?

- **Culturally Diverse Clients**

Job coaching, writing resumes, and business letters for culturally diverse communities are the norm in personal service industries. Immigrants come from all over the world to set up businesses or work in them in the U.S. You'll find software in most major languages sold in the US, and computer products catering to the needs of people from around the world available in major U.S. cities.

Products continue to be built overseas and locally. The wide varieties of books, videos, courses, and software about training and hiring people are available. Products are designed and manufactured in the US and abroad. Import and export of computer parts is a huge industry worldwide. For example, most of your computer hard disks are assembled in Asia.

Cultural diversity in the workplace includes the entertainment industry's use of computers for special effects. Most computer animation for the entertainment television and film industry is currently created by computer special effects in Europe and Asia. Corporate desktop animation and special effects for ad agencies are created mainly in the U.S.A. through multimedia desktop video.

Facing the reality of growing cultural diversity, employers still look for patterns familiar to American corporate values. Employers want information they can understand quickly when reading your resume. What are the most important points an immigrant new to North America can emphasize in a resume or cover letter? As a job coach, you can show similarities and differences to American corporate and educational equivalents in how you present clients to employers.

- **Names and Gender on Resumes**

If you are foreign to the cultural diversity of the United States, you may have to state your gender in the job overview section on your resume. The average North American may not know your gender by the spelling or sound of your name. This especially applies to some Eastern European, Middle Eastern, African, Indian, Far Eastern, Pacific Island, Native American and Australian Aboriginal names.

- **Translate Skills Into Company Values**

Picking from among your client's many abilities is difficult, so be sure to list only those skills that are highly valued by the company. Look at the job description and briefly explain how your client's best skills apply. You're client will be hired for performance of skills highly valued by the employer. Identify what your client does best in terms of what the employer values most.

- **Which Industry Needs Your Client's Skills?**

Look for niches where your competencies can best be used. Sort your experience into categories. Sort your educational courses or technical training into categories which are similar to American levels of education. Clarify and explain where needed.

Call a few employers or human resource managers and ask them what job descriptions and job responsibilities in your computer specialty sound most familiar to average American employers. Decide which foreign work experiences translate into American job descriptions.

List the experiences most similar to American job descriptions of duties. Translate your job responsibilities into statements that most American employers would find familiar.

- **In What Country Will Your Client Work?**

As a job coach, find out whether your client has traveled to areas where that individual would like to live and work. Then decide whether there is enough industry growth in that area in your client's special field. Send your client's resumes to companies in that area. It's best to attend a few professional conventions with your client in the chosen geographic area to network with people in the same specialty. By making business contacts or networking, you and your client may find some good tips about working in that area and may make contacts to find more clients.

- **Be Logically Convincing**

Customize the style, clarity, and content of a resume by stating skill level. Use statistics to verify how good your client's skills are. Convince the employer that your client's foreign skills translate into experience familiar to and valued by an American corporation or institution. Quantify the skills in the resume as in the following examples:

- "Word processing speed is 90 words per minutes with zero errors, specializing in statistical keyboarding and data entry on XYZ computer using ABC software.
- "Two years experience operating NMB computers in the biotech industry."
- "One year experience in database management using Paradox Software on an IBM PC."
- **Immigration Status**

Include on your client's resume whether the individual's visa is that of a student or a resident alien, or whether your client is waiting to become a citizen.

It's important to know that your client is legally in the country and has a work permit or "green card" and how long your client intends to remain in the USA, if not a permanent resident.

List your client's immigration status at the end of the resume without causing undue attention to it. You can ask your client to elaborate at the final interview or after your client is hired. The employer wants to know if it's legal to hire that person.

State your client's English language proficiency level. The employer wants to know you understand and speak English well enough to handle the job. If you have a heavy accent, take some speech coaching to improve it. Include any training taken in the U.S. Explain that your former jobs in the U.S. or elsewhere, required fluency in spoken and written English.

- **Immigrants Wait Longer to Find Work**

It may take a new immigrant longer to find a job than someone who has lived, studied, and worked in the U.S. for many years. Your clients may be even offered less pay if they are not yet US citizens. They may be rejected for a job because they don't have the right level of security clearance. This should be fought legally. Age first and then mobility, not ethnicity is the determiner of how many weeks your client may have to wait to find employment. Do your clients drive cars, or ride public buses to work? What are the clients' disabilities and accessibility needs?

- **An Edge**

Include cost-cutting points on your client's resume which give an extra edge. Target a niche, a specialized corner of the computer industry. Focus. Don't let your resume try to be everything to everybody. Like an older worker, the new immigrant also must find an edge and carve a niche in the computer industry.

An edge is a strategy which focuses on an employer's greatest need. For example, inform an employer how your client will save the company time and money because skills can be qualified and quantified by the following statements…." Then proceed to write statements with input from your client that actually qualify and quantify some of your client's skills.

Layout the reasons as you qualify and quantify how each skill solved problems and achieved measurable results. Make sure the reader can follow the results step-by-step. Emphasize clear, easy-to-understand writing in plain language, even when technical skills are emphasized.

The human resources department interviewer may be a generalist, even though the employer is technically-trained. As a job coach, you'll be listing company-valued details.

CHAPTER 11

The Right Job

This chapter is designed to increase your client's self-awareness. Now that you've learned how to handle your client's resume, as a job coach, it's time to find out which job is the best-fit match for your client. Your goal in running an online resume-writing service is to write a dynamic resume. As a job coach, you'll need to help your client show with words on paper that he (or she) is in command of himself (or herself).

A job coach and resume writer often is like a literacy volunteer, helping people to know themselves better with the help of many resources. Know how to ask directions, and then offer information.

If your resumes frequently bring back form letters which state, "Your credentials are impressive, but they don't fit our requirements at this time," perhaps you're not applying to the business which *profits* from what you do best. Maybe you're not writing your resume according to your personality preferences. Or you targeted the wrong job.

Are you still mailing resumes to any company listing familiar job descriptions? Would you like more power to choose the job that works for you? The personality questionnaire you're about to take in this chapter applies specifically to career choices within the computer industry.

The questions ask for your preferences for the type of work you feel most comfortable doing in the computer industry. After you answer the questions, you can use the answer sheet to self-score the personality type preference classifier to find out what type you are.

Then you can look under the four letters of your type. You'll see a list of the job titles recommended for each type according to the comfort level you feel doing the tasks required in those jobs.

The preference classifier you'll take in this chapter is a tool for understanding our normal differences in the way we gather information, and that's all it's supposed to predict. It will help you appreciate normal differences between all types of people working in the computer industry.

Be Aware Of Preference Differences and Similarities At Work

Different people need different work-related experiences to thrive in a career. After taking this preference 'quiz,' you'll begin to apply type effectively to analyze which tasks feel more comfortable to work at for long periods of time.

Perhaps you won't feel so much like a round CD-Interactive laser disk in a square floppy disk drive. Which job is the right job for you? The answer is, the right job is the one that works for you.

What Interests Come Naturally?

Look for comfort in doing the tasks. Ask yourself what skills are most easy to learn and to practice? What comes naturally? What's harder to do, so hard, in fact, that you become depressed and irritable or stressed out and exhausted from doing them all day?

Whether you're sending your resume to a corporation or already work in a paid job, employers are going to ask, "Why do you mind doing things our way?" When you do mind, it's because your preferences are different from your employer's.

In this chapter, you'll find a preference sorter. It's a classifier which may help you understand better the way you make decisions and solve problems. Use this preference classifier to empower yourself and those with whom you work.

How Can You Use Your Personal Strengths To Improve Teamwork?

The preference classifier will reveal your personal strengths. You'll learn how to apply knowledge about personality preferences to improve teamwork on your job.

You'll appreciate personality type differences on a variety of jobs. And you'll learn how to apply understanding of personality type in a small way—in niches related to selected computer industry job requirements.

There's A Place for Everyone to Earn a Living

You'll learn to see the wonderful gifts of all the types, because all types are needed in the computer industry. There's a place for everyone: from the computer illustrator using software to create cartoons for greeting cards to the financial database manager who uses applied artificial intelligence to design software which forecasts stock market trends.

What Corporations Employ All Skills?

Which tasks would you rather be doing at work? Computer industry personnel differ in their work preferences as they do in their job tasks. Some like to analyze. Others are artistic. There are those who like to sell and talk. Some like to train or teach.

Do you like to work alone using computers as a tool to express or reflect inner thinking or feeling? Would you prefer to use computers as a tool to do other jobs—such as architectural drafting or industrial design?

People who work in the computer industry are there to make life run faster and easier through newer technology. They find computer solutions attractive.

When Standard Behavior No Longer Works

You apply your knowledge of type when your standard behavior no longer works on the job or at home. Once you see your type, use it ethically. Don't let it prejudice you against co-workers with different types and different needs from their work than you have.

Use your knowledge of type to give your co-workers straight information. You'll find people at work who get great pleasure out of filling in the details and grounding you in practicality. Other types may feel that their daydreams for the future are being wasted by attention to details in the present.

Detail-oriented people are clear and precise. They look for common sense. You may wonder why employers so often give the more creative, imaginative, and visionary work to people impatient with details, common sense, and usefulness. Detail-oriented people are just as imaginative in practical ways that use common sense.

What Are Your Client's Real Preferences?

Knowing your client's abilities and preferences give you the added responsibility to use such information fairly. Certain preferences can change or amplify under stress. Or your client could be hiding actual personality traits in order to be more desirable in a career that demands such qualities and offers better pay, hours, duties, or location.

Which Way Does Your Client Approach The Tasks?

Real preferences are those your client feels like choosing when your client no longer has to prove anything or when the individual is not under pressure. Don't let your knowledge of personality classifiers or pop psychology quizzes and innovations give you any biases towards your clients or co-workers.

People do have different preferences regarding which skills they'd select to use all day at work. You and your clients actually prefer the type of work that reflects the way that work influences health, stress levels, and compatibility. Personality and work styles are shaped by the environment, by brain chemicals, genes, familiarity with skills, job experience, and also by the way you and your clients innately relate to people, data, and objects.

List of Recommended Jobs

Job titles change as technology changes. Look into evolving job titles such as biomedical informatics technicians in DNA testing and genetic database management, forensic or 'accident' reconstructionists in legal-oriented event reconstruction, RSS news feed Web content 'syndication' specialist (online content producer), MP3 audio file or online streaming video podcaster, and telecommunications publicists writing video news releases for the Internet.

New jobs are created each year whose titles never existed the previous year. Here are some job titles that you can match your preferences to when you research what job duties are required for the long term.

Are any of job descriptions you research from these job titles possibly the right fit with your client's preferences and abilities? What type of job enhances your client's health and sense of joy of living?

The job recommendations below represent only a fraction of those which exist in a variety of industries. Job titles here today are gone with the passing years, and new job titles take their place. Technology changes what skills the work force uses on the job each year.

- Accountant, data manager, computer security investigator, auditor, software engineer, attorney, economist, career military and civil service computer administrator. Business information technologist, numerical control specialist. Comptroller of financial databases. Law office administrator and paralegal. Medical software transcriber and medical records technician, software manufacturer's representative, applied mathematician. Financial operations manager.

- Computer-aided drafter, computer-aided manufacturing specialist and robotics technician. Computer repair technician, and business computing programmer, applied systems analyst. Systems engineer, astronaut: virtual reality specialist. Defense and weapons computer simulations instructor. Traveling computer security specialist. Information systems consultant, defense weapons vendor or designer.

- Real estate software sales, computer program radio talk show host, computer marketing personnel, peripheral retailer, wholesaler, importer of computer products, design automation publicist, auditor, traveling software distributor. Cable or satellite TV multimedia producer, interactive learning materials designer, digital animator, wireless telecommunications manufacturer's representative. Promoter of new hardware and software, skills, cosmetics, textiles, music, art, self-help, nutrition, or cleaning products.

- Law office administrator, paralegal, computer security specialist, computer lawyer, investigator, manager, business information technologist, data communications engineer, programmer, information retrieval specialist, database manager, records manager, numerical control manager, robotics engineer or technician, accountant, financial programmer, marketing manager, banking programmer or systems analyst, insurance database specialist, wholesaler, international database manager, executive recruiter, broadcasting multimedia executive, hospital and health services administrator, computer science and information systems instructor, production and operations manager, public administrator, logistics specialist, insurance investigation, systems engineer.

- Local area network specialist, telecommunications equipment technician, organizer, word processor, desktop publisher, teacher, librarian, medical software technology designer, telephone company craftsperson, communications technicians, switching machine operator, computer operator, data-entry clerk, secretary, paralegal, applied computing programmer. Applied computing specialist, records manager, court reporter, wireless telecommunications equipment technician, nurse-practitioner, healthcare, oral history transcriber, personal historian, visual anthropologist, documentarian, video producer, medical records administrator. Data communications specialist, telecommunications technologist, computer science education specialist.

- Medical transcriber, Braille transcriber, medical records librarian or administrator, healthcare computing operator, word processor, secretary, bookkeeper, computer illustrator and crafts person. Computer software fashion designer. Satellite TV or Internet sales, Computer repairer, computer peripheral retail sales clerk or manager. Medical records technologist and medical records software manufacturer's sales representative. Desktop publisher. Mail-order customer service manager. Preschool use of computers specialists (games for teaching preschool), computer illustrator, Midi synthesizer music composer or vendor, exhibit designer.

- Software talent agent, computer laser light show performer, sports computing specialist, nurse practitioner manufacturer's software representative, retail computer store sales clerk, virtual reality entertainment retailer, computerized theatrical production specialist, software video producer, computer animation advertising agency representative, public relations account executive, traveling computer sales, computer music (Midi synthesizer and special effects) performer,

- physical therapy and rehabilitation computer trainer or sales representative, software fashion designer, merchandiser, nurse practitioner and trainer, vendor, computer camp counselor and travel agent.

- Database manager, medical administrative assistant, nurse, medical records software technician, programmer, computer store retail manager, sales and customer representative, communications technician with phone company, telecommunications sales representative, computer animation advertising

account executive, publicist, professional associations convention planner, computer professional association national organizer, special events planner, Peace Corps organizer, trainer, nurse-trainer, business education teacher, and/or office information systems manager.

- Computer illustrator and designer, animator, technical writer, software user manual writer, teacher, courseware designer, instructional technologist, on-line librarian, tape librarian, ergonomics designer and researcher, biomedical computing specialist, interactive fiction writer for CD-Interactive/CD-ROM.

- Electronic publishing consultant and color desktop publishing specialist, mediator, human resource manager, outplacement director, personnel consultant, recruiter, exhibit designer.

- Freelance writer, freelance editorial illustrator, computer press columnist/journalist, grant proposal writer, software user manual writer, computer career book author, cartoonist, desktop animator, desktop video script writer, courseware designer, newsletter designer, writing teacher, consultant, computer camp counselor, organizational development specialist, electronic publisher.

- Counselor, computer camp resort recruiter, techno-stress psychologist, computer personnel researcher, computers for the physically handicapped trainer, vendor, ergonomics vendor, professional speaker, career book writer, computer press journalist/columnist, temporary agency recruiter, organizational development specialist, outplacement interviewer, convention and event planner, publicist, trade show and exhibit manager, cruise ship computer room social director, courseware designer, personnel agency manager, small business opportunities columnist/author, publisher, corporate training video producer, animator.

- Public speaker, nurse, physician, geneticist, trainer, teacher, computerized job bank counselor, retail salesperson, manufacturer's representative, interactive multimedia producer, audience tracker, organizational development consultant, office manager, recruiter, human resource development manager, event planner, computers and society researcher, computers and human interaction researcher, traveling seminar specialist, public relations account executive, video producer, computer graphics presentations designer, health care para-professional, Total Quality Management trainer, traveling salesperson and manufacturer's representative. Web administrator, Computer personnel researcher, corporate or educational trainer, online facilitator-university courses.

- 'Automata' and 'computability' theorist, biomedical computing programmer and systems analyst, computer architect, design automation specialist, documentation analyst, symbolic computing and mathematics researcher, software engineer.

- Neuropsychopharmacologist, nutritional genomics researcher, DNA-driven genealogy reporter, forensic DNA test technician, bioinformatics database manager, forensic geneticist, genetics counselor, biotech computer specialist, biomedical engineer, information broker, competitive intelligence specialist, computer security investigator, software manufacturer and designer, object-oriented programmer, documentation analyst, financial analyst, applied artificial intelligence financial forecaster, trend forecaster, economist, computer science educator, neural networks and fuzzy logic programmer/designer, software engineer, electronic publishing vendor, molecular biology software developer.

- Computer architect, numerical mathematician, robotics engineer, measurement and evaluation computing specialist, simulation specialist, software engineer, computational linguistics researcher, educational researcher, securities analyst, systems analyst, programmer, scientific programmer, operating systems specialist, programming languages designer, microprogramming researcher, software designer, computer game programmer, biomedical computing programmer, automata and computability theory researcher, trend forecaster, atmospheric and environmental forecaster, satellite technician or tracker, mathematician, systems analyst, software engineer, educational researcher, biostatistician, numerical control robotics researcher, inventor, electronic engineer, technical writer/science writer, graphics designer.

- Instructional technologist, marketing research manager, labor trends forecaster, economist, inventor, software engineer, designer, multimedia and presentation graphics designer/producer, electronic publisher, wireless communications developer, telecommunications network engineer, technical public speaker, organizational development specialist, outplacement consultant, entrepreneur, 'intrapreneur,' dog trainer, manufacturer's representative, traveling salesperson, computer camp owner, digital imaging photographer, special effects designer, corporate animator, public relations account executive, advertising agency account executive, promotion director, data communications vendor, documentary film maker/training films,

- Web master, programming languages designer, hardware, peripherals, and robotics designer, virtual reality designer, computer and video games programmer/designer, systems analyst, physician's training video producer, independent contractor, computer marketing consultant.

- Data manager, organizational development researcher, visual anthropologist, documentarian, personal historian, oral historian, tape transcriber, bioinformatics database manager, general manager, entrepreneur, operating systems director, career military officer, lawyer, computer security director, design automation researcher, programmer, systems analyst, organizer, planning director, time management trainer, software developer, hardware importer/exporter, computerized genetics researcher, environmental investigator, electronic engineer, software engineer, systems analyst, venture capital broker/banker, executive recruiter, analog/digital circuit engineer, fundraiser, marketing analyst, wireless electronic security wholesaler, weapons systems specialist, public speaker, wireless communications technician, hardware design engineer, network switching software engineer.

What Work Environment Does Your Client Prefer?

Does your client want to be in the corporate world, in academic training, or in the arts or sciences and technology? What would your role be—an administrator, trainer/researcher, artist/writer/editor, or an assistant supporting business, technology, education, or science leaders?

There's a niche industry for all the preferences.

What niche makes the most comfortable fit with your client's preferences, capabilities, and the way others see your client's performance? Discuss and examine your client's preferences. Understand why your client prefers the type of job duties that are comfortable in the long run. Ask your client to visualize how he or she would play at work. Ask the client whether he or she enjoys certain job duties when your client has to repeat tasks every work day.

Select Action Verbs That Describe What Your Client Does at Work

Match your client's preferences with the character of the organization where your client would choose to work if hired. Select those action verbs and preferences that emphasize your client's best qualifications or what your clients have done or would do on a job. Finally, include in your client's resume or cover letters any of your client's preferences that you want to use to direct attention to the type of job your client wants.

The next chapter contains sample resumes which you may use as a guideline to check against your client's skills and volunteered information. At the end of the chapter there's an employer tracking form for keeping records of when and where your resumes were sent. Frequently, it's the balance of not too many follow-up calls and letters that motivate employers to give interviews. Once a month follow-up calls are fine. Weekly contact is seen as interruptive to an employer's busy schedule.

Writing resumes is all about packaging your client as information that offers solutions to problems. People seek work for a variety of reasons, but it takes as much ego-strength to turn down a promotion as it does to climb the ladder. Expand your resume-writing enterprise with job-coaching skills.

CHAPTER **12**

What Looks Great to Employers?

Use the sample resumes at the end of this chapter as guides or templates to inspire you as a job coach and also as a writer of business correspondence and resumes. The resume templates or samples can help you observe details about the many different niches in various industries. Use them to check against your client's work history.

To which companies will you ask your client to send resumes with cover letters, and after the interview, send follow-up letters? If you're looking for names of firms, you can find listings of companies in the U.S. or Canada in business directories and phone books found at your public library.

Look in the industrial directories found in public and university libraries. Industrial directories contain addresses of major corporations and various smaller companies. For a quick listing to help your technical job-seeking clients, you can find excellent databases of U.S. software, hardware, and on-line companies.

Create a database for your contacts. Look at *Fuch's Address Book for Windows* at the Web site: http://www.sharewarejunkies.com/00zwd8/address_book.htm. The Address Book allows you to create a contacts database (address book J) with fields such as; name, title, company, address, phone and fax numbers, e-mail addresses, and notes. Keep a record of all your corporate contacts to help you run your career coaching business.

Just as important as getting a list of current computer companies to send your client's resumes to is designing the visual appearance of each client's resume.

The design and layout really is important. Always use a desktop-published or word-processed resume. However, most employers and employment agency and services owners prefer the desktop published resume laser-printed on good resume-quality paper to the word-processed resume. The resumes you'll find at the end of this chapter also are intended to be used to help you organize and balance the visual design.

The golden strategy of resume writing is: Do unto employers as *they* would have you do unto them. Value their company's needs.

Observe how qualifications listed on the sample resumes match with the needs of the company. Describe the character of the company to your client. Or have your client research the company's characteristics. Does the company's character match well with your client's skill experience, niche abilities, and personality preferences?

Will the job requirements influence your client's health and stress level in a positive or negative way in a long-term situation? As a resume writer or job coach, your goal will be to help your client obtain an interview with a company that would not offer a job detrimental to the long or short-term health status of your client.

No employee wants to stay in a job that is making the worker ill emotionally or physically. For example, an introvert forced to deal with the energy-draining activity of talking to many people all day or repeatedly having long phone conversations with strangers is more apt to wear out the introvert. A job talking face-to-face or on the phone would be better filled by an extrovert who is energized by people and people-related activity. Is your client healthier when working alone? Is your client energized by people or drained?

Does your client feel more stressed and anxious when dealing with customers all day? Would your client like to work alone in a laboratory instead or online at home, perhaps writing or researching facts?

At the end of this chapter, you'll find record keeping pages to help you track your clients' resumes. Follow up jobs and employers' requests for people with specific or niche skills as new openings occur in any company. To help you create your own templates, you'll find sample resumes here that follow some evolving fields from digital media to biomedical technology and beyond. Job titles change with the times.

Web designer today as a job title, didn't exist thirty years ago. Sales representatives and technicians today can have sub-titles such as cell phone specialist or sales manager or wireless communications technician.

A medical technologist twenty years ago today may specialize in working with DNA testing or manage genetic databases with titles such as bio-informatics technologist. Job titles evolve with the duties.

The generalist jobs also gain new titles, such as literacy specialist evolving to online facilitator, and gerontologist to "adult communities' playography designer" or environmental designer of senior residences. Generalists need a specialty or niche to apply skills in practical ways. And specialists need to shift into generalist roles when required deal with what's in front of them at the moment. Below are some job titles reflecting new advances in technology that *require moving between specialist and generalist roles* within a work day.

- Activities Director/Assisted Living
- Artificial Intelligence
- Biotech Computing
- Biotech Medical Writer
- Communications Analyst
- Computer-Aided Design
- Computer Convention/Events
- Computer Graphics
- Computer/Digital Journalism
- Computer Law
- Computer Operations
- Computer Security
- Computer Technology/Repair
- Database Management
- Data Entry Operations
- Desktop Publishing
- Desktop Video/Animation
- Digital Special Effects
- Document Production Manager
- Drafting/Medical
- Drafting/Engineering
- Educational Technologist
- Facilitating Online University Courses
- Fashion Design/Software
- Information Systems Analyst
- Interactive Fiction Writing
- Marketing Communications
- Marketing Management
- Medical Records Technology
- Medical Transcription
- Multimedia
- Network Systems Engineering
- Neural Networks
- Numerical Control
- Personnel Management
- Programming
- Quality Assurance
- Robotics Technology
- Sales and Marketing
- Scientific Programming
- Software Engineering
- Software Talent Agent
- Software Test Manager
- Software Writing
- Systems Analysis
- Systems Engineering
- Tape Librarian
- Technical Illustration
- Technical Writing
- Technical Training
- Tutoring
- Video computer games design
- Video/Teleconferencing
- Virtual Reality
- Wireless Communications
- Word Processing

*   *   *

Paring Down Words

What looks great to employers when they first gaze at a resume or cover letter? Keep the cover letter to one page or one-half page. Be brief and pleasant. When typesetting a resume, set your font size to Times Roman 12. Do not typeset in size10 font to squeeze the resume onto one page. Use only one column on a resume. The majority of resumes longer than a page are discarded.

Pare down words until you get a resume of one page, if possible. Never send a resume that's longer than one and a half pages unless is absolutely necessary for a special job that requires all that reading time. Few employers will read more than a page. A resume averages one 20-second reading or glance at the first paragraph.

If you want a word to stand out, don't use bold italics. The name of a periodical article or book can be italicized or underlined in a resume if you're including the title of an article or book written by the job applicant.

Always include a cover letter, and after the interview, a follow-up letter. Put the current dates on the cover and follow-up letters, not on the resume. Keep sentences short in a resume. Use *powerful* action verbs to describe what your client did on the job—how your client performed at work. Action verbs take less time to read. Stay away from adjectives to describe skills and achievements.

Remember that the human brain/eye is hardwired to notice what is different about a resume or any other visual presentation. Make your client stand out in a crowd in a pleasing, positive way that doesn't take up more time to notice. Positioning your client first in the reader's visual impression is important.

As a job coach and a resume and business-letter writer, help your clients to be memorable and make an impact in a *positive*, outstanding way. Specifically, that way would save the interviewer's time.

What you write for and with your client has a goal of making it easy for the interviewer to understand and remember. To stand out in another person's memory, words need to be pared down to the bare bones. You pare down words by substituting powerful action verbs for descriptive adjectives. These action verbs show the way your client's skills and personality are applied to increasing productivity and income.

Action verbs show how your client *saved time and money* by *solving problems* and achieving detailed *results* that any resume and cover letter reader can *follow step-by-step*. Show how your client offered *benefits* and advantages through effort and efficiency. The person hired is the person who will cost the employer the least amount of money in the long run. Below you'll find numerous resumes that you can use as templates or for inspiration as far as layout and the use of action verbs.

Choose from the list of action verbs that follow the resumes. Now, let's look at a few sample resumes to use as templates or for inspiration when you write resumes for your own clients. Remember to balance the layout of the resumes. Your goal is to use plenty of white space and contrasting (black) lettering on resumes and business letters. When readers first look at the page, the type and white space should be in balance. Now, let's look at some of these resume templates and/or sample resumes.

⋆   ⋆   ⋆

ARTIFICIAL INTELLIGENCE/NEURAL NETWORKS

Your Client's Name
Your Client's Street Address
City, State, Zip Code
Phone Number
Email Address
Web site address

JOB OVERVIEW

Permanent employment desired as an applied artificial intelligence finance database manager specifically in stock market trend forecasting. Goal: To become part of a growing software development company.

SOFTWARE/HARDWARE

C++, C, Pascal, Basic, Novell, Unix kernel, GUI, SCSI interface development in C, on IBM AS 400 hardware, and IBM PC.

EDUCATION

B.A. in Economics with applied mathematics minor, Unversity of Chicago, December 1992. Second minor in computer science and information systems.

SOFTWARE EXPERIENCE

December 2005–Present
MEREET INVESTMENT SOFTWARE DESIGN, INC., Chicago, IL.

Database Manager, Software Designer, and Programmer
Identified a particular stock market situation and environment as the only one resembling a known period in history. Applied artificial intelligence tools to stock market forecasting.
Designed forecasting software. Produced videos and gave seminars.

RESPONSIBILITIES

* Automated investment advisory service.
* Developed software within a closed network.

* Created an end product of presentation software.
* Designed and developed data management software.
* Coordinated with national database to obtain quotes.
* Developed technology including the following:
  *Statistical processes.
  *Extrapolation and trend analysis.
  *Pattern matching to historical development of indicators.
  *Neural networks expertise system and heuristics.
  *Measured breaks in stock market prices for changes in direction.

BIOTECH INFORMATICS TECHNICIAN

Your Client's Name
Your Client's Street Address
City, State, Zip Code
Phone Number
Email Address
Web site address

JOB OVERVIEW

DNA bio-informatics database management responsible for document control and archives meeting government requirements for DNA testing and genetics research within a biopharmaceutical or DNA-testing company developing innovative products.

SOFTWARE/HARDWARE

Lotus 123, dBase, Paradox, Excel, Word Perfect, PowerPoint.
IBM-compatible PC.

DOCUMENT CONTROL EXPERIENCE

October 2000–2005
LOMBOCHE PHARMACEUTICALS, INC., Pendleton, CA.

Clinical Documentation Specialist
* Responsible for document control for clinical studies.
* Maintained department archives to meet FDA requirements.
* Tracked and reported study status.
* Maintained all pharmaceutical documentation in databases using a variety of dBase and spreadsheet software.
* Prepared pharmaceutical documentation for FDA audits.
* Utilized medical terminology extensively.
* Administrative support activities included heavy use of word processing software and spreadsheets.

June 1974-October 1979
ST. MICHAEL'S HOSPITAL, Oceanside, CA.

Medical Records Technician and Transcriber
* Coded medical records and transcribed medical terminology in medical records department of an acute care hospital.
* Operated IBM 129 computer.

EDUCATION

B.S. in Genetics with minor in health sciences, San Diego State University, June 2005.

A.S. Biomedical Technology, American College, San Diego, 2000
Certificate in Medical Transcription and Medical Office Administration, Mesa College, San Diego, June, 1972.

References Sent Upon Request

PHARMACEUTICAL AD COPYWRITER

Your Client's Name
Your Client's Street Address
City, State, Zip Code
Phone Number
Email Address
Web site address

OVERVIEW

Seeking a permanent staff position as an advertising medical writer with a pharmaceutical company, medical advertising agency, or computer corporation specializing in medical software, video, and multimedia presentation technologies.

SUMMARY OF QUALIFICATIONS

* Gather information.
* Reshape information.
* Sell information in a variety of formats.
* Design information to meet different needs.
* Information is my most valuable resource.

RELATED SKILLS

* Interpreted complex clinical research and development data into simple-to-understand marketing support materials.
* Interpreted, wrote, and edited: monographs, presentations, video scripts, sales aid layouts and clinical/marketing research claims support materials.
* Managed projects from inception to completion.
* Authored seven self-help and nutrition books published by major New York publishers.
* Wrote many multimedia computer presentation graphics scripts.
* Wrote medical advertising copy for a variety of advertising agencies within Fortune 500 international health care firms.

EXPERIENCE

1964–Present: Independent contract medical writer,
A.J. Smith Medical Writing Productions, (self-employed), Wilmington, DE.

EDUCATION/TRAINING

Bachelor of Science Degree
English Education
New York University, NY, 1964

Continuing Education in Medical Writing
American Medical Writer's Association
Continuing Education Seminars, 1992

COMMUNICATIONS ANALYST

Your Client's Name
Your Client's Street Address
City, State, Zip Code
Phone Number
Email Address
Web site address

GOAL

To obtain a permanent position as a communications analyst in a large-scale LAN/WAN information systems and services department managing and troubleshooting network projects.

· OVERVIEW

* Six years of LAN/WAN experience with an in-depth knowledge of interconnect technologies.

* Technical and working knowledge of synchronous/asynchronous protocols, TCP/IP and SNA network methodologies.

* Three years hands-on experience with bridges, routers, 10base Tcabling systems, modems, MUXes, and telephone company services (T1, 56k).

* Six years experience with network test equipment (LanAlyzer, Firebird).

SOFTWARE

* Knowledge of Microsoft, Lan Manager, Novell, Unix, DOS, and Email.

EXPERIENCE

January 1987–Present: Communication Analyst, Able Data, Inc., Bloomington, MN. Managed the Information Systems and Services Department of a large-scale LAN/WAN corporation. Troubleshooter on network projects.

EDUCATION

Bachelor of Science
Information Systems
Certificate in Telecommunications
Borne Computer College
Bloomington, MN, 1986

Associate in Sciences
Computer Science and Information Systems
Bloomington Community College, 1983

DIGITAL GRAPHIC ILLUSTRATION & COMPUTER-AIDED DESIGN

Your Client's Name
Your Client's Street Address
City, State, Zip Code
Phone Number
Email Address
Web site address

OVERVIEW: Eight years of increasingly responsible positions as a technical illustrator, with in-depth exposure to AUTOCAD engineering graphics, design, and drafting. Focus on blue-print reading, dimensioning, tolerancing, assembly drawing, and air brush illustration. Four years experience designing special effects. Seek a position as a computer-aided designer in industrial design.

ABILITIES

* Detail drawing of complex concepts in engineering graphics.
* Assembly drawing and cutaways.

* Airbrushing.
* Presentation graphics design on Macintosh computers focusing on multimedia presentations and video.
* Computer applications on Cadds 4x computers.
* Technical illustrations in Freehand and Illustrator software.
* Computer tracing from originals.
* Macintosh production and traffic management.
* Desktop publishing with PageMaker/In Design, Illustrator, and PhotoShop software, specializing in color separations.
* Strong paste-up and design using AUTOCAD software.
* Computer illustration with Coreldraw! on IBM-compatible computers. Finished designs using line or airbrush.
* Corporate computer animation, special effects, and desktop video using the Amiga computer, Video Toaster, and camera.

ACHIEVEMENTS

* Developed detailed, cutaway drawings of computer hardware.
* Designed drafting blue prints of hardware using AUTOCAD software.
* Illustrated parts brochures with Adobe software on the Macintosh.
* Created six award-winning corporate animation videos focusing on special effects.

EMPLOYMENT

June 1985–Present: Technical Graphics Artist and Computer-Aided Designer/Drafter, Creative Media Technical Advertising Agency, Buffalo, New York.

EDUCATION

Associate in Applied Science
Technical Illustration and Desktop Video
Brooklyn Community College, 1985

References mailed upon request.

CONVENTION/EVENTS PLANNER

Your Client's Name
Your Client's Street Address
City, State, Zip Code
Phone Number
Email Address
Web site address

OVERVIEW: Experienced computer and electronics events planner seeks affiliation with convention, trade show, and exhibit planning agency or national association of computer professionals.

ABILITIES

INSTITUTIONAL

* Trade show, exhibit, and convention planner with Mann College Annual Job Fair.
* Knowledge of exhibit design and booth sales.
* Public relations, tours, and press conference planning.
* Site selection and budgeting.
* Coordination and organization from inception to completion of medical trade shows, exhibits, conventions, conferences, meetings, seminars, workshops, and job fairs with institutional and hotel sales and catering managers.
* Sold 500 booths at annual Medical Equipment Dealer's convention.
* Personnel interviewing, screening, and hiring of exhibit designer's crew and carpenters.

EXPERIENCE

June 1992-September 1993: Sales Manager, convention and conference space, Mann Computer College, Hagarstown, MD.

June 1987-May 1992: Exhibits Designer and Events Planner, Glentackie Technical Events Planning Agency, Chevy Chase, MD.

VOLUME

Average annual exhibit booth sales of $600,000 1992–1993.
Average annual exhibit booth sales of $350,000 1987–1992.

EDUCATION

Certificate in Events Planning
Certificate in Desktop Publishing
Baltimore Community College, Adult Continuing Education Div.,
Baltimore, MD., 1987

References sent upon request.

COMPUTER GRAPHICS

Your Client's Name
Your Client's Street Address
City, State, Zip Code
Phone Number
Email Address
Web site address

EDUCATION
Associate in Applied Science
Commercial Art
San Diego City College, 1980

OVERVIEW: Thirteen years of increasingly responsible positions as a staff ad agency graphic designer. Focus on heavy advertising agency brochure, print, greeting card, calendar, and electronic design. Seek a position as a staff illustrator in the advertising department of a large corporation, or as a staff illustrator/graphic designer/desktop publisher or desktop video producer with a major advertising agency.

ABILITIES
* Detail drawing of complex concepts in advertising design.
* Illustration of children's books and editorial text.
* Heavy airbrush illustration.
* In-depth exposure to CorelDraw—compatible computers.
* Design multimedia presentation graphics on Macintosh using Adobe Illustrator, Photo Shop, and Freehand
* Computer tracing from original art.
* Ad agency traffic management, routing, and media buying.
* Desktop publishing with PageMaker software, with either the MAC or IBM.
* Specialist in creating color separations on the computer.
* Corporate computer animation, special effects, and desktop video

ACHIEVEMENTS
* Designed all editorial illustrations for newspapers.
* Illustrated ads for brochures with Adobe software on the Macintosh
* Created an award-winning corporate animation video training film on health tips for truckers

EMPLOYMENT

<u>**June 1980–Present:**</u> Graphics Designer, (Staff Artist/Illustrator) Barnett Public Relations and Advertising Agency, San Diego, CA.

References sent upon request.

JOURNALISM

Your Client's Name
Your Client's Street Address
City, State, Zip Code
Phone Number
Email Address

JOB OBJECTIVE:

Working journalist covering fitness, health, and medical industry, including pharmaceutical trade journals seeks an editorial position on a medical trade journal publication or trade newspaper. Staff reporter available with additional freelance experience seeks general reporter assignment. Excellent command of and experience in digital journalism online content production techniques, RSS news feed syndication management, online podcasting news narration experience, and Web content management.

EDITING EMPLOYMENT:

2004–Present: Freelance magazine writing, popular consumer fitness magazines including the following:

Medical Fitness   12 articles published—2005
Health and Mind   10 articles published—2004
Health for All Magazine   5 articles published—1998

CITY REPORTING:

1980–2004: Reporter, The Daily XYZ. Covered local business news for the Daily XYZ, an urban daily newspaper with a circulation of 300,000 in a city of 750,000.

FREELANCE WRITING

1963–1980: Full-time freelance reporter: national magazines. Wrote over 100 published business articles.

PROFESSIONAL ASSOCIATIONS

* American Medical Writers Association

* Computer Press Association.
* American Society For Professional Journalists.

EDUCATION

Bachelor of Arts in Journalism Education
School of Education, New York University, NY, 1963

Reference letters and published article clips available upon request.

CHAPTER 13

How Job, Life, & Executive Coaches Find Current Employer and Client Contacts

Job coaches, like their clients are looking for innovations in career searching. Are your clients willing to try new search techniques to interest employers? Then show your clients why they can target smaller companies and where and how to find these smaller companies. That's part of your role as a coach, beyond the usual role of writing and formatting resumes. As the larger corporations downsize to cut costs, smaller businesses are less likely to lay-off as frequently, according to a recent poll taken by the American Management Association (New York).

The AMA poll reported that 38 percent of companies employing 10,000 or more had planned to layoff workers in 1993. In contrast, small companies with l00 or fewer workers planned to lay off only seven percent of their employees.

Technology in the world economy now focuses on the growth of export trade businesses. Your client's resume will have a better chance if sent to divisions of companies that show growth.

Therefore, seek out those small to midsize firms that are growing fast. Check a company's growth rates before mailing your resume by looking at Hoover's Handbook of American Business, (Reference Press Inc.) The handbook charts 10-year sales and earnings growth and total debt ratio on more than 500 major employers, according to Capell's article, "Hiring Demand Shows Signs of Life," in Managing Your Career.

Other reference books you need to look through before sending out your resume include the Bond Guide, published by Standard & Poor's. You can find these reference books in any major public or college library. The monthly Bond Guide is a booklet that rates thousands of corporate bonds based on whether a company can pay principal and interest by the due date.

If you see a corporation rated less than BB, then think it over for a long time before you send your resume to a company that has lower bond ratings due to its lack of ability to pay principal and interest when due. It's far better to try networking your resume with the same sources used by professional job researchers.

Use trade journals to network with others in your field. Most major public and college libraries maintain a current collection of trade journals listing companies and names of key personnel in management. Use this information for networking.

Read the trade journal's help wanted classified advertisements. Many trade magazines also run a category for positions wanted advertisements placed by job seekers.

An excellent index to trade journals and industry-oriented magazines, (organized by industry) including those for the computer industry, is listed in Gale's Directoy of Publications, (R.R. Bowker). Computer industry professional and business associations are included with other types of associations in The Encyclopedia Of Associations. These reference books are in your public and university library.

If you're looking for a job in the computer mail order business, for example, you'll find reference books in the library listing the small to medium-sized high growth companies as well, such as Dell Computer Corporation, a pioneer in the computer mail-order business. Sometimes, when you can't find such information in your public or college library, you can turn to university placement directors for this type of information for a small fee, if you're not a student. Many offer such information sources and databanks to the public as well as to their students.

Try Investext. It's a computerized anthology, a CD-ROM data base of professional analysts' reports. You'll find it at Information Access Company, 362 Lakeside Drive, Foster City, California 94404. (Call toll free, 1-800-227-8431.)

Investext is available on-line through many computerized news services, or you can find it on CD. Information Access Company also offers The General Business File. This data base contains full-text articles taken out of trade magazines as well as full-text stock analysts' reports.

If you want to obtain the names, addresses, and phone numbers of top executives in major corporations so you can direct your resume to a particular person in your field, your library contains The Greenwich Register, (Hunt-Scanlon Publishing Company). By checking these reference books or data bases, you can send your resume to the company most likely to be hiring in your niche.

How you present your resume is as important as getting it to the person who has the authority to hire you. More than a decade ago, according to Kevin Collins, in "Does Your Resume Stand Out," Managing Your Career, Spring,

1993, telling an employer "what you've learned on your last job" rather than only stating "what you've done" sets your resume apart from the rest.

The entire computer industry has the same credo—"faster, smaller, and easier to use," according to Denise Hergatt's February 1993 article, "Computer Specialists," in the <u>California Job Journal</u>. This is true whether you're looking for a job in a high-growth area such as computer-aided software engineering or writing adventure fiction for compact disk interactive multimedia producers. The best way to put your resume in the right hands still is to get involved. Build a team of business contacts by joining industry groups in your specialization. Track the trends.

*   *   *

What Facts Will References Report?

Are you concerned whether you should write "references upon request" at the bottom of your resume? Former employers may be required by law to report only the dates you worked for a particular firm, the job title, and description of your job duties. Your references may be no longer allowed to comment on your job performance.

For example, if an en Smith did a wonderful job, but answers a request for references with name, job title, description of duties, and dates worked for Mary Jones, it could be misinterpreted that something was wrong with Mary Jones because the former employer held back comment on Ms. Jones's performance. To equalize everyone's references, all your past employers are allowed to report about your former jobs are the name, rank, and serial number type responses, specifically, your job title, description of duties, and dates worked.

Back in the early 1990s, according to career consultant, Connie Baher, U.S. Business Communications, San Diego, California, in that decade reported (at a presentation), about an excellent strategy for job seekers in a tight market. The strategy was to *adopt your favorite company.* It works great. Learn all you can about the firm by asking for information instead of asking for a job.

Baher suggested asking for perspective on a company. For example, introduce yourself to a company by stating, "I'm not looking for a job. I'd like to know more about your organization."

The hidden job market is active. Eighty percent of the jobs available are not advertised. Finding a job is largely social.

Baher emphasized that the hidden job market includes tips you get from your lawyer, doctor, accountant, tax preparer, or business associates who have a variety of clients who may have additional referrals or know of jobs soon to open in their client's workplaces. Today, most employers don't have time for informational interviews, but adopting a company and researching it in the library and by networking at professional association meetings and conventions still works well.

Network for the hidden job market with your same-age peers who attend those business mixers, socials, conferences, and seminars sponsored by your local chamber of commerce or by professional associations, trade shows, and trade journal publishers and advertisers in your field of interest.

Job leads can be found by calling the businesses that advertise in the business publications and trade journals. These include the magazines of the computer industry and related industries, such as video, graphic design, technical communications, interactiave multimedia, audio, public relations, advertising, marketing, technical training, instructional design, software, robotics, artificial intelligence, engineering, database management, and electronic music periodicals.

In the backs of the latest books on your field of interest you'll usually find a bibliography of the newest periodicals. Advertisers in trade periodicals usually are eager to tell you who their peers are and who they hire.

Employers hire those most like themselves in age, education, and background. People in the emerging ends of the computer industry such as interactive multimedia hang out with their same-age peers unless they're seeking a mentor or an internship.

Branch out in the methods you use to find job leads from business contacts and close friends. If you're coming from outside the company you adopt or walk in off the street, you'll be hired if there's no one inside the company to hire for that job.

Companies really like to hire as much as possible from inside the company in order to give employees the feeling that they're working towards goals and advancement within the company. It tends to keep them in the firm longer.

Sometimes the emerging technology is so new that no one has much experience in it, and the doors are wide open to the inexperienced.

Emerging digital technologies offer many branches of entry to the older worker with fresh ideas in creative, expressive, or software design jobs. Some of the creative jobs include writing fiction for interactive multimedia, CD, DVD, computer games, or desktop video training and education scriptwriting.

Interactive multimedia also opens the doors wide to the computer illustrator, educational or adventure/suspense scriptwriter, instructional designer, and genre novelist. Such creative people may feel shut out of the Hollywood scriptwriting or animation art market due to extreme age discrimination against emerging mature writers and artists.

Discrimination by Hollywood-type agents and producers is especially directed against older emerging scriptwriters, novelists, or artists who didn't break in or move to Hollywood when they were young because they were home raising families or supporting themselves in other work and studying their craft at night. A good resource is the International Documentary Association's 18-minute video, "The Hollywood Grey List," on old age job discrimination against Hollywood scriptwriters. The video is available for rental from the organization.

To counteract old age discrimination against persons in the arts, the computer industry now offers a future in multimedia, particularly, interactive multimedia to writers and artists who can work with computers and video instead of only video tape or film.

The computer industry's new interactive multimedia emphasis combines telephone lines, personal computers, fax machines, modems, local and wide area networks with home VCRs or video cameras, cable, satellites, electronic music, animation, scriptwriting, adventure stories, and games. Instructional courseware design combines software with video conferencing equipment and brings distance teaching into homes or links schools around the globe. Job opportunities are being created for people in all stages of personal growth, from teenagers to the elder-heroes.

Interactive multimedia is so new that there are not yet stereotypes, myths, or prejudices against the older creative writer, software designer, or animation artist as there is in the Hollywood scriptwriting arena. So the older creative writer or artist can feel at home in front of a computer that combines creative writing, animation, graphics, text, and music imagery.

Elder-heroes appear as superheroes in instructional design of software that challenges the imagination in users of all ages. Therefore, if you're over fifty years old and your career is about creative expression, think imaginative or educational software for home computers and for instruction as entertainment. Think hypermedia.

If you're under 25, virtual reality, computer games, and courseware design also were made for your techno-generation. In interactive multimedia, we are all one. You're not an old or young writer, designer, or marketer. You are what you offer. So offer the freshest, most profitable idea acquired through lifelong hands-on training.

Skills are important. After your clients are hired, they can ask for tuition reimbursement plans to can learn more the job and keep on growing educationally. Show your clients how they can keep skills current at their employer's expense if tuition reimbursement is offered. If your clients lose their jobs, at least the new skills will be transferable and competitive.

Losing a job no longer carries the stigma it did twenty years ago because today it is so common to have frequent turnover. Temporary or contingency work is growing rapidly. The average worker now goes through eight or more jobs in a lifetime, often wondering, "Why was I hired or not hired?"

According to Connie Baher, (from the early 1990s presentation) you're hired mainly for two reasons:

1. To be the solution to an employer's problem.
2. If you're the lowest risk possible of all job applicants.

Those hired pose the least risk and solve the most problems. You're hired for the company's reasons, not yours. However, it truly helps if you persist in showing your enthusiasm and say, "I'm so eager to work for this company that I made it my business to learn all about your firm and the benefits and advantages of your products."

What other skills can you as a job coach learn from your clients? They'll show you how to make yourself the lowest risk possible. Low-risk works also work in temporary jobs for the company, serve an internship, apply as freelancers, independent contractors, intrapreneurs, volunteers, or offer to help the company in new and creative ways.

Also, the lowest possible risk has done a similar type of work before. It's a lower risk to hire someone with a high-school education who has done accounts payable clerking before than to take on an unemployed M.A. level English teacher with self-taught word processing skills and wonder whether that person will make mistakes when entering data due to lack of enthusiasm about the job duties.

It's even harder to hire the lowest risk applicant when the unemployed professional with only a slight or new knowledge of computer skills begs for the job, is a homeless single parent, is facing covert age discrimination from other employers, or is in a financial emergency crisis. In the end, the person who does get hired is the one who poses the lowest risk to the employer's investment in the applicant's salary.

If your client earns $30,000 annually, for example, as a technical writer, the employer may risk an investment of more than $200,000 in salary and benefits until it is known whether your client will work out beyond a probation period. That's why the individual who is the lowest possible risk to the employer is hired. Benefits paid by employers often exceed the salary.

Look for open doors in emerging technologies so new that few have any experience with which to compete against your client. Encourage your clients to explore startup businesses if no other paid work can be found after a specified period of trying.

How have your clients "adopted" corporations? Adopting works best when the client is about to join in partnerships with larger firms to develop new products, services, or applications. Adopt a company that will get your client in on the ground floor of a venture. Focus on what your client does best. As a job coach, emphasize what you do best.

Watch the new start-ups closely and ask how your clients can serve on their teams. Observe the financial impact of new deals. When the financial deals are good, they don't make a lot of noise.

Look at companies developing products that allow people to improve health over the long term and corporations that help students to complete homework assignments, watch better entertainment, listen to healing music, and play in harmony with others and the environment.

The living room is a learning center. The workplace is a training center. Learning has become entertainment. The joy of play leads to technical or human relations job skills.

Training leads to production. These are the goals of new job coaches. As you practice career coaching with practical, common sense, you help your potential clients move closer to excellence. Your clients think they run on a competitive edge, but as a job coach you know that all your clients are watching how you emerge on a cooperative curve.

APPENDIX A

Resume Tracking Follow-Up Worksheets

For mass mailings, use or copy this handy form for your files.

Date_____

Company_____

Name_____

Address_____

_____

_____

Phone_____

Interview_____

Interview Comments:_____

_____

Follow-up Letters_____

Job Offer_____

Referrals_____

Related Information_____

_____

Quarterly Follow-up_____

Results_____

For mass mailings, use or copy this handy form for your files.

Date_____

Company_____

Name_____

Address_____

_____

_____

_____

Phone_____

Interview_____

Interview Comments:_____

_____

_____

RESUME TRACKING FOLLOW-UP WORKSHEETS

For mass mailings, use or copy this handy form for your files.

Date_____

Company_____

Name_____

Address_____

_____

_____

Phone_____

Interview_____

Interview Comments:_____

_____

Follow-up Letters_____

Job   Offer_____

Referrals_____

Related Information_____

_____

Quarterly Follow-up_____

Results_____

For mass mailings, use or copy this handy form for your files.

Date_____

Company_____

Name_____

Address_____

_____

_____

_____

Phone_____

Interview_____

Interview Comments:_____

_____

_____

RESUME TRACKING FOLLOW-UP WORKSHEETS

For smaller mailings, use or copy this handy form for your files.

Resume Tracking
Interview or Follow-up History
Name_____

Date _____

_____

Title_____

_____

Organization_____

_____

_____

Address_____

_____

_____

_____

Phone_____

_____

Mailed on:_____

COMMENTS

Follow-Up Letter Mailed	Reject Job	Accept Job
Date_____	_____	_____
Name_____	_____	_____
Title_____	_____	_____
Organization_____	_____	_____
Address_____	_____	_____
_____	_____	_____
_____	_____	_____
_____	_____	_____
Phone_____	_____	_____
Mailed On:_____	_____	_____

RESUME TRACKING FOLLOW-UP WORKSHEETS

For smaller mailings, use or copy this handy form for your files.

Resume Tracking
Interview or Follow-up History
Name_____
Date _____

_____
Title_____

_____
Organization_____

_____
_____
Address_____

_____
_____
_____

Phone_____

_____

Mailed on:_____

COMMENTS

Follow-Up Letter Mailed   Reject Job   Accept Job

Date_____   _____   _____
Name_____   _____   _____
Title_____   _____   _____
Organization_____   _____   _____

Address_____   _____   _____
_____   _____   _____
_____   _____   _____
_____   _____   _____

Phone_____   _____   _____

Mailed On:_____   _____   _____

APPENDIX B

Career-Related Source Books:

<u>The Brand Gap: How to Bridge the Distance Between Business Strategy and Design,</u> Marty Neumeier, New Riders, Berkeley, CA 2005.

<u>Burn Out,</u> How to beat the high cost of success. Freudenberger, Dr. Herbert J., Ph.D. Bantam Books, Inc., NY, 1981.
Career Planner:High Tech, G. Golter & D. Yanuck, VGM Career Horizons, c. 1987.

<u>Careers In Computers,</u> L. Stair, VGM Career Horizons.

<u>Careers Without College, (series), Computers,</u> L. Williams & P.Gunder.

<u>The Complete Negotiator,</u> Nierenberg, Gerard I. The Berkeley Publishing Group, Inc., NY, 1991.

<u>Do What You Are (Discover The Perfect Career For You Through The Secrets of Personality Type),</u> Tieger, Paul D. and Barbara Barron-Tieger. Little, Brown and Co., Boston, 1992.

<u>Getting A Job In The Computer Age,</u> H. Goldstein & S. Fraser, Peterson's Guides, c. 1986.

<u>Gifts Differing,</u> Isabel Briggs Myers. Consulting Psychologists Press, Inc., Palo Alto, CA., 1980

<u>Guerrilla Marketing,</u> Levinson, Jay Conrad. Houghton Mifflin Co., Boston, MA, 1984.

<u>High Paying Jobs In Six Months Or Less,</u> Over 100 Career Opportunities Which Can Pay Over $20,000 A Year, Anne J. Cardoza and Suzee Vlk, Monarch Press, Simon & Schuster, NY 1984.

Homecare Services Careers, (including the electronic home response and software industry, technicians, therapists, and home nursing), Anne deSola Cardoza, VGM Career Horizons, Lincolnwood, IL., 1993.

In The Chips, How To Use Your Computer To Make Money, Anne Cardoza and Suzee J. Vlk, Simon & Schuster, Computer Book Division, NY, 1985.

Life Types, Hirsh, Sandra and Kummerow, Jean. Warner Books Inc., NY, 1989.

New Directions in Career Planning and the Workplace, Kummerow, Jean M., Ed. Consulting Psychologists Press, Inc., Palo Alto, CA., 1991

Please Understand Me (Character and Temperament Types), Keirsey, David and Marilyn Bates. Prometheus Nemesis Book Co., DelMar, CA., 1984.

Positioning, (How to be seen and heard in the overcrowded marketplace.), Ries, Al, and Trout, Jack. Warner Books, Inc., NY., 1986.

Positioning: The Battle For Your Mind, Mc Graw-Hill, NY, 1986.

Robotics, Anne Cardoza and Suzee J. Vlk, Tab Books, Inc., 1985.

The Robotics Careers Handbook, Anne Cardoza and Suzee J. Vlk, Arco Publishing, Inc., NY, 1985.

Survival Games Personalities Play, Delunas, Eve, Ph.D. Sunflower Ink, Carmel, CA., 1992

Type Talk At Work, (How the 16 Personality Types Determine Your Succews On The Job.), Kroeger, Otta with Thuesen, Janet M. Delacorte Press, Bantam Doubleday Dell Publishing Group. Inc., NY, 1992.

Type Talk, Kroeger, Otto with Thuesen, Janet M. Delacorte Press, Bantam Doubleday Dell Publishing Group. Inc., NY, 1988.

Winning Tactics For Women Over Forty, Anne deSola Cardoza and Mavis B. Sutton. Mills & Sanderson Publishers, Bedford, MA, 1988.

Working Together, Isachsen, Olaf, Ph.D and Berens, Linda V., Ph.D. Neworld Management Press, Coronado, CA, 1988.

The Character of Organizations, (Using Jungian Type in Organizational Development), Bridges, William. Consulting Psychologists Press Inc., Palo Alto, CA, 1992.

APPENDIX C

Marketing Research Web Sites

The Market Research Industry

—http://www.asiresearch.com/mri/mri. htm

Market Trends

http://www.wsa.com/wsa/directories/ membership/MarketTrend/info.html

Center For Research In Marketing

—http://www.csom.umn.edu/ CSOM/MktgCenter/MktgCenter.html

Carlson School of Management. University of Minnesota. CenterFor Research In Marketing.

Frost & Sullivan

—http://www.best.com/~fs1/

Center for Latin American Capital Markets Research—
http://www.netrus.net/users/gmorles/ index.html

Market Research—
http://msowww.anu.edu.au/~dfk/ accesories/research/research.html

Ethridge & Associates, Marketing Consulting and Research—
http://www.ethridge.com/

Ethridge & Associates, L.L.C. is a premier marketing consulting firm specializing in helping business and political clients develop winning marketing campaigns.

The CAPRA Index—
http://www.dnai.com/~camp/

The CAPRA Project is a marketing research information service, founded in 1984.

Finance Club Links—
http://www.infobahnos.com/~jason/4fin. htm

TD Marketing Research, Inc. Home Page/Index—
http://www.well.com/user/tdmktg/

W-Two :International Business Planning,Marketing Research, Demographic Trends,…—
http://www.spidergraphics.com/wtw/

E-Marketing Home Page—
http://www.america.net/~scotth/ mktsite4.htm

HP EuroJobs: Manufacturing, Research & Development, Marketing—
http://www-europe.hp.com/JobPosting/ Manufacturing.html

Student Market Research In Europe
http://www.lookup.com/Homepages/63 338/mega/business/students.html

DEKALB Genetics Corporation—
researcher/producer/marketer of hybrid corn, sorghum, sunflowers, varietal soybean & alfalfa seed. Seed, agronomy, biotech & breeding info.—
http://www.monsanto.com/monsanto/us _ag/layout/seed/dekalb_corn/default.asp

Appendix D

List of Published Paperback Books in Print Written by Anne Hart

1. Predictive Medicine for Rookies: Consumer Watchdogs, Reviews, & Genetics Testing Firms Online

ISBN: 0-595-35146-8

2. Popular Health & Medical Writing for Magazines: How to Turn Current Research & Trends into Salable Feature Articles

ISBN: 0-595-35178-6

3. Writing 45-Minute One-Act Plays, Skits, Monologues, & Animation Scripts for Drama Workshops: Adapting Current Events, Social Issues, Life Stories, News & Histories

ISBN: 0-595-34597-2

4. Cutting Expenses and Getting More for Less: 41+ Ways to Earn an Income from Opportune Living

ISBN: 0-595-34772-X

5. How to Interpret Family History and Ancestry DNA Test Results for Beginners: The Geography and History of Your Relatives

ISBN: 0-595-31684-0

6. Cover Letters, Follow-Ups, and Book Proposals: Samples with Templates

ISBN: 0-595-31663-8

7. Writer's Guide to Book Proposals: Templates, Query Letters, & Free Media Publicity

ISBN: 0-595-31673-5

8. Search Your Middle Eastern and European Genealogy: In the Former Ottoman Empire's Records and Online

ISBN: 0-595-31811-8

9. Ancient and Medieval Teenage Diaries: Writing, Righting, and Riding for Righteousness

ISBN: 0-595-32009-0

10. Is Radical Liberalism or Extreme Conservatism a Character Disorder, Mental Disease, or Publicity Campaign?—A Novel of Intrigue—

ISBN: 0-595-31751-0

11. How to Write Plays, Monologues, and Skits from Life Stories, Social Issues, and Current Events—for all Ages.

ISBN: 0-595-31866-5

12. How to Make Money Organizing Information

ISBN: 0-595-23695-2

13. How To Stop Elderly Abuse: A Prevention Guidebook

ISBN: 0-595-23550-6

14. How to Make Money Teaching Online With Your Camcorder and PC: 25 Practical and Creative How-To Start-Ups To Teach Online

ISBN: 0-595-22123-8

15. A Private Eye Called Mama Africa: What's an Egyptian Jewish Female Psycho-Sleuth Doing Fighting Hate Crimes in California?

ISBN: 0-595-18940-7

16. The Freelance Writer's E-Publishing Guidebook: 25+ E-Publishing Home-based Online Writing Businesses to Start for Freelancers

ISBN: 0-595-18952-0

17. The Courage to Be Jewish and the Wife of an Arab Sheik: What's a Jewish Girl from Brooklyn Doing Living as a Bedouin?

ISBN: 0-595-18790-0

18. The Year My Whole Country Turned Jewish: A Time-Travel Adventure Novel in Medieval Khazaria

ISBN: 0-75967-251-2

19. The Day My Whole Country Turned Jewish: The Silk Road Kids

ISBN: 0-7596-6380-7

20. Four Astronauts and a Kitten: A Mother and Daughter Astronaut Team, the Teen Twin Sons, and Patches, the Kitten: The Intergalactic Friendship Club

ISBN: 0-595-19202-5

21. The Writer's Bible: Digital and Print Media: Skills, Promotion, and Marketing for Novelists, Playwrights, and Script Writers. Writing Entertainment Content for the New and Print Media.

ISBN: 0-595-19305-6

22. New Afghanistan's TV Anchorwoman: A novel of mystery set in the New Afghanistan

ISBN: 0-595-21557-2

23. Tools for Mystery Writers: Writing Suspense Using Hidden Personality Traits

ISBN: 0-595-21747-8

24. The Khazars Will Rise Again!: Mystery Tales of the Khazars

ISBN: 0-595-21830-X

25. Murder in the Women's Studies Department: A Professor Sleuth Novel of Mystery

ISBN: 0-595-21859-8

26. Make Money With Your Camcorder and PC: 25+ Businesses: Make Money With Your Camcorder and Your Personal Computer by Linking Them.

ISBN: 0-595-21864-4

27. Writing What People Buy: 101+ Projects That Get Results

ISBN: 0-595-21936-5

28. Anne Joan Levine, Private Eye: Internal adventure through first-person mystery writer's diary novels

ISBN: 0-595-21860-1

29. <u>Verbal Intercourse</u>: A Darkly Humorous Novel of Interpersonal Couples and Family Communication

ISBN: 0-595-21946-2

30. <u>The Date Who Unleashed Hell</u>: If You Love Me, Why Do You Humiliate Me?
"The Date" Mystery Fiction

ISBN: 0-595-21982-9

31. <u>Cleopatra's Daughter</u>: Global Intercourse

ISBN: 0-595-22021-5

32. <u>Cyber Snoop Nation</u>: The Adventures Of Littanie Webster, Sixteen-Year-Old Genius Private Eye On Internet Radio

ISBN: 0-595-22033-9

33. <u>Counseling Anarchists</u>: We All Marry Our Mirrors—Someone Who Reflects How We Feel About Ourselves. Folding Inside Ourselves: A Novel of Mystery

ISBN: 0-595-22054-1

34. <u>Sacramento Latina</u>: When the One Universal We Have In Common Divides Us

ISBN: 0-595-22061-4

35. <u>Astronauts and Their Cats</u>: At night, the space station is cat-shadow dark

ISBN: 0-595-22330-3

36. <u>How Two Yellow Labs</u> Saved the Space Program: When Smart Dogs Shape Shift in Space

ISBN: 0-595-23181-0

37. The DNA Detectives: Working Against Time

ISBN: 0-595-25339-3

38. How to Interpret Your DNA Test Results For Family History & Ancestry: Scientists Speak Out on Genealogy Joining Genetics

ISBN: 0-595-26334-8

39. Roman Justice: SPQR: Too Roman To Handle

ISBN: 0-595-27282-7

40. How to Make Money Selling Facts: to Non-Traditional Markets

ISBN: 0-595-27842-6

41. Tracing Your Jewish DNA For Family History & Ancestry: Merging a Mosaic of Communities

ISBN: 0-595-28127-3

42. The Beginner's Guide to Interpreting Ethnic DNA Origins for Family History: How Ashkenazi, Sephardi, Mizrahi & Europeans Are Related to Everyone Else

ISBN: 0-595-28306-3

43. Nutritional Genomics—A Consumer's Guide to How Your Genes and Ancestry Respond to Food: Tailoring What You Eat to Your DNA

ISBN: 0-595-29067-1

44. How to Safely Tailor Your Food, Medicines, & Cosmetics to Your Genes: A Consumer's Guide to Genetic Testing Kits from Ancestry to Nourishment

ISBN: 0-595-29403-0

45. <u>One Day Some Schlemiel Will Marry Me</u>, Pay the Bills, and Hug Me.: Parents & Children Kvetch on Arab & Jewish Intermarriage

ISBN: 0-595-29826-5

46. <u>Find Your Personal Adam And Eve</u>: Make DNA-Driven Genealogy Time Capsules

ISBN: 0-595-30633-0

47. <u>Creative Genealogy Projects</u>: Writing Salable Life Stories

ISBN: 0-595-31305-1

48. <u>Power Dating Games</u>: What's Important to Know About the Person You'll Marry

ISBN: 0-595-19186-X

49. <u>Dramatizing 17th Century Family History of Deacon Stephen Hart & Other Early New England Settlers</u>: How to Write Historical Plays, Skits, Biographies, Novels, Stories, or Monologues from Genealogy Records, Social Issues, & Current Events for All Ages

ISBN: 0-595-34345-7

50. <u>Problem-Solving and Cat Tales for the Holidays</u>: Historical—Time-Travel—Adventure

ISBN: 0-595-32692-7

51. <u>801 Action Verbs for Communicators:</u> Position Yourself First with Action Verbs for Journalists, Speakers, Educators, Students, Resume-Writers, Editors & Travelers

ISBN: 0-595-31911-4

52. Writing 7-Minute Inspirational Life Experience Vignettes: Create and Link 1,500-Word True Stories

ISBN: 0-595-32237-9

53. Large Print Crossword Puzzles for Memory Enhancement: Neuron-Growing Stimulation for the Age-Wise Brain

ISBN: 0-595-35663-X

54. Tracing Your Baltic, Scandinavian, Eastern European, & Middle Eastern Ancestry Online: Finnish, Swedish, Norwegian, Danish, Icelandic, Estonian, Latvian, Polish, Lithuanian, Greek, Macedonian, Bulgarian, Armenian, Hungarian, Eastern European & Middle Eastern Genealogy (All Faiths)

ISBN: 0-595-35773-3

55. 32 Podcasting & Other Businesses to Open Showing People How to Cut Expenses: Get Higher Quality for Less Money

ISBN: 0-595-36083-1

56. Middle Eastern Honor Killings in the USA: (A Thriller)
ISBN: 0-595-36066-1

57. Infant Gender Selection & Personalized Medicine: Consumer's Guide

ISBN: 0-595-36539-6

58. Writing, Financing, & Producing Documentaries: Creating Salable Reali Video
ISBN: 0-595-36633-3

59. How to Turn Poems, Lyrics, & Folklore into Salable Children's Books: Using Humor or Proverbs
ISBN: 0-595-36735-6

**60. Where to Find Your Arab-American or Jewish Genealogy Records: Also: Mediterranean, Assyrian, Iranian, Greek & Armenian:
ISBN: 0-595-37325-9

Index

978-0-595-37100-6
0-595-37100-0

www.ingramcontent.com/pod-product-compliance
Lightning Source LLC
Chambersburg PA
CBHW020728180526
45163CB00001B/157